Leek Trade c.1830-1930

A source book of trade and business in Leek and surrounding areas c.1830-1930, using letterheads, adverts and directories

Vol. I A-H

From the collection of the late
Stuart Hobson

with notes by
Ray Poole

CHURNET VALLEY BOOKS
1 King Street, Leek, Staffordshire.ST13 5NW 01538 399033
www.thebookshopleek.co.uk

© Churnet Valley Books 2003
ISBN 1 897949 79 0

All rights reserved. Any use of this book in any form needs the permission of both author and publisher.

INTRODUCTION

here was once a popular statement in the printing industry to the effect that "a firm was only as good as s letterheading", and, conversely, that a firm's printed stationery said much about that firm. It is a certain ct that a letter from a company is often the first contact one has with that company, so it is important that his first impression should create a good image immediately. And if one has transacted any business with company it is always reassuring when the account is presented on a neat and attractive billhead - the nmediate feeling of confidence and well-being, as it were, that one has been dealing with a firm of some pute, and one that knows its business.

First impressions count. Die-stamped stationery was expensive but much sought after, for it created very high standard. By this intaglio method, a finely-engraved copper or steel plate produced an image hich stood out in relief on the paper or card. This was particularly important in the case of business ards, for when the representative presented his fine, ivory-white die stamped card the buyer would gently un his finger over the surface, and if he could feel the letters in relief a good impression of the firm would e created immediately. Companies jealously guarded their original plates, which could be re-engraved if ecessary to incorporate changes, and these were usually wrapped in waxed paper to prevent rusting. Die tamping was also used for letterheads, but was not suitable for book work.

The intaglio process of printing from a finely engraved plate was also used to produce a flat image. This allowed a sharp impression of any pictorial or design features to be printed very clearly. Indeed, the mages were often much more crisp and sharp than those produced by the traditional letterpress method, vhere the solid type used was subject to wear and tear. The letterpress process was, of course, more lexible, for it used moveable type, and small alterations could easily be made, whereas the solid engraved late would have to be re-engraved if any changes were necessary.

Commercial letterheadings and other printed ephemera of trade reveal a great deal about the social history of a place. Beautifully designed stationery, the epitome of the skill and craft of the engraver, speaks of prosperity and solidarity. This is certainly true with regard to Leek's burgeoning silk industry, which, in the middle and later Victorian years, was bringing much wealth and commercial prosperity to he town. The well-designed stationery items of the major silk manufacturers reflect this, and a number of letterheads incorporate an artist's impression of the extent of their factories, the trademarks of their products, and often a list of their various services - almost a catalogue in miniature. It is interesting to note that many of the larger companies deemed it unnecessary to print their full address on their heading - after all, everybody recognised them, and knew exactly where they were.

Tradesmen, too, if they could afford it (and many of them could), preferred to have a heading with style. This was particularly important for printers who were able to display the best features of their art and craft in their own stationery, a fine advertisement for their services. It follows, then, that some of the best designed letterheads are those of printers. Many printed headings for tradesmen and shopkeepers were again almost miniature catalogues, listing in great detail and effusive terms the goods and services provided. And it was strangely warming to have a firm "respectfully solicit your earliest attention" whether it be in paying your bill, or perhaps visiting their new showroom! Sometimes a major national company would supply a firm with billheads dominated by their own name, trademark or brand name, and the local shopkeeper would then be able to have his own details overprinted in the small space available.

We hope the mainly Victorian and Edwardian printed ephemera collected here, will give an image of that age in Leek - an age of great advances in the prosperity and civic development in the town, and an age of gracious living, of Darracq motorcars, White May Lamp Oil and Pinet's Boots, of Armour's Extract of Beef and Edwards' Desiccated Soup, of Black and Green's Tea, Provost Oat Biscuits and Hudson Soap, and of gas mantles with such evocative names as Ironclad, Welsbach, Veritas and Volker.

It was the age of the afternoon tea-shop, where ham sandwiches and cream scones could be consumed at a leisurely pace. There were several such establishments, and they managed to preserve an air of Edwardian gentility into the 1950s. However, the 20th Century has taken its toll on the businesses represented in this book. Very few of the factories, shops or tradesmen remain in the same form today, and even the old Leek Urban District Council has been absorbed into the larger authority, the Staffordshire Moorlands District Council. Modern industrial trends, economic circumstances and international trade have decimated the silk and textile industry, and shopping habits have tended towards the edge-of-town hypermarkets and city centre shopping malls. No longer do people go to their local grocer or corner shop for a pound of cheese and say "Put it on my bill." In this age of technology, the machine-printed till receipt, or the computer-realised invoice has replaced for ever the stylish, hand-written bills of yesteryear.

Trade directories have also been used to collate much of the material presented here. From the late 18th century through the Victorian and Edwardian years directories were published, usually annually, and whilst they were by no means comprehensive, being dependent upon the support of traders taking listings, they do give a good picture of the development of trade during that period of great expansion.

White's Directories of Staffordshire for 1834 and 1851 are the best of the early county directories, with a very comprehensive Leek section. Local almanacs were also produced. Thomas Mark, printer and stationer, published his own almanac for a number of years, followed by the Leek Commercial Directory during the later Victorian years. These included much useful local information, and the names of businesses or shops were usually classified according to the appropriate trade or profession.

Later county directories were much larger and more comprehensive, with businesses listed alphabetically. These included the Post Office Directory, Slater's Directory and Kelly's Directory, which is still published today, though not on a county basis.

These letterheads, billheads and other items, including several trade directories, were collected by the late Stuart Hobson who was Head of Mathematics at the Sixth Form College in Stoke. He had a great interest in and knowledge of fine and old books and was also an avid collector of printed and written ephemera relating to Leek and North Staffordshire. Unfortunately he died in 1999. His wife Barbara Hobson kindly allowed us to use his collected ephemera before it was sold. This book is dedicated to Stuart's memory.

Ray Poole, Leek

This work will be produced in three volumes, approximately covering 1830-1930.

Volume I -   Names A-H, the 1838 map of Leek, and two directory sections for Leek, from Parson and Bradshaw's, 1818, and White's Directory, 1834.

Volume II -   Names I-Q, Slagg's 1862 map of Leek, the Leek section of White's 1851 Staffordshire Directory, and Slater's 1862 Leek Directory.

Volume III - Names R-Z, Pattersons 1908 Town Map of Leek, and several Leek Town Directories, including 1876, 1898, 1916 and 1934.

Volume I

Names A-H
The 1838 map of Leek
Two directory sections for Leek
Parson and Bradshaw's, 1818
and White's Directory, 1834

The Congregational Church, Derby Street, 1863.

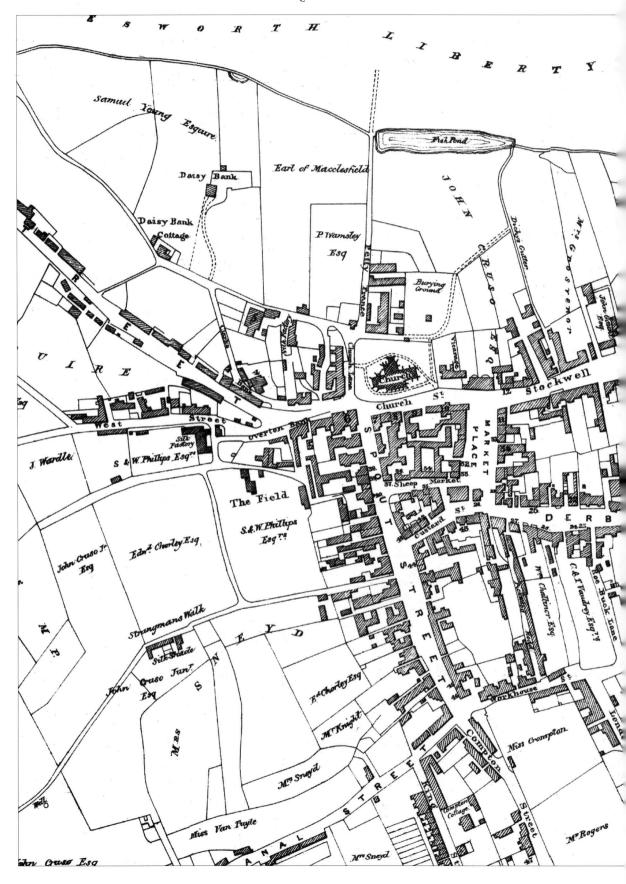

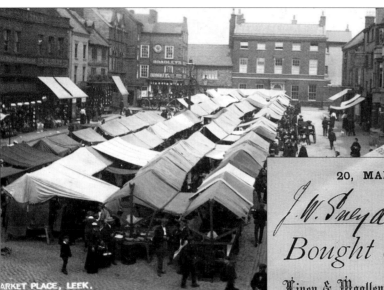

MARKET PLACE, LEEK.

Leek Market Place was the site of many retail businesses at the end of the 19th century, as well as the important weekly Market and Butter Market.

"Chasers" for overdue accounts were usually polite but firm!

20, MARKET PLACE,

Leek, *Aug.t 23* 190*2*

J. W. Sneyd Esq. Basford Hall

Bought of John Adams,

Linen & Woollen Draper, Silk Mercer, Haberdasher,

HOSIER, &c.

FUNERALS COMPLETELY FURNISHED.

To a/c Rendered — 17 8 2

Dear Sir,

I shall esteem it a favor if you will oblige me with your cheque for above on or before Wednesday next, as I am leaving Town for some time and am about handing over my accounts for collection to my Solicitor

I am

Yours Obediently,

Jno Adams

WETLEY ROCKS BREWERY,

NEAR LEEK.

CELEBRATED FOR

BITTER BEER,

As recommended by several Medical Men in the Potteries and District.

PRICE:

54s. PER BARREL,

AND

27s. PER KILDERKIN,

Or in smaller Casks suitable for family trade.

Orders may be sent either direct to the Brewery, or to Mr. JOHN JONES, Cellerhead, Stoke-on-Trent; Mr. ALFRED GROSVENOR, Old Hall Terrace, Hanley, the Agents.

JOHN ADDERLEY,

PROPRIETOR.

Small, private brewers proliferated during the Victorian era. Many pubs brewed their own beer, with a brew-house in the pub yard. John Adderley's brewery was at Wetley Rocks. The advert suggests that a kilderkin was equivalent to half a barrel.

For all that is Best in Radio try

HARRY ALLCOCK,

15a, Fountain St.

(OPPOSITE BROUGH'S LODGE.)

The following are recommended as outstanding sets of the season for trouble-free reception and good tonal quality with high selectivity :- Cossor & "Radio for the Million " Kits, Osram, Lotus, Pye, Ultra, Ekco and - Phillips.-

Ekco All-electric Model £15 15s.

....

All the latest in moving coil speakers, components, etc.

DANIEL ALLEN,
CABINET MAKER, UPHOLSTERER,
AND UNDERTAKER,
Manufacturer of and Dealer in
EVERY DESCRIPTION OF FURNITURE,
Picture and Picture Frames, Mirrors,
BRASS & IRON BEDSTEADS, CARPETS & COCOA
Matting, Mattresses, Perambulators, &c.,
21, MARKET PLACE, LEEK.
ALE AND PORTER STORES.

CABINET & UPHOLSTERY MANUFACTORY ; GLOBE YARD

This small advertisement for Daniel Allen is an example of the Victorian practice of using a different type style for each line.

Messrs. E. Allen & Co., Silk Manufacturers, Britannia Mills, West Street, Leek ; and 10, Higgin Lane, Wood Street, London, E.C.

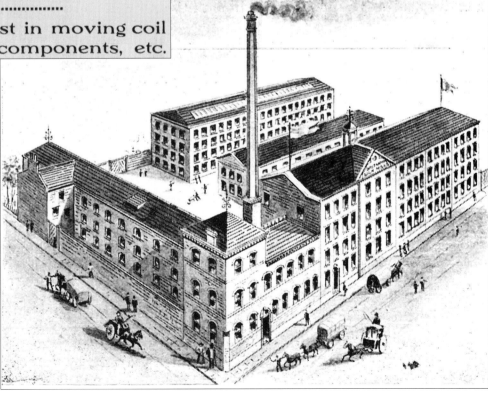

Britannia Mills of E. Allen & Co was on the corner West Street where the Tax Office is now

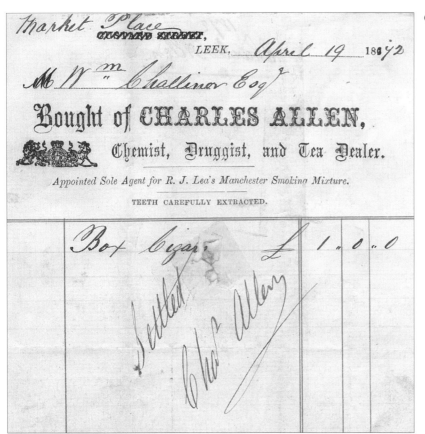

Market Place
~~CUSTARD STREET~~,

LEEK, *April 19* 186 7 2

M *Wm Challinor Esq*

Bought of CHARLES ALLEN,

Chemist, Druggist, and Tea Dealer.

Appointed Sole Agent for R. J. Lea's Manchester Smoking Mixture.

TEETH CAREFULLY EXTRACTED.

Box Cigars   £ 1 . 0 . 0

Settled
Chas Allen

Charles Allen was first listed in Kelly's 1868 Directory. Many chemists also traded as tea dealers, and it is interesting to note that Charles Allen also extracted teeth!

The business was probably situated at the Derby Street end of the Market Place.

North Staffordshire Railway waggons in Leek Market Place in front of the Bird in Hand, late 19th century.

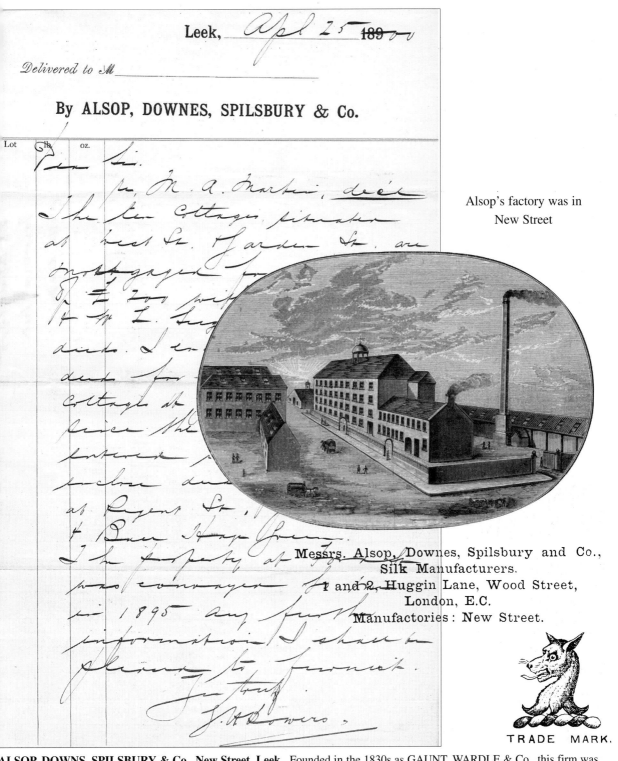

Leek, Apl 25 189

Delivered to M _____

By ALSOP, DOWNES, SPILSBURY & Co.

Lot	lb.	oz.

[handwritten letter]

Alsop's factory was in New Street

Messrs. Alsop, Downes, Spilsbury and Co.,
Silk Manufacturers.
1 and 2, Huggin Lane, Wood Street,
London, E.C.
Manufactories: New Street.

TRADE MARK.

ALSOP, DOWNS, SPILSBURY & Co., New Street, Leek. Founded in the 1830s as GAUNT, WARDLE & Co., this firm was a medal winner at the Great Exhibition of 1851, and similarly at the later exhibition in 1862. The firm's main products were sewing silks, machine silks, silk and mohair braids and bindings and mohair and cotton boot and shoe laces. The 'Leek and District Illustrated' of 1896 claimed that Alsop, Downs and Spilsbury were perhaps the largest manufacturers of hand-made buttons, a speciality of the moorlands area, which was a considerable cottage industry at the time. The firm employed about 200 persons. The New Street Works were acquired by CLEMESHA, BROS. & BIRCH Ltd. in 1907.

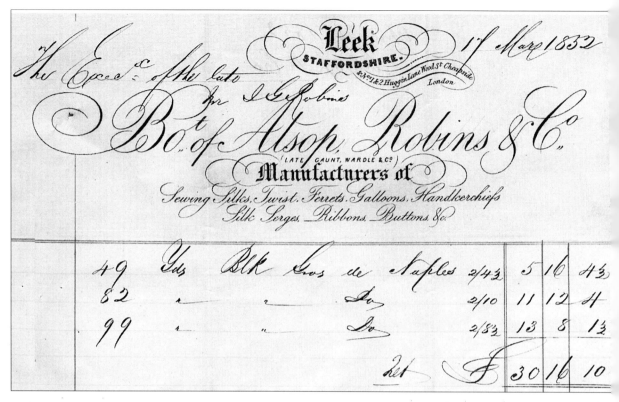

This earlier heading is a further indication that the firm was formerly Gaunt, Wardle & Co. The firm's products - ferrets, galloons, handkerchiefs - were much in demand in the Victorian era. The name of Alsop is commemorated in Leek in the Cottage Hospital, which was officially known as the Alsop Memorial Hospital.

Below: Stockwell Street.

BROOK STREET,

LEEK, _Xas_ 190_2_

M_r_ Grace

✦ Dr. to JOHN AMSON, ✦

ENGINEER AND MACHINIST.

Brass and Iron Founder.   Steam and Hot Water Pipe Fitter.
Repairs of all kinds punctually attended to.   Dealer in New and Second-hand Machinery.
All kinds of Old Machinery Bought.   Best price given for any quantity for cash.

Date	Description	s	d
Oct 23	Boring Flange and chasing	1	0
	1 - 1" ½ tee 1/5 1 - 2" sock 8	1	11
	1 - 2" nif 6° 1 - 2" Plug 8	1	2
	Screwing pipes	1	0
Nov 15	Screwing pipes		8
28	Cutting Girder 2 sums	2	6
	Repairing Boiler stand	1	0
	Drilling Girders	2	0
Dec 4	Drilling Plate, ½		8
	2 saws		8
		12	7

FOR BICYCLE REPAIRS,
HEATING APPARATUSES,
IRON & BRASS CASTINGS,
STEAM & GAS ENGINES,
Try J. AMSON,
DUKE STREET IRON WORKS,

Satisfaction ✦ Guaranteed.

JOHN AMSON, Brook Street, Leek.
John Amson, and later James Amson, provided a light engineering service from the workshop in Brook Street until the post-War (WW2) years - about 1950.

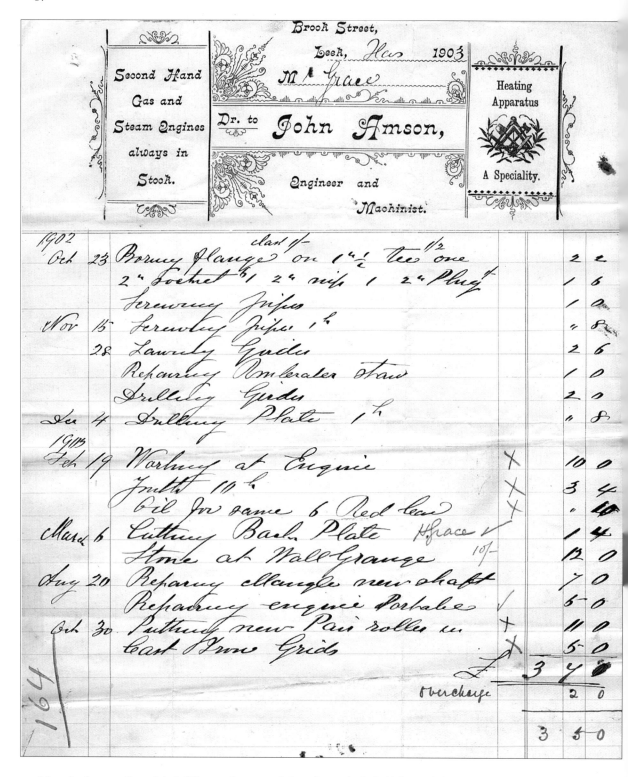

Brook Street,

Leek, *Nov* 1903

Mr *Grace*

Dr. to **John Amson,**

Engineer and

Machinist.

Second Hand
Gas and
Steam Engines
always in
Stock.

Heating
Apparatus

A Speciality.

1902				
Oct	23	Boring flange on 1"½ tee one	2	2
		2" socket 1 2" nip 1 2" plug	1	6
		Screwing pipes	1	0
Nov	15	Screwing pipes 1"	"	8
	28	Lawing Guides	2	6
		Repairing Umbrellas stand	1	0
		Drilling Girder	2	0
Dec	4	Drilling Plate 1"	"	8
1903				
Feb	19	Working at Engine	10	0
		Smith 10"	3	4
		oil for same 6 Red lead	"	10
Mar	6	Cutting Back Plate H Grace	1	4
		Stone at Wall Grange 10/-	12	0
Aug	20	Repairing Mangle new shaft	7	0
		Repairing engine Portable	5	0
Oct	30	Putting new Pair rollers in	11	0
		Cast Iron Grids	5	0
			£3 7 0	
		overcharge	2	0
			3 5 0	

164

Many businesses allowed their fellow traders extended credit, particularly if the work-load was relatively light. This bill
represents a whole year of small jobs done by John Amson for Grace's, the builders.
The 'annual settlement' was an accepted trade practice at the time - this would not find favour today.

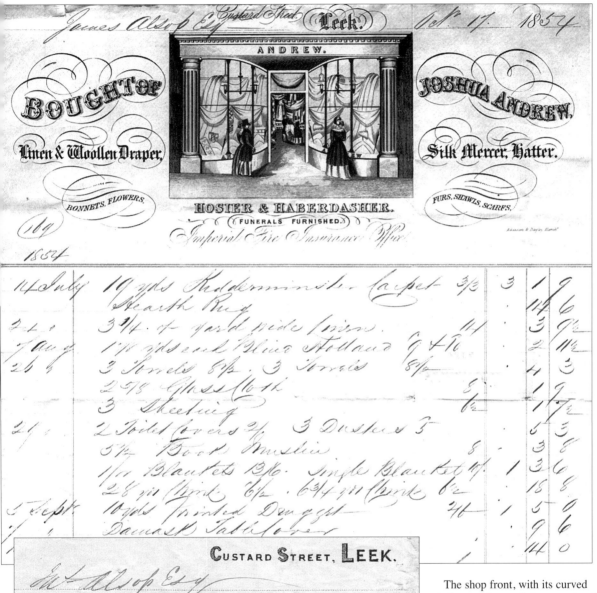

The shop front, with its curved windows and central doorway, is still recognisable today in Stanley Street. This old established business later moved to 14 Market Place, as shown by the 1888 heading on page 16.

Joshua Andrew's original shop was in Custard Street (now Stanley Street). Like many traders, this firm also offered a funeral service.

14. Market Place.   Leek   August 18th 1888

M Representatives of W & C Smith

Funeral Expenses.

Boᵗ of Joshua ~~Andrew~~ Bayley Late

Linen & Woollen Draper, Silk Mercer.

HABERDASHER, HOSIER & GLOVER.

FAMILY MOURNING, FUNERALS FURNISHED.

1888

	£ s d
May 31ˢᵗ 1 Shirt 5/11 17½ Crape 5/6 3½ Silk 3/11	5 15 10½
4½ Shroud Flannel 1/10. 18 Invitations 4	14 3
12 Wadding 3. Shroud making —	
putting on & paying woman 21/-	1 4 0
14 Hatbands 10½ 2 Silk Gloves 1/4½	15 0
1 Kid 2/11. 8 Cashmere 3/6. 2 Taffeta 10½	1 12 8
14 Dents Gloves 3/11 . 1 Taffeta 1/4½	2 16 2½
Mr Wood at Grave 2/- 2 Bearers 3/-	8 0
Hat 1/3 Harrod 1 Gloves 3/11	5 2
5 Drivers Gloves 10½ 1 Gloves 1/2½	5 7
2 Gloves 2/11½ 1 Gloves 2/11½	8 10½
1 Gloves for Miss Walker 2/11	2 11
6 Ribbon for Rosettes for Shroud 4	2 0
8 Nuns Cloth (Crape) 2/-	16 0
£	15 6 6½

Recᵈ Aug 18/88

15 6 6½

Jos. Bayley

With Thanks

Joshua Andrew later became Joseph Bayley who adapted Andrew's headings for his own business.
The items listed on this invoice are an indication of the trappings of a Victorian funeral.

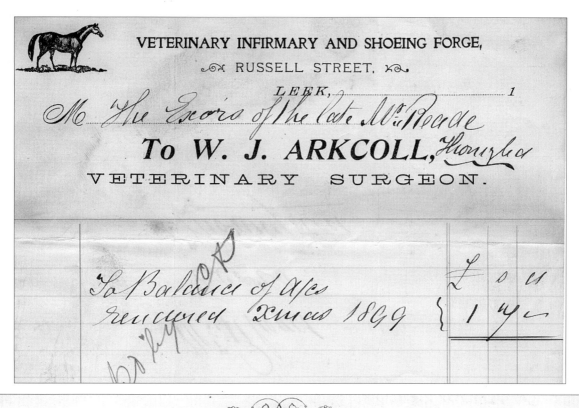

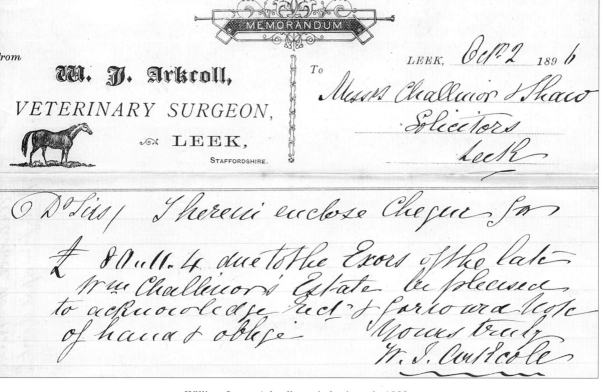

William James Arkcoll was in business in 1888.
He was followed by George Spencer Arkcoll at the same address (1921 Directory).

TELEGRAPHIC ADDRESS: "ARMSTRONGS, LEEK."

4, Gaunt Buildings, DERBY STREET,

LEEK.....*March 14th* 191*1*

M~r~ *Wm Brookes*

98 Mill St

Dr. to ⚹ ARMSTRONG BROS.

Up-to-Date Tailors & Gent.'s Outfitters.   TERMS: STRICTLY CASH.

1910					
Nov	8	Suit	1	5	6
		Cash Rec'd		9	0

This traditional family firm also supplied school uniforms. Bespoke tailoring, as opposed to "off the peg", was always in demand, and this invoice indicates a made-to-measure suit for £1-5-6 to which the customer has paid a deposit of 9/-.

This small, home-based business allowed customers to bring their own material for tailoring - a custom whereby George Arnold would not have to carry stocks of material at his terraced home.

GEORGE ARNOLD,
TAILOR, CARPET MAKER, &c.,
No. 13, HORTON STREET, LEEK,

Begs respectfully to inform the Inhabitants of Leek and vicinity than Gentlemen finding their own material can have any kind of garments made up on the shortest notice.

NOTE THE ADDRESS:—

13, HORTON STREET, LEEK.

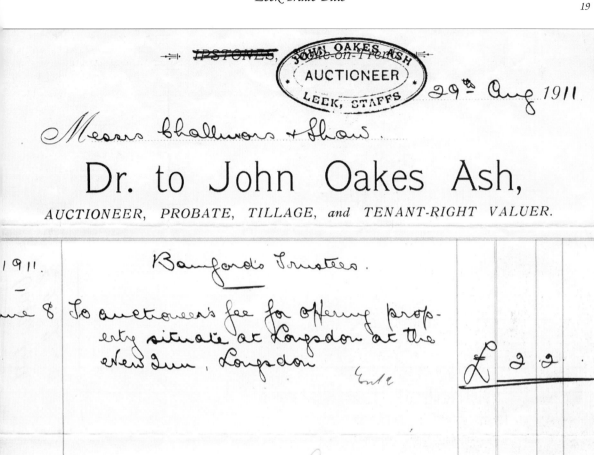

~~IPSTONES,~~ Stoke-on-Trent

JOHN OAKES ASH
· AUCTIONEER ·
LEEK, STAFFS

29th Aug 1911

Messrs Challinors + Shaw.

Dr. to John Oakes Ash,

AUCTIONEER, PROBATE, TILLAGE, and TENANT-RIGHT VALUER.

1911.

Bamford's Trustees.

June 8 To auctioneer's fee for offering property situate at Longsdon at the New Inn, Longsdon
£ 2 2

Recd 22/11 J.O. Ash
with Thanks

JOHN OAKES ASH,

Auctioneer

—AND—

APPRAISER,

IPSTONES, CHEADLE.

**Cheshire Cheese Inn, and Smithfield Offices,
Leek, on Wednesdays.**

Oakes Ash had an office in Leek Cattle Market, listed in Kelly's 1904 Directory. The present Bury and Hilton estate agents were previously Bury, Hilton and Oakes Ash.

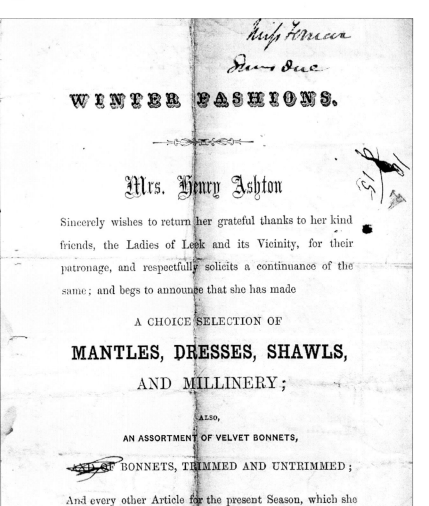

WINTER FASHIONS.

Mrs. Henry Ashton

Sincerely wishes to return her grateful thanks to her kind
friends, the Ladies of Leek and its Vicinity, for their
patronage, and respectfully solicits a continuance of the
same; and begs to announce that she has made

A CHOICE SELECTION OF

MANTLES, DRESSES, SHAWLS,

AND MILLINERY;

ALSO,

AN ASSORTMENT OF VELVET BONNETS,

BONNETS, TRIMMED AND UNTRIMMED;

And every other Article for the present Season, which she

It is interesting to compare this
genteel, polite approach to direct
advertising with the "hard sell"
methods of today.

Mary Ann Ashton's address was
19 Market Street.

Many ladies operated a
millinery and
dressmaking service from
their own homes, and
usually built up a circle
of regular customers.

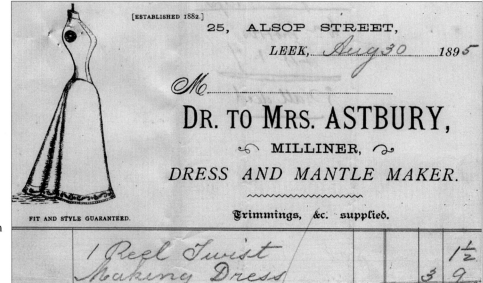

[ESTABLISHED 1882.]

25, ALSOP STREET,

LEEK, *Aug 30* 1895

M

DR. TO MRS. ASTBURY,

MILLINER,

DRESS AND MANTLE MAKER.

FIT AND STYLE GUARANTEED.

Trimmings, &c. supplied.

1 Reel Twist		1½
Making Dress	3	9
	3	10½

116

LEEK, *Dec 19th* _____ 19 0 1

STAFFORDSHIRE.

~✳* MEMO *✳~

FROM

The Associated Trimming Weaver's Society.

To *Mr Thos. Robinson.*

Dear Sir,

Will you kindly explain why the Trimming Weavers Society was not invited to the Meeting held at the Town Hall Tuesday the 17 inst, to discuss alterations in Working Hours. We cannot understand why we were ignored in the matter. We are by far the largest Trade Union in Leek, and you must excuse us for thinking we have a right to a voice in any alteration of Working Hours,

The textile union was a strong voice for the workers in the industry. This letter from the secretary William Bromfield politely but firmly registers a protest about the union's apparent exclusion from a meeting on working hours.

THE ASSOCIATED TRIMMING WEAVER'S SOCIETY

As industries expanded generally so did the need for trade unions, and the Leek textile industry was no exception. The Associated Trimming Weaver's Society (the apostrophe is rather singular!) was one of the early local trade unions. Established in 1871, its first secretary was Charles Swain, who had experience in union work in Manchester, although he was a native of Leek. William Bromfield took over as secretary in 1907, and supervised the Federation of the seven separate textile unions to form the Amalgamated Society of Textile Workers and Kindred Trades in 1919. He remained as secretary until 1942, and became MP for Leek in 1918.

And Now . . .

ARKIRECTO

The Latest and Greatest of all constructional toys

No Nuts! No Bolts! No Screws!

And yet THE ARKIRECTO SYSTEM enables you to build Engineering and Architectural Models of every conceivable kind. Realistic in appearance. Easy to Dissemble. All parts can be used over and over again.

● **Youngsters will have it!**
● **Fathers will want it!**

100% BRITISH

SETS FROM 2/6 to 52/6
Packed in Attractive Boxes & Cabinets

MECCANO

Complete Outfits from 1/- to 385/-

Spare parts kept in stock.

AEROPLANE CONSTRUCTION SETS.

Complete outfits 5/-, 9/-, 15/-, 16/6, 25/-

Aeroplane Hangars 4/11 & 6/9

Hangar Outfits 9/6 each.

DINKY BUILDER OUTFITS,
For the Kiddies. 6/- & 7/6

No 1 for general construction including wheel toys and No. 2 for making groups of realistic miniature furniture.

TELEPHONE 169

S. W. BAILEY,
COMPLETE SPORTS OUTFITTER,
30, STOCKWELL ST. LEEK

S.W. Bailey, in Stockwell St from the 1930s, moved to Derby St in the 1950s, and eventually to Stanley Street until 1980s.
Below: Stockwell Street - the photographer would be standing just outside Bailey's old shop

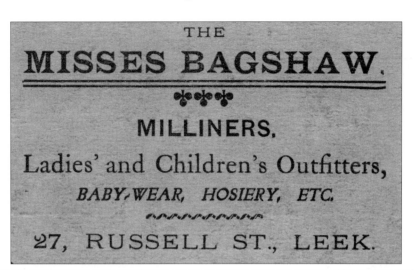

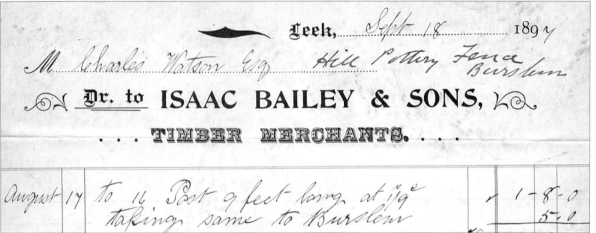

Isaac Bailey's address was Ball Haye Green.

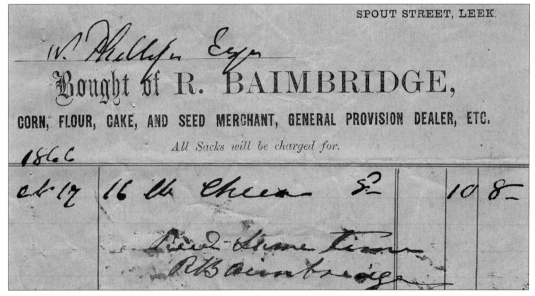

Spout Street was the original name for St. Edward Street.

St. Edward Street before High Street and Strangman Street were constructed. Stanley Street is seen leading off to the right by the public house. Sheep Market leads off to the right further up, opposite the site of the present High Street.

W. Barker in St Edward Street had a wonderful mix of trade - coal merchant and tax collector!

MEMORANDUM.

FROM

W. BARKER,

ASSISTANT OVERSEER AND COLLECTOR

OF POOR RATES AND GOVERNMENT TAXES.

COAL MERCHANT.

Agent for the Calidonian Insurance Office: Established 1805.

68, St. Edward Street, Leek, ... *Decr 8* 189*2*

Dr Sir

Will you oblige by forwarding me the poor Rates you pay for to day or to morrow I am behind with the Union Calls & have been fast at home near a fortnight bad with Bronchitis

				4 . 11 . 4½
£ .	1 : 18 : 4½	27	6 .
to re	1 . 4 . 4½		4 : 17 : 4½
	: 2 . 6		

J. BALL,

Grocer & Provision Dealer,

Sheep Market, Leek.

Highest Quality

Bacon - Ham - Cheese
Fine Blended Teas.
Coffee.　　　　Cocoa.
Dried Fruit. Tinned Fruit.
Preserves.　　Mincemeat,
and many Special

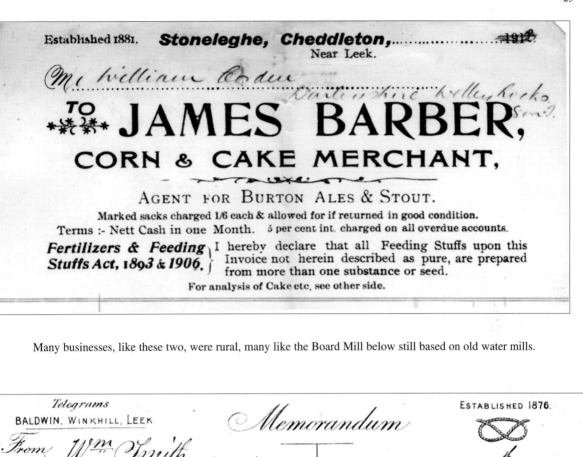

Established 1881.   **Stoneleghe, Cheddleton,**..................1912
Near Leek.

Mr William Corden

TO JAMES BARBER,
CORN & CAKE MERCHANT,
AGENT FOR BURTON ALES & STOUT.

Marked sacks charged 1/6 each & allowed for if returned in good condition.
Terms :- Nett Cash in one Month.   5 per cent int. charged on all overdue accounts.

Fertilizers & Feeding Stuffs Act, 1893 & 1906. } I hereby declare that all Feeding Stuffs upon this Invoice not herein described as pure, are prepared from more than one substance or seed.

For analysis of Cake etc. see other side.

Many businesses, like these two, were rural, many like the Board Mill below still based on old water mills.

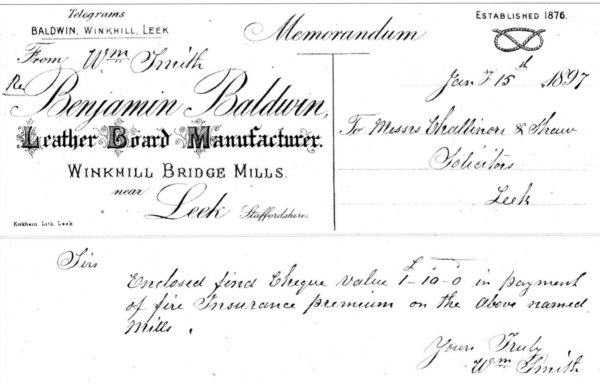

Telegrams
BALDWIN, WINKHILL, LEEK

Memorandum

ESTABLISHED 1876.

From Wm Smith

Re **Benjamin Baldwin,**
Leather Board Manufacturer.
WINKHILL BRIDGE MILLS.
near *Leek* Staffordshire.

Kirkham. Lith. Leek

Jan 15th 1897

To Messrs Challinor & Shaw
Solicitors
Leek

Sirs

Enclosed find Cheque value £1-10-0 in payment of fire Insurance premium on the above named Mills.

Yours Truly
Wm Smith

See also John Hargreaves page 238.

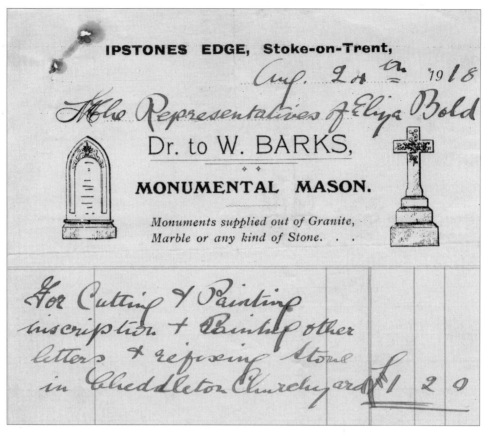

IPSTONES EDGE, Stoke-on-Trent,

Aug. 2nd 1918

The Representatives of Elija Bold

Dr. to W. BARKS,

MONUMENTAL MASON.

Monuments supplied out of Granite,
Marble or any kind of Stone. . .

For Cutting & Painting inscription + Painting other letters + refixing Stone in Cheddleton Churchyard £1 2 0

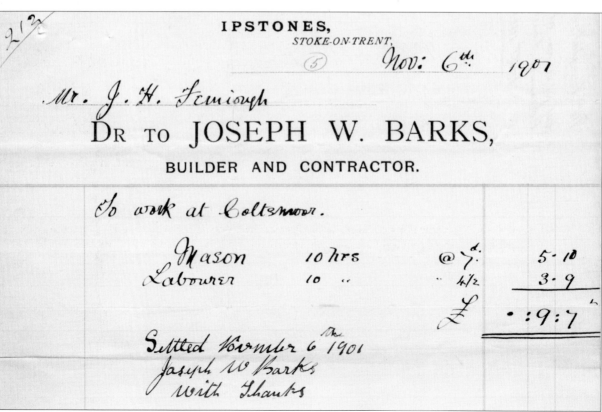

2 / 2

IPSTONES,
STOKE-ON-TRENT,
⑤   Nov: 6th   1901

Mr. J. H. Femiough

Dr to JOSEPH W. BARKS,

BUILDER AND CONTRACTOR.

To work at Coltsmoor.

Mason	10 hrs	@ 7d.	5 · 10
Labourer	10 "	" 4½	3 · 9
		£	· : 9 : 7

Settled November 6th 1901
Joseph W Barks
with Thanks

44

BUXTON ROAD,
LEEK, Aug 1883

M J Grace

⊁✠ Dr ∴ to ∴ Mathew ∴ Barlow, ✠⊱

BUILDER AND CONTRACTOR.

DEALER IN EVERY DESCRIPTION OF BUILDING MATERIALS.

1880			
Oct 16th To 30 Fire Brick 2/6		2	6
1881			
Mar 5th To 1 Cask of Romon Cement 11/		11	
„ 26th To 1 Bagg of Plaster 6/6		6	
May 7th To 12 Red Roof Tiles 8/	..	..	8
„ 21 To 3 Pecks of Keens Cement 1/6		4	6
Oct 1st To 1 Round Chimney pipe W.G		4	..
Nov 19th To 9 Valley Tiles @ 2½		1	10½
1883			
Feb 24th To 11 Capped Ridges @ 7		6	5
Aug 15th To 9 do do @ 7		5	3
	£	2	2 2½

This little bill represents the supply of building materials to Thomas Grace over a period of three years! Extended credit appears to have been a normal trade practice in those days, particularly between fellow traders.

C. WILFRED BARNETT,

STANLEY STREET, LEEK,

SOLE LOCAL AGENT FOR

WOLSELEY, HUMBER, MORRISS COWLEY, MORRISS OXFORD, BEAN, and STANDARD CARS.

CARS FOR HIRE.

B.S.A., Norton, A.J.S., New Imperial, Douglas, New Hudson, Levis, Royal Enfield, Motor Cycles.

B.S.A., Royal Enfield, New Hudson, Campion, Cycles

Any make Motor Car, Motor Cycle, or Lorry supplied to Order,

TELEPHONE 156.   GARAGE :—SNEYD STREET.

Barnett's garage was towards the bottom of Stanley Street where the present health shop is situated now.

C. WILFRED BARNETT, Motor Agent.

Sole local agent for the World Famous Morris Oxford and Cowley, Humber, Bean, Standard, Hillman, Daimler, Wolseley, Fiat, and Citroen cars.

COMMERCIAL VEHICLES.

MORRIS **8** cwt,. **10** cwt., **1** ton and **30** cwt. Lorries and Vans.

BEAN **12** cwt. and **30** cwt. Lorries and Vans.

MOTOR CYCLES.

A.J.S., Norton, B.S.A., Douglas. Enfield, New Imperial, Sunbeam and Levis.

PEDAL CYCLES.

Royal Enfield, B.S.A. Sunbeam and Campion.

Morris Oxford Saloon.
Unprecedented Value £250.

Any make of MOTOR, CAR. COMMERCIAL VEHICLE, MOTOR CYCLE or CYCLE supplied to order for Cash or by arrangement.

PETROL, OIL, GREASES, TYRES, ACCESSORIES of every description from Stock or by Return Rail.

REPAIRS & OVERHAULS to Cars, etc., of every description.

Stocks of New and Second-hand Cars and Motor Cycles always on hand for Sale.

DEPOT :—
Stanley Street, LEEK.

Tel. **156**
Day or Night.

GARAGE :—
Sneyd St., LEEK.

Central Show Rooms near Railway Station, Stoke-on-Trent.
Also Regent Street, Eccles, Manchester.

By Royal Letters Patent.

Xmas 1901

M Executers of the late Mr John Bradly

Derby Street

Dr to *Barnfather Bros.*

90 Gold & Silver Medals awarded for Excellence.

Prize

Carriage Builders.

STOKE-ON-TRENT, LEEK & ECCLES, MANCHESTER.

1901		£	s	d
May 31st	To amount of a/c rendered	-	19	10
July 5th	To cutting fincing & putting on 1 tyre	-	3	-
	To rivetting with 10 revits & pounds & touching up	-	1	8
		1	4	6

Settled
May 27. 1902
W Barnfather
With thanks

BARNFATHER Bros. Carriage Builders, 9 Haywood Street, Leek.
The ornate, elaborate billhead reflects the reputation of this highly-regarded firm of carriage builders. William & James Barnfather had works in Stoke Newington, Stoke-on-Trent and Eccles, as well as Leek. Founded in the 1870s, they took great pride in the painting of coats of arms to a high degree of accuracy, and won many prizes in open competitions. The fact that such a high quality firm was operating in Leek is another indication of the prosperity of the town at that time. The premises stood on the corner of Haywood Street and Shoobridge Street, and included extensive showrooms and workshops.

LEEK ⁖ & ⁖ STOKE.

Aug 24 1896

Mr W Prince Esqr Exectr

24 First Prize
Medals
Awarded.

24 First Prize
Medals
Awarded.

| HAYWOOD STREET, | | STOKE ROAD, |
| **LEEK.** | DR. TO W. & J. BARNFATHER, | **STOKE-ON-TRENT.** |

PRIZE ✦ CARRIAGE ✦ BUILDERS.

CENTRAL SHOW ROOMS:—TWO MINUTES FROM STOKE STATION.

1895		£	s	d
June 14	To 1 Pair of India Rubber Break Blocks		8	6
Nov 11	To new felloeing wheels round with 16 felloes	1	12	-
	To 1 Pair of Patent Steel Tyres	1	5	-
	To Varnishing Felloes 4 Coates		7	6
	To 1 new Wrought Iron lifting Jack for Wheels	-	15	-
	To 1 Pair of Rubber Break Blocks		8	6
	To Cleaning oiling & washering wheels		3	6
1896	To repairing Foot Rest	-	1	6
June 6	To tightening Tyres	-	7	-
	To 1 Pair of Rubber Break Blocks	-	8	6
June 24	To 1 Bottle of Varnish		1	-
		5	18	0

The invoice also tells us much about trading practice in the late 19th century - this is a full year's trading, June 1895 to June 1896, sent two months later (August) and paid a further three months later (November)! Cash flow in those days did not seem to be a problem!

RUSSELL STREET,

LEEK, *Mar 17.* 1892

Mrs Bestwick's Executors

Dr. to JOSEPH BARR,

PLUMBER,

GLAZIER AND GAS-FITTER.

1891			
June 25	Property 5 Russell St Repairing burst pipe & tap	2	6
Oct	Property 47 & 92 Grove St Repairing water taps	1	-
	11 Park Rd Repairing burst pipe	2	6
15	Ball Haye Rd Repairing taps	1	-
Nov 1	72 Grove St To papering bedroom 7 pieces paper	2	4
	Size, Paste & Time	4	-
Dec 30	84 Grove St. Repairing water pipe Lead pipe, Time & solder	2	6
Feb 11.	Ball Haye Rd Repairing burst pipe Lead pipe, Time & solder	3	6
		19	4

Settled 22/4/92
J. Barr

MEMORANDUM.

Barr £ 2.10.0

From

J. BARR,

Plumber, Gas-fitter, Painter & Glazier

ELECTRIC BELLS, SPEAKING TUBES,
&c., FIXED TO ORDER.

30, RUSSELL STREET,
LEEK.

To

LEEK, *Dec* 3rd 1894

Mrs S. Grace

Compton School Outhouses
To fixing lavatory basins. 1 New one
with taps + waste pipe and a stop tap
complete. 1 Draw-off tap & Stop tap
in infants W.C. for the sum of Two pounds
ten shillings.
£2 - 10 - 0

J Barr

RUSSELL STREET,

Leek, _____ May _____ 19 29.

M Iss. Magnier. Bradnop.

Dr. to JOSEPH BARR,

PLUMBER and DECORATOR.

GAS AND ELECTRIC LIGHTING.

ELECTRIC BELLS AND TELEPHONES FIXED AND REPAIRED.

Terms, Quarterly.   Estimates st

1929½

Jan 11. To repairing ball tap at property Cromwell Terrace.	
Time etc.	
Apl 2 To repairing bursts at property Kiln Lane,	
1" lead pipe. 2/6. 2-½" joints. 1/6.	

RUSSELL STREET   720

PLUMBING
PAINTING
GLAZING
PAPER
HANGING

RUSSELL STREET,
LEEK, *Dec 8* 190 8

M *W Challinor Esq/*

Dr. to JOSEPH BARR,
DECORATOR AND GAS=FITTER.

Electric Bells and Telephones Fixed and Repaired.

Dec.	Late Hoods house Property H Dishley Junction Road.			
	Drawing Room. To whitening Ceiling cornice & frieze, stripping & papering walls & Painting woodwork.			
	Bedroom. To Papering ceiling & walls Painting woodwork.			
	Bath Room & W.C. To whitening Ceilings & Coloring walls &c.			
	To limewashing Cellars Coal place &c.			
	To painting in Hall Staircase &c.	6	19	-
	1 New galvanized cylinder with Hand hole for cleaning out &c.	2	2	-
	1 New pull Chain To W.C.		1	6
	Time 10 hrs J Barr.		7	6
		£ 9	10	-

Settled 7/09
J Barr

ONE PENNY

Joseph Barr's shop was 30 Russell Street.
This very detailed memorandum gives a full specification for a painting and decorating job.

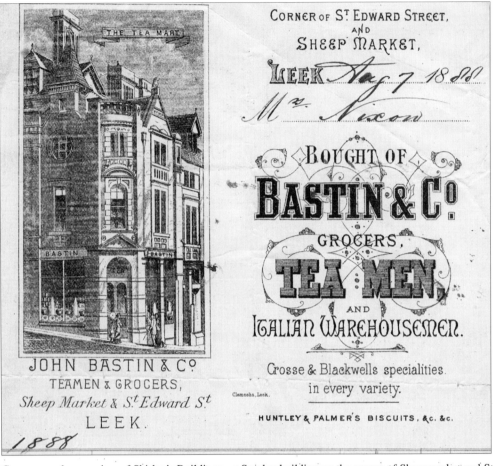

BASTIN & Co. were early occupiers of Shirley's Buildings - a Sugden building on the corner of Sheepmarket and St. Edward Street, built in 1875. The elaborate billhead indicates that John Bastin & Co. are the proprietors, and Kelly's Directory of 1892 also lists a Mary Bastin, grocer, at 38 St. Edward Street. This business was later taken over by Mr. E. Green, who built up a considerable reputation as a grocer and cheese factor. The architecture is still recognisable as the building which stands on the corner of Sheepmarket and St. Edward Street, an Indian restaurant at the time of writing, and at one time a Boots' store.

Barrow's printing works made a speciality of memorial cards. In Victorian times most families marked the death of a relative by sending these cards to family and friends, who often collected them. The firm was also well-equipped to meet the needs of the silk industry for pattern cards. Machine ruling was a method whereby pens would be set to rule the required number of cash columns on ledger paper which would then be bound into cash books and ledgers.

ESTABLISHED 1826.

ST EDWARD STREET, *Leek Exmas 41*
(LATE SPOUT STREET,)
AND LONDON MILLS,
LEEK, STAFFORDSHIRE.

W Challinor Esqr

Dr. to **H. D. BAYLEY,**
(*Late Beardmore*)

Silk Machinist, Agricultural Implement Maker, Hot Water Apparatus, Steam and Gas Fitter,

Wrought Tubes, Plain or Galvanized, Palisading, Iron Gates, Hurdles and Strained Wire Fencing, Fancy Wire Work, &c.   Agent for Mowing and Reaping Machines, Haymakers, Horse Rakes, Thrashing Machines, Horse-Power Works, Chaff Cutter, Pulpers, Mills, Winnowing Machines, Ploughs, Cultivators, Hoes, Drills, Chain Harrows, Steam Engines, Pumps, Hydraulic Rams, &c.

1891   ☞ *All kind of Implements procured to order from the leading Makers Carriage free, at List Prices.*

		£	s	d
To acct Rendered —		3	12	2½
Dec 2 Rep piston Making valve Joint 3/			3	0
4 Grinding pump Clacks 3/3			3	3
23 & 25 fitting pipe to from pump to				
well fitting new Rings in Cylinder				
2½ Days 12/6 · 1 Day 7/ · 1 Day 6/		4	0	6
40 feet of ½" Steam pipe 3½"			11	8
4 ½ sockets 1/ · 1 nut 3½" 2 Screws ½			2	5½
2 nipples 6" one Copper Rose 2/6			3	0
2 ½ Taps Keys 12/6 · 1 file 1/4			13	10
2 Bolt Lever 6"				6
6 new Brass Rings for piston 3/6 each 1. 1. 0				
Allowance 1/ —			1	0
Repairs to Engine & Boiler —		£ 7	12	5

settled
Feby 22/2
H D Bayley

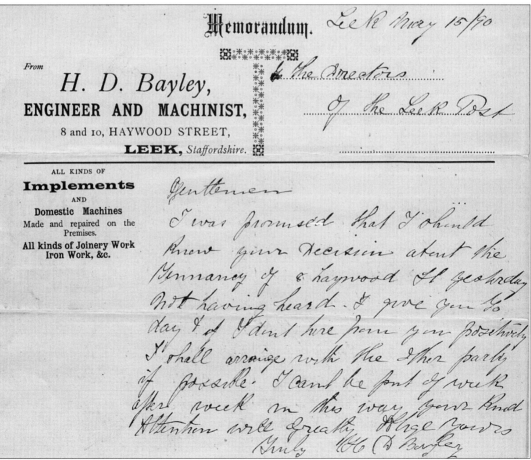

8 & 10 Haywood Street Mill, LEEK, Staffordshire.

To To Directors of Leek Post

Dr. to H. D. Bayley,

Engineer and Machinist, Agricultural Implement Maker, Hot Water Apparatus, Steam & Gas Fitter.
WROUGHT TUBES AND FITTINGS ALWAYS IN STOCK.

Agent for Mowing and Reaping Machines, Haymakers, Horse Rakes, Thrashing Machines,
Horsepower Works, Chaff Cutters, Pulpers, Mills, Winnowing Machines,
Ploughs, Cultivators, Hoes, Drills, Chain Harrows, Steam Engines, Pumps, Hydraulic Rams, &c.
☞ *All kinds of Implements procured to Order from the leading Makers, Carriage Free, at List Prices.*
ALL SORTS OF SILK MACHINERY ON IMPROVED PRINCIPLES.

1890

April 1	To 13 weeks firing	at 3/	1	19	0
	To 13 weeks grease	at 4/6	2	18	6
	To 10 weeks for room	at 3/-	1	10	4
	To 4 3/4 Yrs over time			7	2
			6	15	0

Memorandum. Leek May 15/90

From

H. D. Bayley,
ENGINEER AND MACHINIST,
8 and 10, HAYWOOD STREET,
LEEK, Staffordshire.

To the Directors

of the Leek Post

ALL KINDS OF
Implements
AND
Domestic Machines
Made and repaired on the
Premises.
All kinds of Joinery Work
Iron Work, &c.

Gentlemen

I was promised that I should know your decision about the tenancy of 8 Haywood St yesterday. Not having heard. I give you to day & if I don't hear from you positively I shall arrange with the other party if possible. I cant be put off week after week in this way your kind attention will greatly oblige yours

truly H. D. Bayley

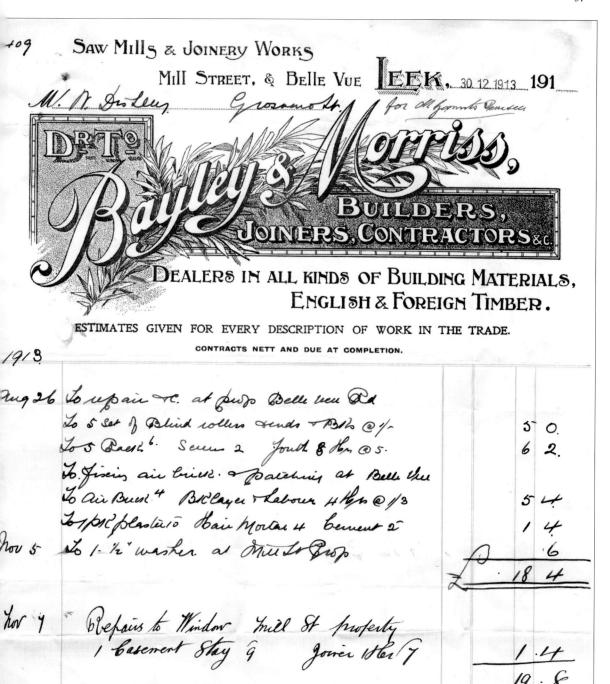

109

SAW MILLS & JOINERY WORKS

MILL STREET, & BELLE VUE LEEK, 30.12.1913 191

Mr N. Dooley   Grosvenor St   for All Garments Premises

DR TO Bayley & Morriss,
BUILDERS,
JOINERS, CONTRACTORS &c.

DEALERS IN ALL KINDS OF BUILDING MATERIALS,
ENGLISH & FOREIGN TIMBER.

ESTIMATES GIVEN FOR EVERY DESCRIPTION OF WORK IN THE TRADE.
CONTRACTS NETT AND DUE AT COMPLETION.

1913

Aug 26	To repair &c. at Prop Belle Vue Rd	
	To 5 Set of Blind rollers Ends & Brkts @1/-	5 0.
	To 5 Back'b. Screw 2 South 8 Hrs @ 5.	6 2.
	To fixing air brick. & Patching at Belle Vue	
	To Air Brick'd Bricklayer & Labour 4 Hrs @ 1/3	5 4
	To 1/2 R plaster'o Hair Mortar 4 Cement 2	1 4
Nov 5	To 1-1/2" washer. at Mill St Prop	6
	£	18 4
Nov 7	Repairs to Window Mill St property	
	1 Casement Stay 9 Joiner 1 Hr 7	1.4
		19.8

This very imposing heading for a building and joinery business is an indication
of the quality of printing which local printers were able to offer.

EAM JOINERY WORKS.
MILL STREET, LEEK,   189

To the Executors of the Late Mr H Hales

To BAYLEY & MORRISS,
CONTRACTORS, JOINERS, BUILDERS, CABINET MAKERS & UNDERTAKERS.

PACKING CASES MADE TO ORDER ON THE SHORTEST NOTICE.

1895

1895		£	s	d
June 15	To one French Polished oak coffin stuffed and Linen with Best Brass Mountings Engraved	3	15	0
	To one Flannel Shroud		7	6
	To Hearse and Pair of Horses To Cemetery		12	6
	To 47 Memory Cards and Envelopes Silvered Bordered		5	0
	To Grave & Burial Fees at Cemetery	£5	1	6
	nett	£ 10	1	6

Received with thanks
by J Bayley for Bayley & Morriss
Aug 26 1895

Bayley and Morris were one of the many local builders and joiners who offered an undertaking service.
It is interesting to note the cost of a quality Victorian coffin with all fittings: £3-15-0.

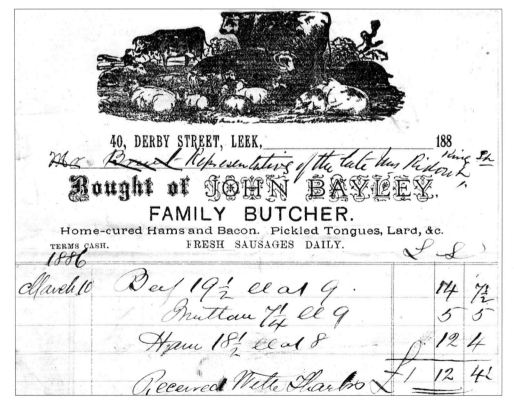

40, DERBY STREET, LEEK,   188

The Representatives of the late Mrs Ridout King St

Bought of JOHN BAYLEY,
FAMILY BUTCHER.
Home-cured Hams and Bacon. Pickled Tongues, Lard, &c.
TERMS CASH.   **FRESH SAUSAGES DAILY.**

1886			£	s	d
March 10	Beef 19½ ℔ at 9			14	7½
	Mutton 7¼ ℔ 9			5	5
	Ham 18½ ℔ at 8			12	4
	Received With Thanks	£	1	12	4½

It was often the custom for butchers in Victorian times to display their meat hanging outside the shop in the fresh air - there would be no vehicle pollution in those days!

JOHN BAYLEY, Derby Street, Leek.
Established in the early 1870s, this butcher had his slaughterhouse in West Street. Mr. Bayley had some considerable experience of the trade before setting up his own business, which occupied a prime site in Derby Street, where he built up a very extensive circle of customers. The shop developed a method of trading whereby no money changed hands over the counter. The customer's requests were supplied by the counter sales staff, and payment was made to the cashier, who sat in a booth at the rear of the shop. This same system of payment operated for many years when the firm continued to trade as Bayley & Son.

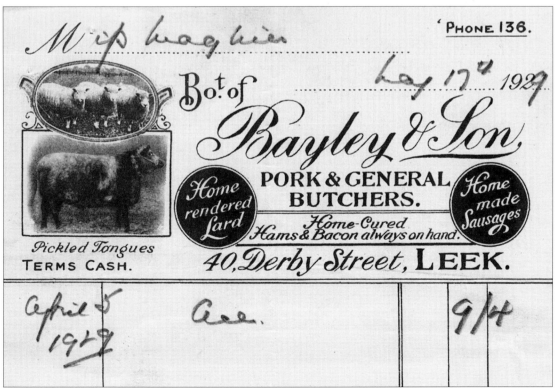

40 Derby Street, Leek,

.................................190

Mr *Dilling*

Bot. of BAYLEY & SON,

PORK & GENERAL BUTCHERS.

Home-cured Hams and Bacon always on hand.   —o—   Pickled Tongues.
Home-rendered Lard.   Home-made Sausages.   TERMS—CASH.

Nov 16/1909	Bag & Kidney 2¼ 7½		1 - 5
Dec 4 "	Bag 6¼	8	4 - 2
4	Steak & Kidney 26	8	1 - 4
	Bag 4½	5½	3 - 4
18	Lard 10	8	5 " 1
22	Bag 2½	8	1 - 5
24	Bag 1½	9	1 " 1½
	Sausage 2½	4	1 " 5½
	Bag 5 3/4	8	3 " 10
	Kidney	4	4
30	Bag 2"	9	1 " 6
Jan 1st/1910	Sausage 1½	7	10½
	Bag 7½	8½	5 " 4
4	Chop	4	4
4	Bag 1½	9	1 " 1½

CHRISTMAS FARE

Once again We have made SPECIAL PURCHASES of

PRIZE CATTLE

From SMITHFIELD CLUB SHOW.

This SHOW has again excelled all Previous Exhibits. It is representative of
the Finest Breeds of Cattle, supplying all the demands of the Present Day for
Quality, as desired by the British Public.

SEE WINDOWS FOR PRIZE CARDS.

SIDNEY BAYLEY,

BUTCHER,

DERBY STREET, LEEK.

J. Brindley Bayley occupied the Derby Street/Market Street corner site.

J. BRINDLEY BAYLEY,

THE PEOPLES' DRAPER.

DRESS MATERIALS.

Always a Special Show.   Novelties in
HOSIERY, BLOUSES, GLOVES,
TIES, LACES, CORSETS, BELTS, ETC.

Every variety of patterns.

DERBY STREET & MARKET STREET, **LEEK.**

Joseph Bayley took over the old-established drapery business of Joshua Andrew, formerly in Custard (now Stanley) Street.

ME

From

JOSEPH BAYLEY,

(LATE ANDREW),

Draper, Milliner & Mantle Warehouse,

SILK MERCER, &c.,

MARKET PLACE,

ESTABLISHED OVER A CENTURY.   Leek.

Shaws solicitors

Leek

policy 1426778 — I have obtained a contract for Repairs for damage done by the fire at 44 Fountain St — I think the neighbours who carried water deserve 2/6 (or The House would have been burned down) Kindly give it your Early attention as its awkward the WC cannot be used the Seat being destroyed Yours Faithfully J Bayley

BRETTLES HOSIERY

DRAPERS | J. BAYLEY & SONS | COSTUMIERS

J. BAYLEY & SONS
THE DRAPERS & COSTUMIERS
⊞ ⊞ LEEK ⊞ ⊞

Joseph Bayley's business later removed
to this address in Derby Street, where it
continued to trade for many years.

Apl 8   19 29

...BY STREET,
...EEK.

...hbourne Rd

BOUGHT OF . . . .

J. Bayley & Sons,
DRAPERS AND COSTUMIERS.

1929

	£	s	d
Coat 68/9	3	8	11
Frock 56/11	2	16	11
4 Harp 4½		1	6
1 7½			7½
1			9
Corset		8	11
2 Hose 2/11		5	10
Gloves		2	3
Vest		11	9
		7	11
		1	3	6
	9	8	10½
	3	15	0
	£ 5	13	10½
		12	6
	£ 6	6	4½

LEEK Jan 25 19 30 ^^3493

Received *from*

Miss Maynier Habrouska

£ 6/6/4½

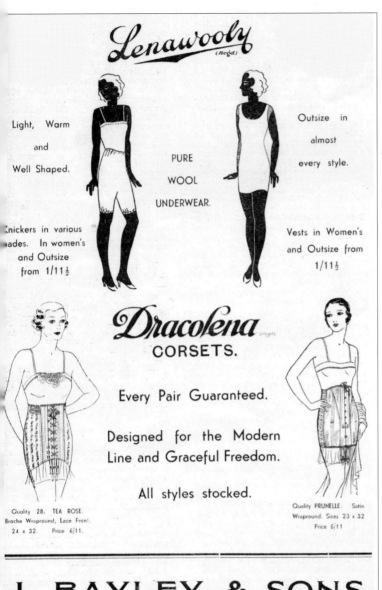

Lenawooly (Regd.)

Light, Warm
and
Well Shaped.

PURE
WOOL
UNDERWEAR.

Outsize in
almost
every style.

Knickers in various
shades. In women's
and Outsize
from 1/11½

Vests in Women's
and Outsize from
1/11½

Dracolena (Regd.)
CORSETS.

Every Pair Guaranteed.

Designed for the Modern
Line and Graceful Freedom.

All styles stocked.

Quality 28. TEA ROSE.
Broche Wrapround, Lace Front.
24 x 32.   Price 6/11.

Quality PRUNELLE.   Satin
Wrapround. Sizes 23 x 32
Price 6/11

J. BAYLEY & SONS,
Derby Street & Sheep Market, Leek.

These adverts appeared in "Leek News" during the 1930s.

*There is a special seasonal
selection of Dance Shoes at
the Benefit Shoe Shop. -*

*The newest designs, exclusive
models - and reasonable prices.*

G 127   6/11
The 1930-31 Dress
Shoes at the Benefit
Shoe Shop are most
appealing. Moderate prices too.

G 128   6/11
Black Satin Court
with dainty brilliant
buckle. - Quality
material and smart
finish.

G 532   6/11
All the new designs
in Tinsels & Brocades. - Here is a
brocade in delightful shades of pink
and blue with silver

G 106   4/11
Very neat Sandal
Bar style in a reliable Black Satin.
See the complete
range of popular
priced dance shoes.

*Comfortable Slippers and charming
Shoes are most suitable and sensible
presents. This week the windows
are replete with these always acceptable gifts. . .   Call To-day*

THE BENEFIT SHOE SHOP
38, Derby Street, LEEK.

The Late 14, Market Place, Leek, Nov 2 1893

Mrs E M Princes Funeral A/c

Bot. of Joseph Bayley

(Late ANDREW)

Linen and Woollen Draper, Silk Mercer,

HABERDASHER, HOSIER & GLOVER.

FAMILY MOURNING. FUNERALS FURNISHED.

1893

June 30	5 Zephyr 7½ 20 Holland 5½ Corsets 5/11		18	2½
July 6	5 Hose 12½ 3/4 Linen 1/9½ 3 Calico 3½		7	5½
" 8	1 Cotton 1 1 Gloves 3/6 4 Rbn 3½ ½ Do 5		3	11½
" "	1 Skirt 4/11 1 Do 2/6 3 Rbn 8½ 2 Shirts 5/11½	1	1	5½
" 11	3 Hdkfs 8 1 Rent 1/11 1 Do 11½ 2 Lining 3½		5	5½
" 19	3/4 Silk 5/9 Marking Frayed Strings 1/6		5	11
" 25	1¼ Gossamer 1/4 Btns 6½ Do 7½ 3 Socks 1/-		5	10
" "	2 P Btns 6½ 1 Hose 2/3 1 Belting 3½ 1 Veil 1/-		4	7½
" "	Rent Shirting 3/6 4 Flannel 11½ 1 Rug 4/11		12	3
28	2 Btns 2½ 2 Do 1 1 Do 2 10 Towelling 5½		5	4
" "	2 Lace 3½ 1 Gloves 1/4 5 Calico 4½ 1 Belting 3½		4	1
31	1 Rbn 5½ 1 Lace 3½ 1½ Silk 2/11½ Hose 1/4		6	6½
Aug 10	1½ Towelling 5½ 1 Gloves 1/8½ 1½ Flannel 1/-		3	11
" 11	1 Rent Muslin 1/11 4 Satteen 6½ 4 Rbn 9½		7	3
" 22	12 Indian Cashmere 2/4 8 Silk Kaken 7½	1	13	0
" "	2 Rbn 1/3½ 4 Lining 6½ 1¼ Silk 5/6 2 Steels 6½		12	8½
" "	18 Braid 5½ 9 Do 4½ 8 braid 1½		12	7
24	1½ Button 5½ 2 Gloves 3/6 2½ Lace 7		9	2
Sep 1	2¼ Belting 3½ 2 Button 6½ 2½ Do 4½		2	9
" 3	3 Shirts 5/11½ 6 Rbn 3½ 4 Cord 1		19	11½
" 12	3 Flannel 1/3 6 Brown Rbn 4½		6	0
" 16	9 Blk Satin Cloth 2/11½ 3 Blue Flannel Jackets 4/11	2	1	4½
" 17	1 Vest 5/- 3 Ornaments 6½ 1½ Rbn 7½		7	7
" 23	1 Squirrel Boas 27/6 Wadding 6	1	8	0
" 24	8 Domett 11½ 12 Rbn 4½ Silk 4		12	2
" "	2 Rugs for Mr Tynney 8/6		17	0
" 28	1 Pr Gloves 3/6 4½ Flase 1 Holland 6½		6	3½

This highly detailed invoice represents a large amount of trading - it appears that a sale was made about 3 times a week! Clearly a very regular customer!

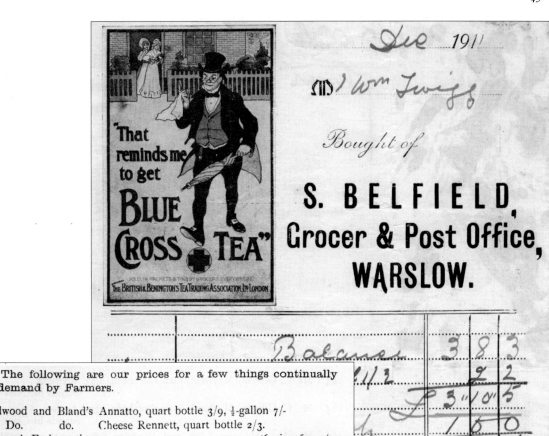

The following are our prices for a few things continually in demand by Farmers.

Fullwood and Bland's Annatto, quart bottle 3/9, ½-gallon 7/-
   Do.   do.   Cheese Rennett, quart bottle 2/3.

Elliman's Embrocation	...	...	...	2/6 size for 1/9.
Mc.Dougall's Sheep Dip	...	...	...	1/- „ 10½d.
Do. do.	...	...	...	3/- „ 2/6.
Day's Red Drinks ...	...	...	...	1/- „ 10½d.
Do. Black Drinks	...	...	...	1/8 „ 1/6.
Do. White Oils ...	...	...	...	2/6 „ 2/2.
Silver Churn Butter Colouring	...	...	6d. „ 4½d.
Do. do.	...	...	...	1/- „ 9d.
Danish Butter Colouring ...	...	...	6d. „ 5d.
Do. do.	...	...	...	1/- „ 9½d.
Tomlinson's Butter Powder...	..	...	6d. „ 4½d.
Do. do.	...	...	...	1/- „ 9d.

Epsom Salts for Cattle, 1d. per lb. 7 lbs. for 6d.
Machine Oils for Carts, etc., 4½d. per pint. 2/6 per gallon.
Best Raw Linseed Oil, 4½d. per pint. 2/6 per gallon.
Saltpetre, lump or powdered, 5d. per lb.
Castor Oil for Cattle, 6d. per lb.
Best Sulphur for Cattle, 3d. per lb.
Turpentine, 5d. per pint.
Carriage Candles, 6d., 8d. and 10d. per pound.
Insect Powder, 6d. size for 4½d.
Condition Powders for Horses, in 1/- Tins.

———

BENTLEY'S DRUG Co.,

(LIMITED,)

SHEEP MARKET, LEEK.

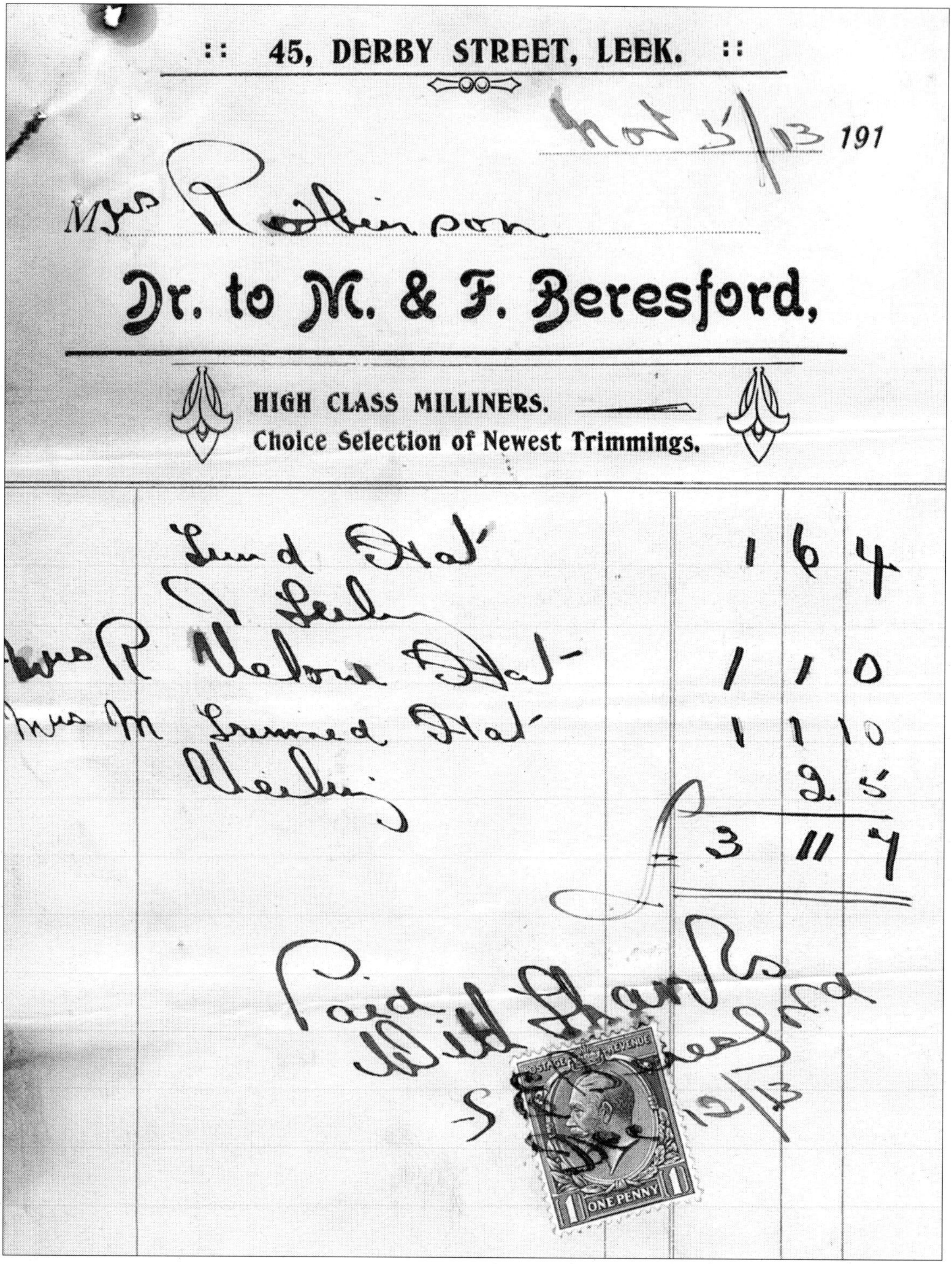

:: 45, DERBY STREET, LEEK. ::

Nov 5/13 191

Mrs Robinson

Dr. to M. & F. Beresford,

HIGH CLASS MILLINERS.
Choice Selection of Newest Trimmings.

	£	s	d
Trimmed Hat	1	6	4
Mrs R Velour Hat	1	1	0
Mrs M Trimmed Hat	1	1	10
Veiling		2	5
	£3	11	7

Paid with thanks M. Beresford

5 Dec 12/13

POSTAGE & REVENUE ONE PENNY

⋆ Memorandum. ⋆

FROM **GEO. H. BERMINGHAM,**
FOUNTAIN MILLS,
Leek.

Telegraphic Address:
"FOUNTAIN, LEEK."

16 *April* 1891

To *J Challinor Esq*

Leek

D' Sir,

I have received enclosed from the Directors
of the Bank for re-signature

Please place the same before my Mother
and M' Gould and return it to me when signed

REGISTERED
TRADE MARK

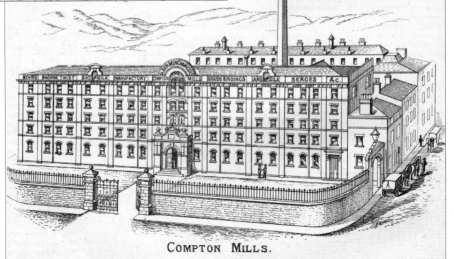

COMPTON MILLS.

TRADE MARK
PAGODA

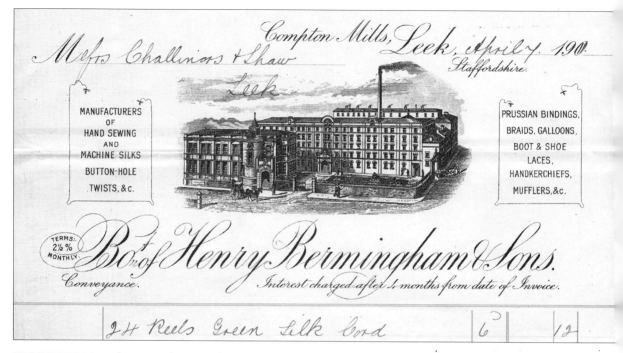

Compton Mills, Leek, April 7 190

Mefrs Challinors & Shaw

Leek Staffordshire.

MANUFACTURERS OF HAND SEWING AND MACHINE SILKS BUTTON-HOLE TWISTS, &c.

PRUSSIAN BINDINGS. BRAIDS, GALLOONS, BOOT & SHOE LACES, HANDKERCHIEFS, MUFFLERS, &c.

TERMS: 2½ % MONTHLY.

Bot of Henry Bermingham & Sons.

Conveyance. *Interest charged after 4 months from date of Invoice.*

24 Reels Green Silk Cord	6	12

HENRY BERMINGHAM & SONS, Compton Mills, Leek. The company was founded in 1832 by Mr. Henry Bermingham, who died in 1845, when the business was carried on by his two sons, Henry and James. Henry became sole proprietor following the death of his brother in 1869. The main products were sewing silks, braids, bindings and fancy trimmings, silk facings and handkerchiefs. The large Compton Mill was aquired by Job White in 1909. The original factory was in Fountain Street.

COMPTON SILK MILLS.

J & H. BERMINGHAM.

Leek, 25 August 1882

Bermingham's original factory was in Fountain Street. It later became part of the Brough, Nicholson and Hall factory complex. Compton Silk Mills eventually became Job White Ltd.

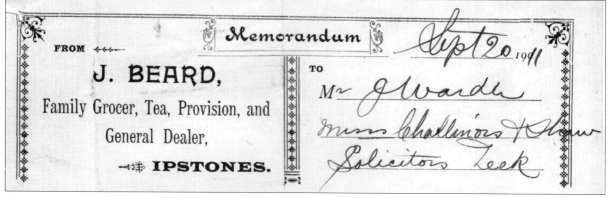

Memorandum *Sept 20 1911*

FROM

J. BEARD,

Family Grocer, Tea, Provision, and General Dealer,

IPSTONES.

TO *Mr J Wardle*

Messrs Challinors & Shaw

Solicitors Leek

7, BALL HAYE STREET,

LEEK, *Jan* – 1892

Miss Mellor

DR. TO WILLIAM BESTWICK,

Iron and Tin-Plate Worker, and General Dealer.

All kinds of Factory Work and Packing Cases done on the premises at shortest notice
and at reasonable prices.

5 *per cent. charged on over-due Accounts.*

W. BESTWICK,

IRON AND TIN PLATE WORKER,

25, RUSSELL ST., LEEK,

AND

MARKET PLACE ON WEDNESDAY.

All orders promptly attended to on the shortest notice.

Below:
Leek looking from Ball Haye Park
showing some of its many textile mills
in the early 20th century.

STOCKWELL STREET ~~AND CHURCH STREET~~, LEEK,

Mʳˢ Alsop april 1st 9 —   1856

BOUGHT OF BEVINS ,
TAILORS AND DRAPERS.

		£	s	d
1 wascot Repairing prefsing & nue button		"	"	10
1 pair mixtin trouser nue Bottoms & Binding Round top & faul down & && nue button hols		"	2	6
1 pair Black trouser faul binding & Seats Repairing & nue Button hols & prefsing all over & & & &		"	2	0
1 Cort 10 hours workmanship & Brade for Binding all Round & flaps & hands & Sowing & prefsing all over & Alpaca for lining		1	5	6
		£ "	10	10

payment recd, i Rent.

Edmund Bevins was a bespoke tailor, offering not only garments made to measure, but also a service for repairs and alterations.

The bill opposite- which is continued on the next page, page 52 - is from William D. Billing, 23 Osborne Street, and represents a large amount of building work for the Challinor family.

Residence
22, OSBORNE STREET.

OSBORNE STREET.

LEEK, *April* 19 1 0

M⌀ J. Challinor

Dr. to W. D. BILLING,
JOINER and BUILDER.

Dealer in BRICKS, TILES, PIPES, CEMENT, PLASTER, & all kinds of Building Materials.

Estimates given for every description of work connected with the Building Trade.

To week ending

1910			£	s	d
Jan 7th	Bricklayer & Labourers time to Repairing Roofs				
	Rebuilding Wall Pointing, & Plastering front (in Cement				
	at M⌀ E Challinor's Stockwell S⌀ 30½ 1/3	1	18	1½
	1 Bag Cement 9/6 5 Barrows Mortar 4/2 16 - 2/4 x 1/4 3 Cakes		16	0
	50 Pressed Brick 3/- Carting 1/-		4	0
Feb 4th	1 Bricklayers & Lab time to Roofs New Drain & manhole				
	Rep⌀ &c at Grindon - 42½ 1/3	2	13	1½
Grindon	25 - 4" Glazed pipes 12/6 2 - 4 x 4 Junctions 3/- 5 - 4" bends 2/4		17	5
	1 - 6" Gully & Iron Grid 4/- 2 Sink waste pipes 2/-		6	0
	1 - Iron Manhole Frame & Cover 10/6 50 tiles 3/6 10 - tile & half 10		13	10
	1 Bag Cement 9/6 Carting 1/- Lodgings 4/-		19	6
Mar 12th	Labourer taking down fences to form gaps. &				
	opening out Water Course at Rider's Fields 50 6	1	5	0
" 5th	Labourers fixing Scaffolding to Gable & Roof at 37½ 6		18	9
	Bricklayer - M⌀ J. Kinsey Ball Haye Green 2 9		1	6
	1 Bag Cement 9/6 Black Sand 9/6 -		8	0
" 12th	Bricklayer to Stripping roof retiling pointing				
	Chimneys, Gable & Side rebuilding Scullery Wall 53½ 9	2	1	7½
	Labourer to Floors in house &c & above - 53½ 6½	1	10	1
	" to Above - 53½ 6	1	7	9
	400 ft Tile Laths 5/4 100 Tiles 3/- 12 Tile & Half 1/- 20 ease 1/-		12	4
	120 Pressed Brick 5/- 70 - 6 Quarries 4/3 5 feb 2 lath nails 10½		10	3½
	6 Barrows Mortar & Hair 6/- 6 Blue plinth Brick 9		7	3
	1 Sink waste pipe 1/- 1½ Bag Cement 9/9		10	9
	Joiners making to Making fixing New Windows 1/9 8¾		12	4½
	Apprentice to Scullery & Glazing same 3 4		1	0
	3 ft 6 x 3 13 10 ft x 3 x 2½ 1/5 3 ft x 3 x 2 4½ 9 ft x 2 x 2 9	3	1½
	3 ft 6 x 2 x 1 3 Sash Rails 1/6 Butt & screws 5		8
	3 ft 6 x 6 x 1 4 9 Bottom		11

Residence
22, OSBORNE STREET.

OSBORNE STREET.

LEEK, ...19

M ....

Dr. to W. D. BILLING,

JOINER and BUILDER.

Dealer in BRICKS, TILES, PIPES, CEMENT, PLASTER, & all kinds of Building Materials.

Estimates given for every description of work connected with the Building Trade.

				£	s	d
	— Brought Forward —			19	3 (2)	8 (10½)
Mar 18	Bricklayer at Kinsey's —	6	9		4	6
	Do —	6	6½		3	3
	Labourers taking down Scaffold &c —	13	6		6	6
	50 Roof tile 3/- 6 tile & Half 6 1 Bag Cement 6/6				10	0
	2 B^s Sand 8 1 Barrow Hair Mortar 1/-				1	8
	2 - 6ft lengths 4½ Gutter 3/6 1 Angle 1/- ½ Doz Spout Bolts 3				4	9
	3 lbs putty 4½ 2 lbs Lead paint 10 1 lbs nails 2½				1	5
	12 ft x 2½ x 1 Mould 1/- 1 = 3" Butt hinge 3 1 Axle Pulley				1	6
	3 Blind Cord Racks 1/9 2 Casement Fasten 1/-				2	9
	1 Doz 1½ screws 2 Carting Scaffold &c Kinseys 2/-				2	2
" 24th	Bricklayer & Lab at Repairs to out buildings					
(10/9)	Roofs &c at Mr Bray's Ladderidge	29½	½	1	13	10
	Joiners to Windows in house	20	8¾		14	7
	Apprentice	14	4		4	8
	40 = 6 Quarries 2/6 6 - 1 ft ½ pipes for feeding troughs 12/-				14	6
	5 - B^s Mortar 4/8 1 Bag Cement 6/6 18 yds Sash cord 1/6				12	8
	Clout nails 3 15 ft x 11 x 1¼ 4/3 14 ft x 9 x 1 2/4 15 ft x 2½ x 1¼ 1/3				6	1
	15 ft x 6 x 1 1/10½ for New Barge Boards				1	10½
	62 ft x 5½ x 1 T.&G. 5/2 12 ft x 6 x 1½ Bands 2/-				7	2
	2 lbs Wrot nail 7 4 lbs Lead paint 1/8				2	3
	6 lbs nails 1/3 ½ Doz 3½ Bolts & nuts 6				1	9
	1 pair Wrot Band Hinges 2/- 2 Doz 2" screws 4				2	4
	Carting 2 Loads 3/-				3	0
	Joiners time to making Hanging Doors &c	33¾	8¾	1	4	0½
	Apprentice	28	4		9	4
	Bricklayer & Labourers to Repairs	37	½	1	18	2
April 1st	Joiners time to New Doors —	13	8¾		9	5½

Settled Sept 12/1910 W. D. Billing

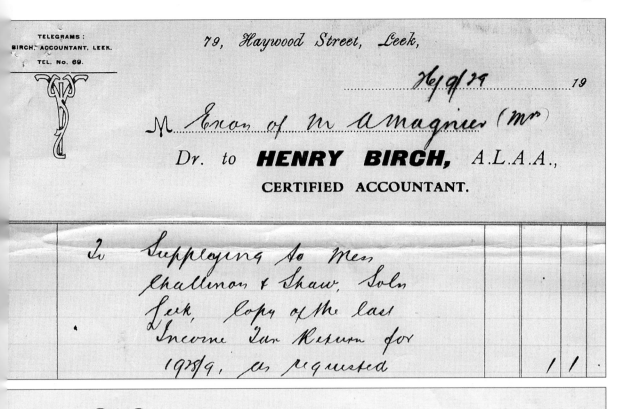

79, *Haywood Street, Leek,*

26/9/29 19

M Exor of M A Magnier (Mr)

Dr. to **HENRY BIRCH,** A.L.A.A.,

CERTIFIED ACCOUNTANT.

To Supplying to Mess
Challinor & Shaw, Solrs
Leek, copy of the last
Income Tax Return for
1928/9, as requested 1 1

WM. BIRCH,
PUBLIC ACCOUNTANT.

PUBLIC AUDITOR
APPOINTED BY THE LORDS'
COMMISSIONERS OF HIS MAJESTY'S
TREASURY
(FOR THE UNITED KINGDOM)
FOR THE PURPOSES OF
THE FRIENDLY AND INDUSTRIAL
SOCIETYS' ACTS.
1876 AND 1893.

TELEGRAMS: BIRCH. ACCOUNTANT, LEEK.

77, HAYWOOD STREET,
LEEK, STAFFS.

Gents.—

Cycles. Cycles.

TAYLOR & BIRCH
**Cycle and Motor
Manufacturers,**
DERBY ST., LEEK,
STAFFS.

Machines Built to Order.
Repairs while you wait.
Enamelling and Plating—
SPECIALITY.
Machines on Easy Payments.
Cycles and Tandems on Hire.
All Accessories in Stock.
GOOD ACCOMMODATION FOR CYCLISTS.

TAYLOR & BIRCH
MANUFACTURERS
CROWN CYCLE,
DERBY ST., LEEK
STAFFS.

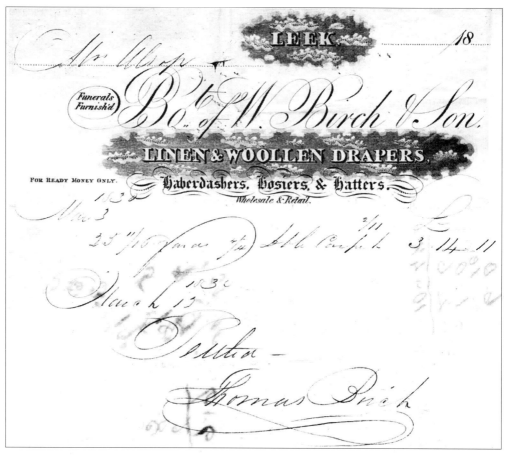

This invoice boldly states "FOR READY MONEY ONLY" suggesting that credit was difficult to obtain from W. Birch & Son. Indeed, it appears that this bill was settled in 10 days! It is interesting to contrast this with other invoices, which show considerably extended credit!

3, *Church Lane,*

LEEK, *June 30th* 18*94*

Messrs *Challinors & Shaw*

To THOS. H. BISHTON,

Solicitor.

1894		*Macalpine & Tymney*				
June	24	To my charge for copy affidavit of Dr C. H Braddon fos 9.			"	30.
		The like copy affidavit of Messrs Macalpine & Hilditch fos 23.			"	7	8.

111

1, Stanley Street, LEEK, *Xmas* 1879

Exrs of the Late Mr Goldstraw

Bought of **J. B. BLADES,**

(LATE C. BLADES,)

DISPENSING CHEMIST,

ASSOCIATE OF THE PHARMACEUTICAL SOCIETY, (BY EXAMINATION,)

Patent Medicines, Wax, Spermaceti, Composition Candles, Spices, Coffees, Genuine Teas,

British and Foreign Wines &c.

Five per cent. interest charged on Overdue Accounts.

July	To account delivered		11	
Aug 6.	Condition Powder 1/– (Dec) Cowslip Wine 1/7 (9) Mass Paste	2	7	6
9.	Calvefat Jelly 1/– (18) Jelly 1/6. (20) Jelly 2/8	5	2	
21	12 lbs Linseed Meal 5/– 2 Cowslip Wine 3/2	8	2	
		£ 1. 7. 5.		

Christopher Blades was one of only four druggists listed in White's 1851 Directory, having made his first appearance in William's Directory of 1846. J.B. Blades first appears in the Leek Commercial Directory of 1883, and continues to trade well into the 20th century.

— Established over a Century. —

MEMO. from

BLADES & SON,

DISPENSING & PHOTOGRAPHIC

CHEMISTS.

. . LEEK.

SOLE PROPRIETORS of— "TONO" the new Tonic, 1s. per bottle   "LEMONELLA," the new Lemon Fruit Drink, 4d.
VELVETTA SKIN CREAM for Soft White Hands, 6d. and 1s.
SULPHUR HAIR RESTORER, 1s. per bottle.   STIMULATING ESSENCE for the Hair, 1s. per bottle.
ETC , ETC

56

5, STANLEY STREET, **Leek,** Jan 1910

Dr Taylor.

J. B. BLADES & SON,

Bought of ~~Johnson & Son~~

Interest charged on
over-due accounts at the rate of
5 per cent per annum.

Family and **Dispensing Chemists.**

Date	Item		£	s	d
July 2	Shampoo 2 (16) Tooth Pd 10			1	
19	Sulphur Lg 4 (aug 24) Corn Rings 6				10
Sept 1	Angier 1/1½ (9) Draught 4			1	5½
13	Sen Lea 1/_ (Oct 19) Angier = 2/6			3	6
Oct 19	Tooth Pd 10 (27) Angier 2/6			3	4
27	Hazeline Snow 1/_ (Nov 5) Loz 4			1	4
Nov 5	Angier 2/6 (12) ditto 2/6 Lg 4½			5	4½
23	Angier 4/6 (25) Corn Rings 7			5	1
Dec 9	Angier 4/6 (21) Lg 4			4	10
		£	1	6	9
	Errors			1	
		£	1	5	9

Received

BLADES & SON
DISPENSING
CHEMISTS
LEEK

May 22/10

J B Blades

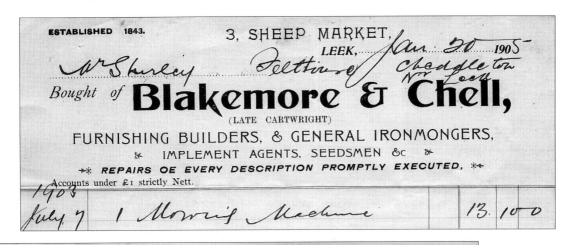

ESTABLISHED 1843.

3, SHEEP MARKET,

LEEK, *Jan. 20 1905*

Mr Shirley   Pethiver   Cheddleton Nr Leek

Bought of **Blakemore & Chell,**

(LATE CARTWRIGHT)

FURNISHING BUILDERS, & GENERAL IRONMONGERS,

IMPLEMENT AGENTS, SEEDSMEN &c

REPAIRS OE EVERY DESCRIPTION PROMPTLY EXECUTED,

Accounts under £1 strictly Nett.

1903			
July 7	*1 Mowing Machine*	*13*	*10 0*

ESTABLISHED 1843.

3, SHEEP MARKET,

LEEK, *Apl. 1902.*

Mr Heath & Lowe.   Builders Bruce St Leek

Bought of **BLAKEMORE & CHELL,**

(LATE CARTWRIGHT).

FURNISHING BUILDERS' & GENERAL IRONMONGERS,

IMPLEMENT AGENTS, &C.

REPAIRS OF EVERY DESCRIPTION PROMPTLY EXEC

Looking down Sheep Market the old-established business of Blakemore and Chell is still trading today on the left on the corner of Dog Lane. It was formerly Daniel Cartwright (see page 101).

We keep abreast of all progress in the science of ~ Boot Repairing. ~

Up-to-date plant and modern methods enable us to execute all repairs with neatness & perfection

JOHN BLORE,

High Class Bootmaker & Repairer,

27, Fountain St.

Leek.

:: NO REPAIR ::
TOO DELICATE.
:: NONE TOO ::
SUBSTANTIAL.

Sewn work a Speciality.
REPAIRS PROMPTLY EXECUTED

St. Edward Street (formerly Spout Street).

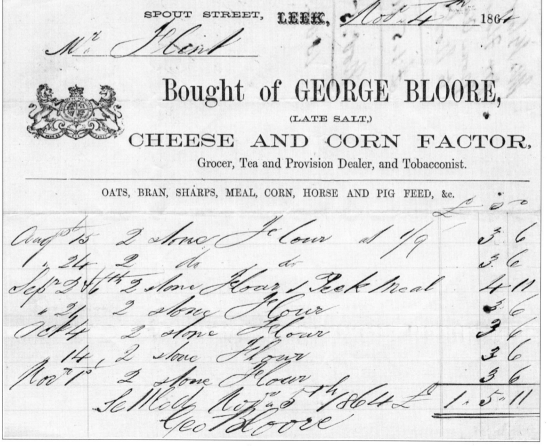

SPOUT STREET, **LEEK,** *Nov. 4th* 186_

Mr *J Kent*

Bought of GEORGE BLOORE,

(LATE SALT,)

CHEESE AND CORN FACTOR,

Grocer, Tea and Provision Dealer, and Tobacconist.

OATS, BRAN, SHARPS, MEAL, CORN, HORSE AND PIG FEED, &c.

			£	s	d
Aug 15	2 Stone Flour	at 1/9		3	6
„ 24	2 do	do		3	6
Sep 2 & 6th	2 Stone Flour 1 Peck Meal			4	11
„ 24	2 Stone Flour			3	6
Oct 4	2 Stone Flour			3	6
„ 14	2 Stone Flour			3	6
Nov 1st	2 Stone Flour			3	6
	Settled Nov 5th 1864		1	5	11
	Geo Bloore				

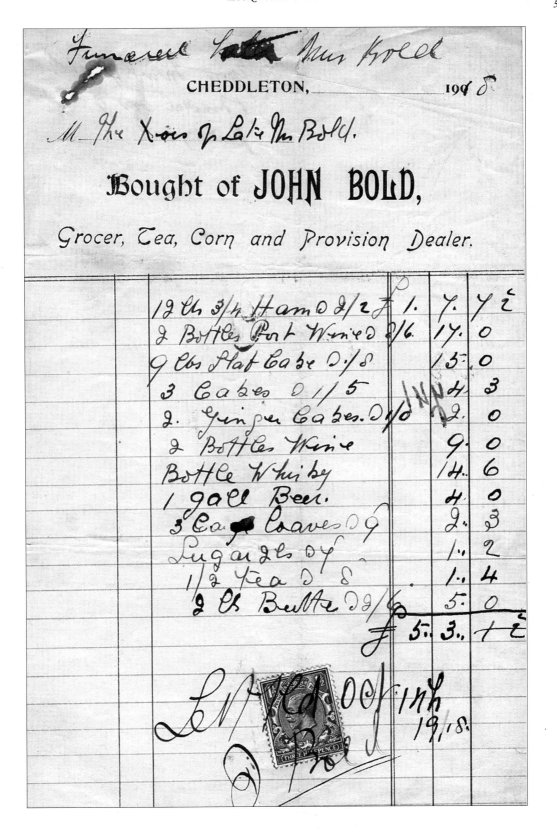

Funeral *Catie* Mrs Krell

CHEDDLETON, _____ 190 8

M— The Xors Of Late Mr Bold.

Bought of JOHN BOLD,

Grocer, Tea, Corn and Provision Dealer.

12 lbs 3/4 Ham @ 2/2 £ 1.	7.	7½
2 Bottles Port Wine @ 2/6.	17.	0
9 lbs Slab Cake @/8	15.	0
3 Cakes @ 1/5	4.	3
2 Ginger Cakes @/0	2.	0
2 Bottles Wine	9.	0
Bottle Whisky	14.	6
1 gall Beer.	4.	0
3 Cap Loaves @9	2.	3
Sugar 2lbs @4	1.	2
1/2 Tea @ 8	1.	4
2 lbs Butter @ 2/6	5.	0
£	5. 3.	7½

Settled Oct 14th
19/18.

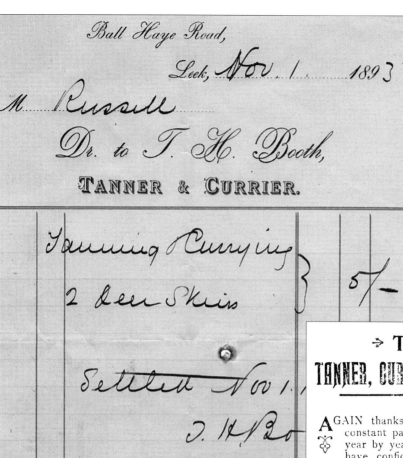

Ball Haye Road,

Leek, Nov 1 1893

M. Russell

Dr. to T. H. Booth,

TANNER & CURRIER.

Tanning Currying } 5/-

2 Deer Skins

Settled Nov 1

T. H. B.

T.H.Booth, whose tannery was in Ball Haye Road, also had a large shop in the Market Place and a warehouse in St. Edward Street.

This very detailed advert makes a very clear and bold statement about the trading practices of T.H Booth.

Below:
Booth's Tannery, Ball Haye Road, after a disastrous fire.

→ T. H. BOOTH, ←
TANNER, CURRIER & LEATHER MERCHANT.

AGAIN thanks his customers for their steady and constant patronage and support extended to him year by year which he takes as a proof that they have confidence in being dealt with fairly and honestly. First, he buys the hides, skins, &c., in the raw state, tans, curries, and sells them direct to the consumer, thus avoiding a middle profit. Second, he does not find it necessary to go to the expense of travelling, as his goods carry their own recommendations with them. Third, his intimate personal acquaintance with a many of the leading tanners in the country, places him in the position of being able to buy direct from them, and consequently to the best advantage, which advantage he always extends to his customers.

HIS STOCK INCLUDES:

ENGLISH & FOREIGN BENDS,
SHOULDERS, BELLIES, RANGES, &c.
ALL KINDS OF
Dressed Leather, Welt Pieces, &c., Machine Strapping.
CLOSED UPPERS OF THE BEST VALUE.
—o—
☞ Boot Laces cut from skins selected and specially prepared. Clarified Cod Liver Oil for medicinal purposes. Cod Oil for Harness and Boots. Neatsfoot Oil. Genuine Curriers' Dubbin.

CLOG SOLES, IRONS & NAILS, WHOLESALE & RETAIL.

THE NOTED AMERICAN BURNISHING INK,
THE LEADING MAKES OF SEWING MACHINE NEEDLES,
AND EVERYTHING CONNECTED WITH THE TRADE.

Postal Address & Manufactory —46, BALLHAYE ROAD, LEEK.
Warehouse—10, ST. EDWARD STREET, LEEK.

QUEEN'S HEAD INN YARD,

Leek,_____186

A. James Alsop Esq.

To W. JACKSON & W. BOOTH,

PLUMBERS, GLAZIERS, GAS FITTERS, PAPER HANGERS, PAINTERS, &c.

Boots Chemists originally had their store on the corner of Sheep Market and St Edward Street - see page 34. The shop then moved to the corner of Derby Street with Market Street (now Chapter One) and later to its present site in Derby Street. Many older people in Leek still remember the lending library at Boots.

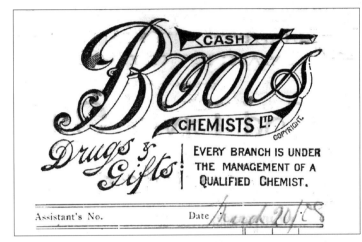

Small scale work here, for a private customer - an indication that even the smallest items were not overlooked by Mr Bostock.

Assistant's No. _____ Date *March 20/* __

Mrs Hudson   *Oct* 1909

❖ Dr. to H. BOSTOCK, ❖

WHEELWRIGHT, JOINER & UNDERTAKER,

ALSOP STREET, LEEK.

ESTIMATES GIVEN FOR REPAIRING AND PAINTING LURRIES, CARTS AND TRAPS.

Repairing neatly and expeditiously executed with well seasoned materials, best workmanship, and at moderate charges.

1909		
Aug 11ᵗʰ *one wood knob to Boiler cupboard*		1½
Sept 24ᵗʰ *To Altering table Timber & Screws etc.*	2	6
	2	7½

The favour of your recommendation respectfully solicited.	RUSSELL STREET & HAYWOOD STREET,

LEEK, *June* 190 *8*

R2424

M *the Excors of Miss C. Robinson*

Bought of C. W. BOTT,
GROCER & PROVISION DEALER.
HOME-CURED HAMS AND BACON.

2 3½ Beef	16	8
Cooking Same		6
3 Currant Loaves	3	6
3 Seed "	3	6
3 Bosc Loaves	3	0
1 lb Tea	2	0
6 " Lp Sugar	1	3
1½ " Savoy Fingers (Bis)	2	3
2 z Mustard		2½
1 bottle + Pickles	1	0
2 " Piccalili		8
5 z Tobacco	1	3
12 lbs. 3 z Ham @ 9	9	2
£	2	4 11½

*Paid with thanks
C W Bott*

Bott's shop, which also became an off licence, occupied a corner site at the Russell Street/Haywood Street junction. In the 1960's it was trading as Victoria Wine.

OPPOSITE PAGE: A good sale! The most expensive items were sugar, bacon and cheese.

36

Stockwell Street, near the Market Place

Leek, May 29th 1911

Ex.tors of Late G H Gould Esqr

DR. TO **HENRY BOWCOCK,**

Wholesale & Retail Corn Dealer, Confectioner & Fancy Biscuit Baker.

. . GROCER, CHEESE AND CORN FACTOR. . .

SACKS CHARGED 1/6 EACH.   N.B. TERMS: CASH IN 28 DAYS

April 29	18 lb Lump Sugar	4	6
	6 lb Demerara	1	3
	6 lb Fine Grain	1	3
	1 lb Best Coffee	1	8
	1 lb Cocoa		5½
	1 lb Wax Candles		4
	3 lb Perfection Soap		9
	Box Starch		5
	¼ Blue		3
	Tin Soft Soap		6½
	½ doz Eggs		6
	2 St Flour		11
	¼ S.R. Flour		6
	Eggs	1	.
	Biscuits	1	4
	½ lb Mustard		10
	2 oz w Pepper		2½
	Salt		1½
	9¼ lb Bacon	6	11½
	7 lb Cheese	4	10
	2 pkts Prov at Oats		11
	2 Tins Evangeline		4
	Doz Matches		3
	4 Scones		3½
	1 lb Vinegar		6
	Sardines		5½
	Metal Polish		2.
		£1	11 9½

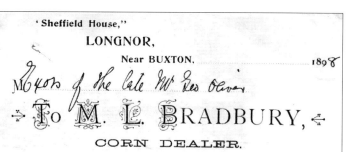

"Sheffield House,"

LONGNOR,

Near BUXTON. 189*8*

To M.L. of the late Mr Geo Oliver

→ *To* **M. L. BRADBURY,** ←

CORN DEALER.

ALE ÷ AND ÷ PORTER ÷ STORES.

All Sacks, Barrels, &c., to be returned when empty, or if kept will be charged for.
INTEREST CHARGED ON OVERDUE ACCOUNTS.

GENERAL DRAPERY ESTABLISHMENT.

THOMAS BRADBURY,

LINEN AND WOOLLEN DRAPER,

33, DERBY STREET,

CORNER OF MARKET STREET, LEEK.

THE LATEST NOVELTIES IN

SILKS, FANCY DRESSES, SKIRTINGS,

Shawls, Mantles, and Jackets.

A large and well-selected Stock of

CARPETS, DRUGGETS, HEARTH RUGS, MATS,

HASSOCKS, ETC.

BLANKETS, SHEETS, COUNTERPANES, QUILTS, TOILET COVERS,

BROAD AND NARROW WOOLLEN CLOTHS.

ALL KINDS OF GARMENTS MADE TO ORDER

OVERCOATS, MACINTOSHES, ETC.,

Hosiery	Hats	Laces	Collars
Gloves	Flowers	Fringes	Fronts
Corsets	Feathers	Shirts	Umbrellas
Bonnets	Ribbons	Ties	Braces

FUNERALS COMPLETELY FURNISHED.

Charities and the Trade supplied on the most liberal terms.

Longnor had been an important market town in the 18th century and was still a busy village with many traders.

BY GOING TO
F. BRADLEY'S
CHEAP DRAPERY ESTABLISHMENT,
2, SHEEP MARKET, LEEK,
YOU WILL FIND IT A GREAT SAVING.
Business conducted on the Principal of
VERY SMALL PROFITS
FOR
READY MONEY ONLY

FUNERAL HOODS AND FALLS LET OUT ON HIRE.

The branch of Bradley's Gents' and Boys' Outfitters, shown below, extended across the North-West corner of the Market Place.

Telegrams:
"BRASSINGTON, LEEK."
TELEPHONE 53.

LONDON MILLS, *Leek, Staffs* Oct. 7 1913

and Golden Bridge Saw Mills, Inchicore, Dublin.

Messr Challinors + Shaw

Bought of H. Brassington & Sons.

TIMBER MERCHANTS, BOBBIN MANUFACTURERS, &C.

GROSS.	DOZ				
		Packing Paper	0.1.12	29/-	10/-

It is interesting to note that Henry Brassington
also had a sawmill in Dublin.
In Kelly's 1888 Directory he is listed as being a
paper merchant and commission agent.

ITALIAN WAREHOUSE
3, MARKET PLACE, LEEK.

H. BRASSINGTON
Would call special attention to his Large Stock of

SALMON IN TINS,
LOBSTER (STAR),
SARDINES, KIPPERED HERRINGS,
BURGESS'S ANCHOVIES,
PICKLES,
GREEN PEAS IN TINS,
KETCHUP,
Jellies, Lemon Juice, Condensed Milk, in Tins,
Biscuits,
PRINCE OF WALES' SALAD SAUCE,
Preserved Ginger,

JAM OF ALL KINDS,
SARDINE OPENING KNIVES
Best Wiltshire Smoked Bacon.

Agent for
W. and A. GILBEY'S
WINES, SPIRITS, &c.

In this very comprehensive advert each line is
printed in a different style - a common practice
in Victorian and Edwardian times.

THOS. BREALEY & SON,
LAND AGENTS & SURVEYORS,
Leek, *17 Dec.* *1894.*

TO

Messrs Challinors & Shaw
Leek

Dear Sirs   *re John Nixon decd*

I have inspected the Stable or Cowhouse on Ashbourne Road, and find it now mainly used as a green grocers Store by Mr Joseph Shingler who pays £8 per Annum for Same which I consider a fair rent the frontage is twenty five feet six inches & the contents 89 yards or thereabouts. I consider the present Value to be One hundred and fifty five pounds —

Yours truly
Thos Brealey

The entrance to Cruso's Yard, just off Stockwell Street.
Brealey's office was just above this, towards the Market Place

THOS. BREALEY & SON,

LAND AGENTS & SURVEYORS,

Leek, 20th Sept. 1899.

Mr Samuel Turnock.

To Thomas Brealey & Son.

1898.

Jany 19. Paid Henry Davenport your
half share of the cost of
Horse Hire taking a Mr Hall
to inspect Dunlee Farm.   3 „ 0

May 18. Paid the Staffordshire Advr
advertising the Farm to let.   4 „ 0

Septr 28. Paid   do   do   7 „ 0

                                                    14 „ 0

22nd November 1899.

Received the above

Thos Brealey & Son

by J W Wooley

Thomas Brealey's office was at 1 Stockwell Street, and he also had an office in Hanley. His nephew, John Brealey, was an architect in competition with the Sugdens, over whom he won the contract for the Butter Market and Fire Station in 1897.

Messrs. Challinors & Shaw.
Leek.

Leek,
18 March 1903

To Thos. Brealey & Son.

1913.		Re Haddon Hall Hydro	£	c
February 11	To	journey to Haddon Hall with Mr. Ferguson & Mr. Sam Smith, taking particulars of the Property for the purpose of drawing up Sale Particulars		
	"	preparing plan of premises & furnishing you with tracing for lithographing with Sale particulars		
	"	Several interviews with you prior to Sale etc. re particulars, easements, fixtures and Sale of furniture.		
	"	attending Sale at Buxton when the Property was Sold for £7000 to Mrs. Hall and Mr. Garlick	7	7
	"	paid cost of hire of Motor, lunch etc & incidental expenses at Buxton	2	10
		Received with thanks Brealey	£ 9	17

13 June 1913

17, Macclesfield Road, and Shop, Clerk's Bank,

Leek, May 10th 1902

Messrs Heath & Lowe

To W. J. BREW,

PAINTER, SANITARY PLUMBER, GLAZIER, PAPER-HANGER, &C.

Terms—2½ Cash. Quarterly Accounts and Contracts Nett.

	£	s	d
By Contract Villas Newcastle Road	100	0	0
Excess Prices for Baths &c	5	6	7½
36 lbs Sheet Lead		7	4½
Balance due from Parker &c		16	0
Goods supplied on Private Acc		4	0
	106 = 14 = 0		
Deductions Heath Plumbers Acc	1	14	0
Gas Fittings not supplied	7	0	0
	8 = 14 = 0		
nett Balance	98	0	0

This debt was contracted by both Partners in Sept 1901, both of whom I hold responsible

W. J. Brew

This advert from the 1927 *Leek Town Guide* shows that W.J. Brew had moved to a shop in St. Edward Street by that time.

─────PRACTICAL─────

Painter & Decorator, Sanitary Plumber, Glazier & Paperhanger,

14, Edward Street, LEEK.

Estimates furnished for every description of Household Decorations and Repairs.

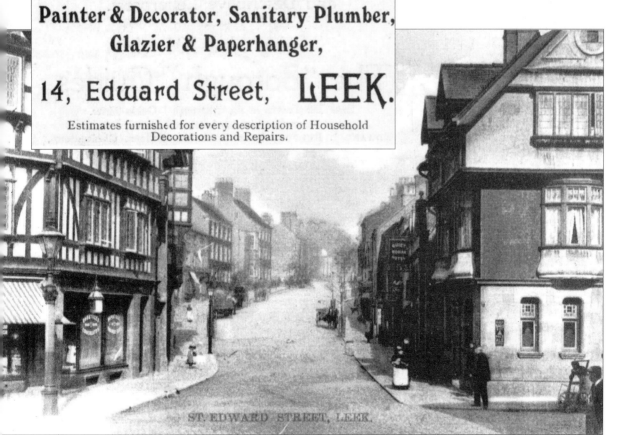

ST. EDWARD STREET, LEEK.

Robert Brindley's Perseverance Steam Saw Mill

Fire!   Fire!!   Fire!!!

Have a good one by burning

R. BRINDLEY & SON'S, Ltd.

COALS, COBBLES

Nuts, and Slack.

Orders received at Offices, 45, Buxton Road,
and at the Depôt, Leek Wharf.

SOLE AGENT at Wharf and Canvasser,
JAS. PORTER, 28, Russell Street

'PHONE 147.

52, DERBY STREET & LEEK WHARF,

July 1st 1927.

Mr E. Jackson, Broad St.

SAM. BRINDLEY,

Coal and Coke Merchant.

~~~~~~~~~~~~~~

ORDERS PROMPTLY ATTENDED TO.

924	Tons	Cwt.	Qrs.	Coals	Price	£	s.	d.
				A/c rend. Dec 30th/24		6	6	1

MARKET-PLACE,

Uttoxeter and Leek, _____ 18__

Mr J Pimlott

Bot of W. Britton & Co.,

WHOLESALE AND RETAIL SHOE MANUFACTURERS,

AND LEATHER CUTTERS.

Pairs.		£	s.	d.
	To Bill del'd	3	0	9
	By A/c	1	1	4
	Balance	1	19	5
	Sept 4/62			

MRS. BROOME'S

LADIES', GENTLEMEN'S, & CHILDREN'S

HOME-MADE

BOOT AND SHOE ESTABLISHMENT,

TOP OF THE

MARKET PLACE, LEEK.

HOME-MADE BOOTS AND SHOES

OF EVERY DESCRIPTION.

Orders and Repairs executed with neatness and dispatch. **Ready closed**
Uppers in great variety. **Elastics put in by Patent Machines.**

In late Victorian times there were many boot and shoe dealers in Leek - no less than 65 listed in the 1898 Almanac. These were the days when people walked everywhere and only the rich could afford carriages. The dyeing and farming industries would also require special footwear - many clogs were made and sold.

2. Stanley Street & Market Place.

LEEK, ... *June* 1913

Mr C. Robinson

Bought of

M. H. BROOKS & SON,

THE CENTRAL DRAPERY & BOOT STORES.

ALL GOODS sold at Lowest Possible Prices for Cash.
Mourning and Special Orders receive every attention.

Clothing Club Tickets taken as Cash.   **Special Dividend Given.**

DRESSES	*1912*					
CALICOES	May 10.	24/	Wht Calico	5	1 - 0½
SHIRTINGS	June 19	5	" "	6½	2 - 8½
CORSETS						
GLOVES						
HOSIERY	July 3	3	" Emb:	4½	1 - 1½
BLOUSES						
		1 pr	Kid Gloves		1 - 11½
SHEETS						
BLANKETS		1 "	Grey "		1 - 0½
FLANNELS						
FLANNELETTES	10	5	Wht Calico	6½	2 - 8½
		2	" "	5	10
UNDERCLOTHING						
PINAFORES		3	" Emb:	4	1 - 0
OVERALLS						
SKIRTS		3	" "	4½	1 - 1½
UMBRELLAS	Sept 7	6	" Calico	6½	3 - 3
PRINTS AND ALL	Nov 19	24/	" Print	6½	1 - 4½
CLASSES OF		3				
DOMESTIC .						
DRAPERY						
LADIES', GENT'S.						
AND . . .						
CHILDREN'S						
BOOTS AND						
SHOES						

NO. 1, SILK STREET, LEEK.

BROOK'S

WHOLESALE AND RETAIL

GASLIGHT, BENZOLINE,

NAPTHA, HAIR OIL,

Lubrication Oil for Machinery, and Fire Lights.

IM BROOKES,

- Joiner and -
Funeral Furnisher,

0, Fountain St.,

32
YEARS
EXPERIENCE
IN THE
BUILDING TRADE.

inery work of every
description, and repairs
to property carefully
and efficiently executed.

FUNERALS
COMPLETELY
FURNISHED.

For sound workmanship and
the best materials at
the keenest price, try

CHARLES BROUGH

Can make Picture Frames cheaper than any house in the trade

Mounts, Memory Card Borders, Rings, Back Board, Corners,

And a great Variety of Mouldings,

AT 48, GROSVENOR STREET, LEEK.

N.B.—SHOW CARDS and PLANS FRAMED on the Shortest Notice

**William Broster and Co.,
Silk Manufacturers, Waterloo Mills,
National Telephone No. 2.   Telegrams:
"William Broster, Leek."**

Waterloo Mill - designed by the architect James Gosling Smith.

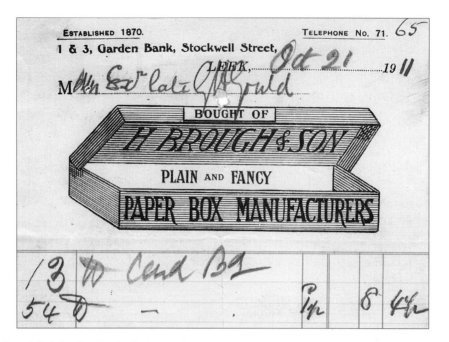

ESTABLISHED 1870.   TELEPHONE No. 71. 65

1 & 3, Garden Bank, Stockwell Street,
LEEK, *Oct 21* 19 11

M *...*

BOUGHT OF

H. BROUGH & SON

PLAIN AND FANCY

PAPER BOX MANUFACTURERS

H. Brough & Son, 1 & 3 Garden Bank, Stockwell Street, Leek. The ingenious design of this letterhead clearly illustrates the services provided to the textile industry by H. Brough & Son. In the Post Office Directory of 1872 Henry Brough is listed as a box maker in Russell Street, but by 1892 (Kelly) Brough & Son are trading from the Stockwell Street address - a workshop at the rear of the row of terraced houses between Union Street and New Street. Brough's continued in a small factory in Union Street for many years.

Show Rooms: Haywood Street & Bath Street.

ART CABINET WORKS,

3, BATH STREET, LEEK, *15 Oct* 189 4

Mess *Challinor & Shaw*

Bought of C. BROUGH & SONS,

Cabinet Makers, Upholsterers & Picture Frame Manufacturers

HAIR, SPRING, AND WOOL MATTRESSES.   ALL KINDS OF WINDOW BLINDS.
Flocks, Feathers, Ticking, Cloths, Buttons, Gimps, &c.

TELEGRAMS SEWINGS, LEEK. | H. T. RUSSELL.   LONDON: 4, CASTLE STREET, FALCON SQ., E.C.
NATIONAL TELEPHONE, N? 36.   PARTNERS | H. R. BRUNT.   NEWCASTLE-ON-TYNE: 4, MARKET ST.
                                      | J. SHORTER.

From *Russell, Brunt & Shorter,*

LATE FYNNEY & COMP?
LATE HENRY BRUNT & C?

Silk Manufacturers,
Leek,
Staffordshire.   CHINA FLAG MAKE

ACME MAKE.

Oct 9 189 6

Mess *Challinors Shaw*

Leek

ESTABLISHED 1880.

LADDEREDGE;

Nov 2ᵈ 1895

Mr W. Roylance

BOUGHT OF JOHN BROWN,

FAMILY GROCER. ETC.

TERMS.

1 Valve Key		3	0
1 Small lid Key			4
2 Rubber rings		1	3
4 Bolts & nutts			8
Red Lead			4
Carting Lead		1	0
One Bucks		1	3
Settled		7	10

Shoeing Forge, St. Edward Street, LEEK.

The Executors of the late Wᵐ Young Oct. 192.8

M *R Brealy Esq.*

Dr. to ...

HARRY BRUNT,

Shoeing and General Smith.

REPAIRS TO AGRICULTURAL IMPLEMENTS A SPECIALITY.

Maker of Ornamental Gates, Railings, Hooping & all other Carriage Iron Work.

Member of the
National Master
Farriers' and
Blacksmiths'
Association.

Registered after
Examination by the
Worshipful Company
of Farriers, London.

Repairing railings & ironworks to property £8 5 8

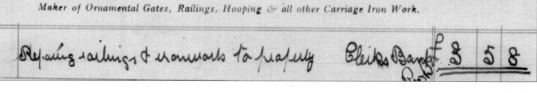

Harry Brunt's address was 9 St Edward Street. The business was formerly Joseph Brunt - see next page.
There was a smithy at the top of St. Edward Street until the late 1980s.

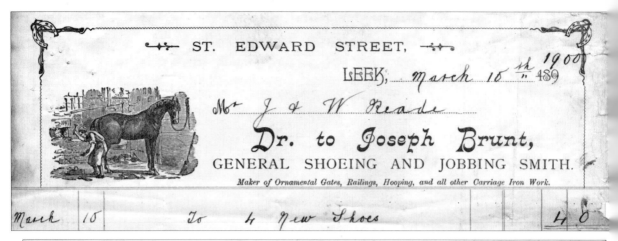

ST. EDWARD STREET,

LEEK, *March 15th 1900* 489

Mr J & W Reade

Dr. to Joseph Brunt,

GENERAL SHOEING AND JOBBING SMITH.

Maker of Ornamental Gates, Railings, Hooping, and all other Carriage Iron Work.

March	*15*	*To*	*4 New Shoes*		*4*	*0*

ST. EDWARD STREET,

Leek, *Midsummer 1882*

M Wm B Badnall Esqr

DR. TO JOSEPH BRUNT,

General Shoeing & Jobbing Smith.

Maker of Ornamental Gates, Railings, Hooping, and all other Carriage Iron Work.

1881 *Dec 22*	*To altering Iron Railings in Stockewell St*	*10*	*0*

❀ MESSRS. BROUGH, NICHOLSON AND HALL, ❀

Silk Manufacturers,

LEEK & CHEADLE, Staffordshire; and 41, Cheapside, LONDON, E.C.

Artist's impression of the factory viewed from Fountain Street

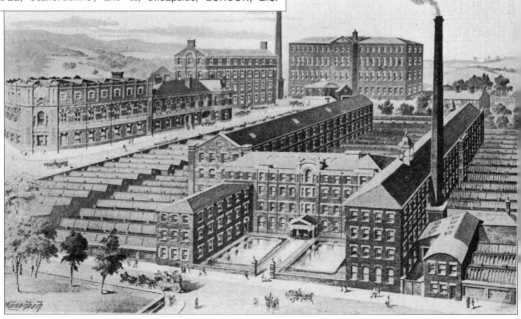

BROUGH, NICHOLSON & HALL Ltd. John Brough started his first silk 'shade' in 1815 in Stafford Street, just off Stockwell Street (the street was appropriately re-named Silk Street), before moving to a much larger 'shade' in nearby Union Street, on the steep slope known as 'Brick Bank'. A weaving shed, or 'shade' was usually a single storey building of a length sufficient to house the looms. Some 'shades' were located in the attics above the workers' terraced houses, a common attic often running above several houses to make the length required for the looms. The *Parsons and Bradshaw Directory* of 1818 lists the firm as 'Baddeley & Brough, silk manufacturers, Stockwell Street'. Following the move to Union Street, John Brough was the sole proprietor until he was joined by his sons, Joshua, James and John, in 1831, when the firm became known as 'J. and J. Brough & Co.' (*Pigot's Directory*, 1835). Joshua Nicholson, a Yorkshireman, had been employed by the firm as a commercial traveller for about twenty years, when, following the death of James Brough in 1856, he became a partner with the surviving brothers, Joshua and John. Another long-serving employee, a Mr. B.B. Nixon, also became a partner at that time, and the firm traded as J. and J. Brough, Nicholson & Co. Soon after this the firm moved to London Mill on Ashbourne Road. In 1868 Joshua and John Brough retired, and W.S. Brough (Joshua Brough's son), Arthur Nicholson (son of Joshua Nicholson), Edwin Brough (John's son) and John Hall (another old employee) became partners in the new enterprise which began to expand in the Cross Street and Fountain Street area. During the 1880s the firm lost three partners, W.S. Brough and B.B. Nixon retired, and Joshua Nicholson died on 24th August, 1885. This was barely a year after the ceremonial opening of the public building that was his great gift to Leek, the Nicholson Institute. Brough, Nicholson & Hall Ltd. continued to expand under the directorship of Arthur Nicholson and John Hall, and there was a royal visit by the Duke and Duchess of York in 1900, following which the new mill on Well Street was named Royal York Mill in their honour. Arthur Nicholson was knighted in 1909. The elaborate letterheading gives an artist's impression of the extent of the Brough, Nicholson and Hall factory complex, dominating the area between Ashbourne Road and Fountain Street and including Cross Street and Well Street, and employing several hundred workers at its height. There was also a factory at Cheadle - Cecily Mills - and a London office.

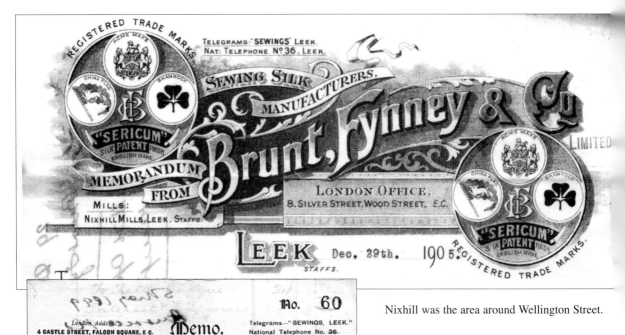

REGISTERED TRADE MARKS

TELEGRAMS: "SEWINGS" LEEK.
NAT. TELEPHONE Nº 36, LEEK.

SEWING SILK MANUFACTURERS,

Brunt, Fynney & Co

LIMITED

MEMORANDUM FROM

MILLS: NIXHILL MILLS, LEEK, STAFFS.

LONDON OFFICE, 8, SILVER STREET, WOOD STREET, E.C.

"SERICUM" SILK PATENT FINISH ENGLISH MAKE

LEEK Dec. 29th. 1905.
STAFFS.

REGISTERED TRADE MARKS.

No. 60

London Address
4 CASTLE STREET, FALCON SQUARE, E.C.

Memo.

Telegrams—"SEWINGS, LEEK."
National Telephone No. 36.

FROM

BRUNT, FYNNEY & COMPANY,

SILK MANUFACTURERS,

LEEK, Staffs,

May 5ᵗʰ 1899

Nixhill was the area around Wellington Street.

Leek. March 7 1852.

Boᵗ ᵒᶠ *George Bull.*

Grocer, Tea Dealer, & Tallow Chandler,

MANUFACTURER OF PURIFIED MOULD & DIP CANDLES, BY HER MAJESTY'S ROYAL LETTERS PATENT.

Also of the Patent Wicked Moulds & Dips, which require no snuffing.

Bull's grocery shop was at the top end of Derby Street, near the Market Place - the row of 4 shops above Challinor and Shaw's offices which Leek people remembered as *"Salt's - Eaton - Ellerton's - Bull"*.

179

Leek,   Decr 29 1870

Miss Goldstraw

Bought of George Bull,
Grocer, Tea Dealer, and Tallow Chandler,
MANUFACTURER OF PURIFIED MOULD AND DIP CANDLES,
By Her Majesty's Royal Letters Patent:
Also of the PATENT WICK'D MOULDS & DIPS which require no snuffing.

1870				£	s	d
		To Amount of A/c Delivered from				
	July 22 1870.	Sep^t 14th A/o inclusive		3	5	7½
Sep^t 27	2 gals	Vinegar ½			2	0
30	6 ℔	Large Sago 3/6			1	9
Oct 5	1½ ℔	Pat Candles 4/-			9	0
14	1 —	Brown Soap 3/4			3	4
	2 ℔	Coffee Berries 1/3			2	6
	1 —	Green Tea 3/9			3	9
15	1 ℔	Lf Sugar 4/9			4	9
19	1½ —	Pat Candles 4/-			9	0
Nov 2	6 ℔	Pat Candles 4/-			3	0
7	1½ ℔	Pat Candles 4/-			9	0
	1 ℔	Green Tea 3/9			3	9
23	6 —	Pat Candles 4/-			3	0
26	2 gals	Vinegar 1/-			2	0
	2 ℔	Coffee Berries 1/3			2	6
	2 ℔	Pat Candles 4/-			12	0
Decr 7	1 ℔	Green Tea 3/9			3	9
9	1½ ℔	Pat Candles 4/-			9	0
				7	9	8½

		£ s d				
Oct 28/70	By Cash 1-0-0					
Nov 18/70	By do 1-0-0			2	0	0

1897
Feb. 15 To Goods — 3 8½

2

2, DERBY STREET, *Leek.* ———— *1894*

Messr. Challinor & Shaw — Leek

Bought of Bull Brothers.

GROCERS. TEA & COFFEE DEALERS & TOBACCONISTS.

1894					
	Forward			13	6½
June 18	1 dz. Matches				2½
July 6	1 tin Enameline				2½
„ 18	3 ozs. ~~Attoney~~ Honey Soap				10
	Blacklead				6
„ 26	6 ozs. S. Soap 1/6	1 tin Enameline 2½		1	8½
Aug. 9	3 dz. Matches 7½	Pipeclay 6		1	1½
„ 15	1 „ Matches				2½
„ 31	1 tin Enameline				2½
Sep. 4	6 ozs. Soft Soap			1	6
„ 11	1 dz. Matches				2½
„ 20	1 tin Enameline				2½
„ 24	1 tin Enameline 2½	1 dz Matches 2½			5
Oct. 16	3 ozs. Soap 10	3 dz. Matches 7½		1	5½
	1 dz. B & M. Matches			1	—
	Forward		£	1	3	4

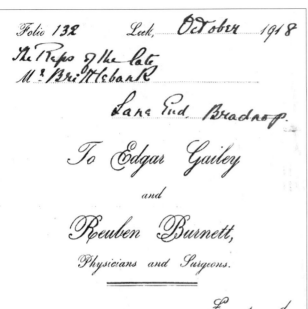

Folio 132   Leek, October 1918

The Reps of the late
Mr Brittlebank

Lane End Bradnop.

To Edgar Gailey

and

Reuben Burnett,

Physicians and Surgeons.

1918. October.

	£	s.	d.
	2.	1.	0

To Professional Attendance,

£2. 1. 0.

The Accounts are rendered half yearly – Midsummer and Xmas.

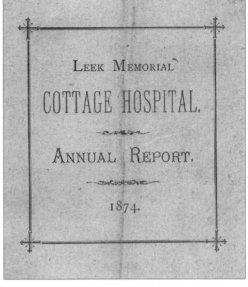

LEEK MEMORIAL
COTTAGE HOSPITAL.
ANNUAL REPORT.
1874.

The town of Leek enjoyed the facility of a cottage hospital in Stockwell Street for 150 years - the Alsop Memorial Hospital. There was also a Workhouse in Ashbourne Road from the 1830s.

The surgery was at Moorland House, Regent Street. The practice later became that of Dr Dyson, who married Dr Burnett's daughter. It is now the Moorland's Medical Centre.

T. Burgess's shop in St Edward Street and, below, his delivery van.

Showroom & Residence 1 & 2, Overton Bank,

WORKSHOP, HAYWOOD STREET,

Leek, _____ Dec. 31st _____ 1901

Mrs. Brealey, Derby Street.

Dr. to W. L. Bullock,

Cabinet Maker, Upholsterer, and Importer of Oriental Goods.

Furniture of every description made to order at the lowest price consistent with good material and sound workmanship.
Art Print, Spring Roller and Venetian Blinds. Pattern Books and Prices submitted on application.

1901		£	s	d
	To Amt. of a/c. rendered		5	0
			9	3½
June 11th	Fix. new cord in staircase window. Cord & line		1	0
June 24th to 29th	Taking bath down, mak. & fix. stand for cistern, cutting joists & plugging walls for plumbers, rep. bath top, fix. lavatory			
	& odd jobs. R.M. 42in. @ 7½d. £1-5-4½ W.B. 6in 4/-	1	9	4½
	10ft of 3½ × 2" 1/0½. 10ft of 9" × 1" 2/1		3	1½
	2 lbs nails 4d. Screws 3d. Holdfasts 4d.			11
	Brass screws & screw caps 1/2. 17ft moulding 1/3		2	5
	2 Blocks ea. 10" × 4½ × 2½ strips & plugs			9
July 1st to 4th	Fix. casings for pipes, bath casing, lavatory & work for plumbers R.M. 22in. 13/3½ W.B. 1/4		14	7½
	Strip 4'-6" × 2" × 1" & D. 21" × 3" × 1"			5
	3ft of 14" × 3/4" 1/-. 2ft of 10" × 3/4" 5d.		1	5
	5ft. moulding, screws & nails			8
" 6th	Making wool flock mattress (tick found)		3	4
	41 lbs. woollen flocks @ 4½d. lb.		15	4½
	Sandpapering & repolishing bath tops			
	Polish & time		5	3
Nov. 15th	Rep. venetian blind, fix. new pulley &.			9

W. L. BULLOCK,
Cabinet Maker & Upholsterer,
HAYWOOD STREET,

LEEK, STAFFS.

Furniture, Antique and Modern; Upholstery, Blinds,
Picture and Showcard Frames, Show Cases, &c.

3, WOOD STREET,

LEEK, *Jany 2 2* 190*9*

M² *Robinson*

Dr. to JOHN BURNETT,

GENERAL CARTER & CONTRACTOR.   FURNITURE REMOVER.

| Jany 19 | Coals 8 . 18 . 2   *at 1/6 per* Ton | 13 | 5 |
| | Weighing | | 8 |

3, WOOD STREET,

LEEK, *June* 189*4*

Mr *J J Smith*

DR. TO JOHN BURNETT,

General Carter and Furniture Remover.

30	6 load stone from ballington to Challinors		6
	removing stone dirt at Challinors 1 day		4
July 2	10 load stone from ballington	10	
2	removing stone sand 3 quarters	5	3
3	9 load stone from ballington	9	
3	removing stone sand 3 quarters	5	3
4	4 load stone from ballington stone sand alf day	3	6
5	14 load stone from ballington	14	
		3 4 0	

JOHN BURNETT is first listed as a General Carter in Kelly's 1892 Directory, and is also listed in the 1912 Directory. Like most of his trade, he would have to be prepared to transport literally anything - from furniture and household goods to stone and building materials.

Mar 12 1892

M Escors of Mrs H Birch

Bought of GEORGE BURTON,

WHOLESALE AND RETAIL CONFECTIONER.

ALL ACCOUNTS DUE 1st OF MONTH.   72 Derby St Leek

1890 Jan 4	To Goods supplied G H Bestwick by her order			5	8
Dec 3/91 to Feb 16/92	To Goods supplied N Bestwick 12 wei at 5/	3	•	•
Feb 18	To Goods for Funeral				
	6 Milk Loaves	at	6	3	•
	3 Large Currant	"	1/-	3	•
	2 " Spice	"	1/-	2	•
	3/4 lb Tea		3/-	2	3
	1/2 " Coffee		1/8		10
	1/4 " Mustard				5
	6 lbs Sugar			1	3
	Pickles & Salt			1	1
	Tobacco			1	0
	3 lb Butter			5	0
	Oat Cakes				6
	4 Bottles Wrights Wine			8	8
					4
				3	8
				16	8
				1	0
	Drink			2	6
	...uits			3	•
	...y & Beef Roasting			1	4
			£	**6**	**3**	**2**

NO TEA TO EQUAL BLACK & GREEN'S

If you are not at present drinking
BLACK & GREEN'S TEA, then do so, and we feel
confident you will be better pleased than with
any other Tea. This, at any rate, is the experience of thousands of our customers. The test
is worth making.

72, Derby Street,

LEEK, Nov 11 1913

Escors of
Mr C Robinson

Bought of

F. L. BURTON,

—— Family Grocer. ——

Prices: 1/4, 1/6, 1/8, 1/10, 2/-, 2/4 per lb.

1912
Mar 18

4 Stone Bay Camel Flour	6	6

From the turn of the century
manufacturers often supplied traders,
especially grocers and animals feed
suppliers, with printed billheads
carrying a blank space for a local
shop's details to be printed.

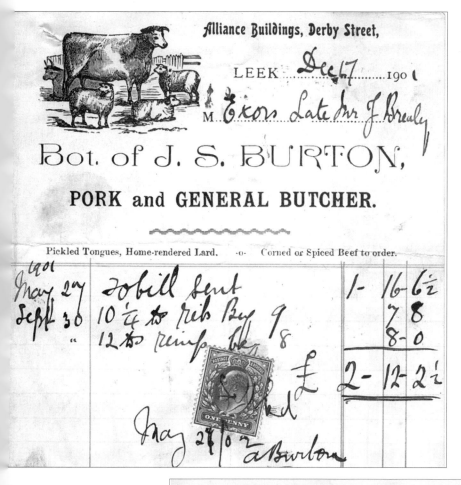

J. S. BURTON, Derby Street.
Stated as Alliance Buildings on his billhead, Joseph Shirley Burton's address was 70 Derby Street. He moved to this address around 1890, but had already been trading for over 20 years. He had his own slaughterhouse, a staff of experienced assistants and maintained a number of carts which were used for local deliveries.

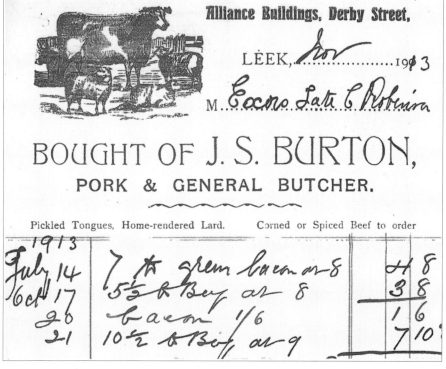

WESTWOOD TERRACE,

Leek,................................ 186

M. the Trustees of Leek Alms Houses

To EDWIN BUTTERFIELD, Dr.

1869		COALS.			SLACK.		AMOUNT.		
		T.	C.	Q.	T.	C.	£	s.	d.
Jany 5	To 8 Tons of Coals @ 13/9 ½ p Ton						5	10	"
1869. Jany 19									

Settled Edwin Butterfield

Many coal merchants operated from home - in fact many did so until very recently - with their depot at the local railway station or wharf.

BOOT & SHOE REPAIRER

J. BUXTON, 14, ST. EDWARD STREET, LEEK.

Only Best English Leather and Driped used.

WORKMANSHIP GUARANTEED

FOUR ROYAL APPOINTMENTS.

ELEVEN PRIZE MEDALS.

PEEK, FREAN & Co's
LONDON
Biscuits and Cakes

Have Obtained Great Celebrity For their purity and Excellence.

Bought of

Leek Cricket Club
July 27 1895

T. CANTRILL,
Wholesale Family Grocer, Baker, & Confectioner,
19, STANLEY STREET,
And 29, ST. EDWARD STREET, **LEEK.**

2 dg Beer	7/-

Paid
T Cantrill
Aug 29/95

...NUFACTURE BISCUITS IN ABOUT 250 VARIETIES AND CAKES OF ALL KINDS.

EDMUND BYRNE,
GILDER,
AND
PICTURE FRAME MANUFACTURER.

DEALER IN

Gilt, Veneered, and Stained Mouldings,
PHOTOGRAPHIC FRAMES AND MOUNTS,
BACK BOARDS, GLASS, RINGS, &c.

Oleographs, Engravings, Lithographs and Prints.

OXFORD FRAMES
IN OAK, GILT, ROSEWOOD, WALNUT, BLACK, AND GOLD.
*Superior Frames (Alhambra pattern) made to order, Gilt in Oil,
Matt, or Burnish.*

PICTURE & LOOKING GLASS FRAMES
REGILT EQUAL TO NEW.

LOOKING GLASS PLATES RE-SILVERED
By new patent process, being impervious to damp.

Photographs, Prints, Plans, and Drawings
Of every description, mounted in a superior manner, and with the
greatest care ; in White or Tinted, Smooth or Rough Surface, Bronze or
Imitation of Gold.

OBSERVE THE ADDRESS :—

56, *St. Edward Street,* LEEK,
Next door to Mr. Maskery, Confectioner.

GOLDEN LION YARD,
CHURCH STREET,
LEEK *June 28* 188*8*

Mr Fowler for
Mr I Challner

at cottage 109 Ballhaye Green

Dr. to WALTER CANTRILL,

Shoeing and General Jobbing Smith.

May 20	*repairing grate*		2	4
	repairing boiler		1	6
			3	10
	Settled June 28 88			
	W Cantrill			

The conglomeration of buildings behind Church Street and the Market Place included many small buildings and workshops. The Golden Lion, which fronted on to Church Street, was a coaching inn, on the turnpike road through Leek.

District Agents for
BIBBY'S CAKES AND MEALS.

TELEPHONE 3YI.

The Corn Stores, *Leek*

1909

Mr W Smith

Bought of

Carding Bros.

Millers & Corn MERCHANTS.

DEALERS IN BURTON ALES & STOUTS.

BRANCHES.
WINKHILL CORN MILL.
WATERHOUSES,
IPSTONES CORN STORES.

WE HEREBY DECLARE THAT ALL FEEDING STUFFS UPON THIS INVOICE, NOT THEREIN SPECIALLY DESCRIBED AS PURE ARE PREPARED FROM MORE THAN ONE SUBSTANCE OR SEED.

5% CHARGED ON ALL OVERDUE ACCOUNTS.   ALL MARKED SACKS CHARGED FOR.

| *Ap 14* | *1 Ton Slag* | | £ 2 | 0 | 0 |

Many corn merchants also had a license to trade in ales and stouts.

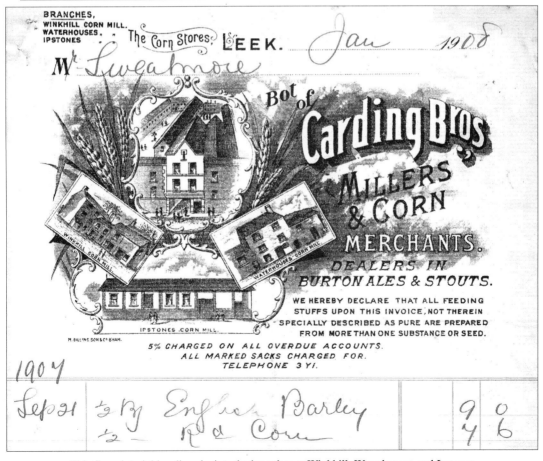

TELEGRAMS:
"CARDING Bros.,
LEEK."

THE CORN STORES,

Exors of the late **LEEK,** 189

Mr Wm Prince Woodcroft.

BOUGHT OF F. & H. CARDING,
CORN FACTORS.

ALL SACKS NOT RETURNED IN GOOD CONDITION WILL BE CHARGED
1/6 EACH.

1896				
Jan 14	1 Bg Roller Old Oats		13	6

BRANCHES,
WINKHILL CORN MILL,
WATERHOUSES,
IPSTONES

The Corn Stores, LEEK. Jan 1908

Mr Sweatmore

Bot of

Carding Bros,
MILLERS & CORN MERCHANTS.
DEALERS IN BURTON ALES & STOUTS.

WE HEREBY DECLARE THAT ALL FEEDING
STUFFS UPON THIS INVOICE, NOT THEREIN
SPECIALLY DESCRIBED AS PURE ARE PREPARED
FROM MORE THAN ONE SUBSTANCE OR SEED.

WINKHILL CORN MILL.
WATERHOUSES CORN MILL.
IPSTONES CORN MILL.
M. BILLING SONS & Co BHAM.

5% CHARGED ON ALL OVERDUE ACCOUNTS.
ALL MARKED SACKS CHARGED FOR.
TELEPHONE 3 YI.

1907				
Sep 21	½ Bg English Barley		9	0
	½ — Rd Corn		4	6

This fine pictorial heading depicts the branches at Winkhill, Waterhouses and Ipstones.
The main depot was in Derby Street, Leek. The address of Fred and Harry Carding's corn stores was 61-63 Derby Street
and 3 Bath Street. The business was later absorbed into the Biddulph & District Agricultural Society.

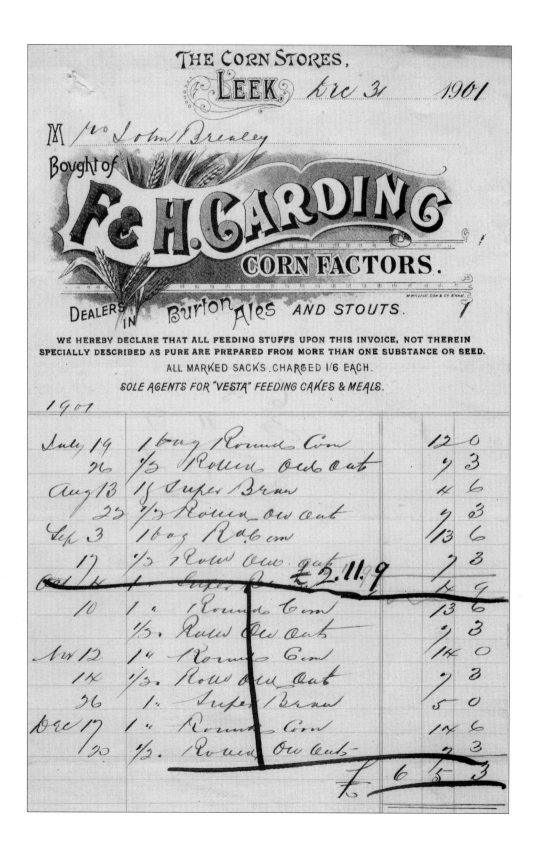

THE CORN STORES,

LEEK, *Dec 31*   1901

M̃ Mr John Brealey

Bought of

F & H. GARDING

CORN FACTORS.

DEALERS IN *Burton* Ales AND STOUTS.

WE HEREBY DECLARE THAT ALL FEEDING STUFFS UPON THIS INVOICE, NOT THEREIN
SPECIALLY DESCRIBED AS PURE ARE PREPARED FROM MORE THAN ONE SUBSTANCE OR SEED.

ALL MARKED SACKS CHARGED 1/6 EACH.

SOLE AGENTS FOR "VESTA" FEEDING CAKES & MEALS.

1901

Date	Description		
July 19	1 bag Round Corn	12	0
26	1/2 Rolled Old Oats	7	3
Aug 13	1 Super Bran	4	6
22	1/2 Round Old Oat	7	3
Sep 3	1 bag Rd Corn	13	6
17	1/2 Rolled Old Oat	7	3
Oct 4	1 Super £2.11.9	4	9
10	1 " Round Corn	13	6
	1/2 Rolled Old Oats	7	3
Nov 12	1 " Round Corn	14	0
14	1/2 Rolled Old Oat	7	3
26	1 " Super Bran	5	0
Dec 17	1 " Round Corn	14	6
20	1/2 Round Old Oats	7	3
		£6 5 3	

3, MARKET PLACE,

LEEK, *Oct 3rd* 18~~90~~00

Mr S. Mottershead. Agent to Lurnock Trustees

Dr. to M. CARDING, F.I.I.B.D..

PLUMBER, GLAZIER, GASFITTER, DECORATIVE PAINTER,
AND ELECTRIC BELL FITTER.

Iron Welded Tubes and Fittings.   Scotch Cast Iron Spoutings of every description.

AGENT FOR THE INCANDESCENT GAS LIGHT Co. Ltd

.1900..   £ - s. d

1900		£	s	d
Sept. 12	Inside. Victoria St.			
	1. Pk. of Adamant 1/- Mortar 6d		1	6
	Man 5 hr @ 8½ 3/6½. App. 5 hr @ 3d 1/3		4	9½
13	2½ Pks of Adamant plaster 2/6. Lime Putty 6d		3	.
	Men 10 hrs @ 8½ 7/1. App. 10 hr 3d 2/6		9	7
14	7½ Clay Damp proof Paint @ 1/-		7	6
	Whiting for ceilings 9d ½ Clay Glue Powder		1	2
	3. Clay Dry colour 1/. Man 10 hrs @ 8½d 7/1		8	1
	App. 10 hr 2/6		2	6
15	10 Clay Paint @ 6d 5/. Man 4 hr. 2/10		7	10
	App 5½ hrs. @ 3d		1	4½
17	21. Pieces of Paper @ 6d 10/6 6 yds of Border 3d		10	9
"	Paste 1/. 5½ Clay Paint 2/9		3	9
	Putty 2d Man 8 hr. 5/8. App 10 hr 2/6		8	4
18	Man 10½ hr 7/5½. App. 10½ h 2/7½		10	1
	" 5 hr 3/6½. 5 hr 1/3		4	9½
		£	4	5	½

This work was in respect
of No 22 Victoria St which
was void and several
tenants refused to take it
unless it was put in order
and Miss M Lurnock
authorized me to have it
put in order. The rent
has also been increased
from 2/10 to 3/ per week.

Market Place, Leek,
Oct 3/00
Received of Mr S. Mottershead
the sum of 4 Pounds
5 Shillings 8
Pence.
FOR M. CARDING,
£ 4 - 5 - 0

J Carding

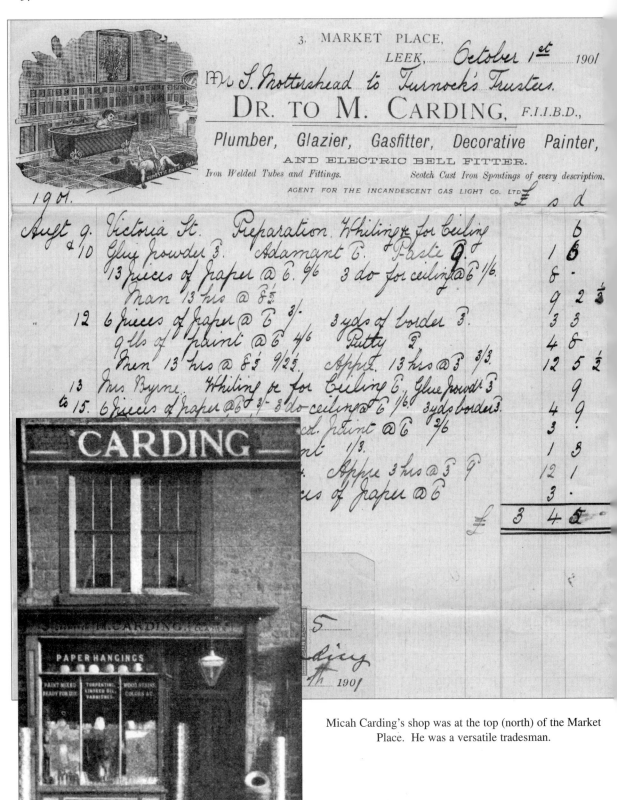

3. MARKET PLACE,

LEEK, *October 1st* 1901

Mr *S. Mottershead to Turnock's Trustees.*

DR. TO M. CARDING, F.I.I.B.D.,

Plumber, Glazier, Gasfitter, Decorative Painter,

AND ELECTRIC BELL FITTER.

Iron Welded Tubes and Fittings.   *Scotch Cast Iron Spoutings of every description.*

AGENT FOR THE INCANDESCENT GAS LIGHT Co. Ltd

1901.			£	s	d
Augt 9	Victoria St. Preparation Whiting & for ceiling				6
& 10	Glue powder 3. Adamant 6. Paste 9.			1	6
	13 pieces of paper @ 6. 7/6 3 do for ceiling @ 6 1/6.		8	·	
	Man 13 hrs @ 8½			9	2¼
12	6 pieces of paper @ 6. 3/. 3 yds of border 3.		3	3	
	9 lbs of paint @ 6. 4/6 Putty 2.		4	8	
	Men 13 hrs @ 8½ 9/2½. Appr 13 hrs @ 3 3/3.		12	5½	
13	Mrs Byrne. Whiting pr for Ceiling 6. Glue powdr 3			9	
to 15.	6 pieces of paper @ 6 3/- 3 do ceiling @ 6 1/6. 3yds border 3.		4	9	
	cd. paint @ 6. 7/6		3	·	
	nt 1/3.		1	3	
	Appr 3 hrs @ 3 9		12	1	
	es of paper @ 6		3	·	
		£	3	4	5

5

ding

th 1901

Micah Carding's shop was at the top (north) of the Market Place. He was a versatile tradesman.

DERBY STREET,
LEEK, ... 18 70

Miss Goldstram

BOUGHT OF

SAMUEL CARDING,

Grocer & Provision Dealer.

Oct 31	1	Sk Flour	1 " 19 " 6
Nov 9	1	— do	1 " 19 " 6
15	1	— do	1 " 19 " 6
22	1	— do	2 " 0 " 6
Dec 2	1	— do	2 " 0 " 0
			£ 9 " 19 " 0
12	2	lb Sugar	4 " 4
13	5	Currants	2 " 1
	1	C Peel	10
			£ 10 " 6 " 3

Samuel Carding was the fore-runner of F. and H. Carding, trading from 61 and 63 Derby Street.

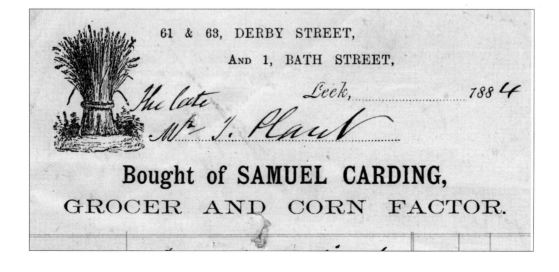

61 & 63, DERBY STREET,

AND 1, BATH STREET,

The late *Leek,* 188 4

Mr J. Plant

Bought of SAMUEL CARDING,

GROCER AND CORN FACTOR.

7, Derby Street, Leek, Feb 7/88
Staffordshire

Mr Challinor

Bot of H. Geo Carr,

Linen & Woollen Draper Silk Mercer,
HATTER, HOSIER GLOVER &c.
FUNERALS FURNISHED.

18   Ex.d

1888	Goods supplied to this Garret		
Feb 6th	8 yds French Merino 2/2	17	4
	14 " Persian Cord 1/2	16	4
	5/2 Lining 6/2, 3 ribb 4	2	11
	4 Bodice Lining 6/2	2	2
	6/2 Braid 1		6/2
	2 doz Butts 3/2, 2 + 3	1	1
	1 Blk Astrachan Jacket	17	6
	1 Hat 2/9, 1 Bonnet 7/2	9	11
	1 Pr Kid Gloves	1	11½
		£3	9 9

This building occupied by H.G.Carr, shown on this billhead, was designed by Leek's Victorian architects, Sugden and Son.

7, Derby Street, Leek, *March 8th, 1888*
STAFFORDSHIRE.

M. Challinor Esqr. *for Miss M. Gaunt.*

Bought of H. G. CARR,

Linen and Woollen Draper, Silk Mercer,

HATTER, HOSIER, GLOVER, &c.

Exd.

FUNERALS FURNISHED.

		£	s	d
Goods as Bill	—	3	9	9
Fur Cape	7/9		7	9
Corsets	8/11		8	11
		4	6	5

Settled with thanks
May 8. 1888.

H. Geo Carr

The upper part of this Sugden
building remains unaltered today.

4, 6 & 8 BROAD STREET,

(36)

Leek, Aug. 10th 1907
Staffordshire.

M the Executors of the late Mrs Smith

Bot of H. G. Carr,

Draper & Silk Mercer.

TELEGRAPHIC ADDRESS:- "CARR LEEK."   C. KIRKHAM, LEEK.   FUNERALS FURNISHED.

| June 28 | To Balance of account as per account rendered | } | 3.19.10 |

according to a/cs rendered
the balance due is £ 3/15/-

H.G. Carr later moved to Victoria Buildings, Broad Street - a block of Tudor-style buildings on the corner with St. Edward Street, designed by James Gosling Smith.

HOPE FOUNDRY.

Leek, Mior 1891
STAFFORDSHIRE.

Mr. W. B. Badnall

W. WOODHEAD,
LATE

Bought of Woodhead & Carter,

Iron & Brass Founders Millwrights, Engineers, &c.

			Cwt.	qr.	lbs.	@	£	s.	d.
May	26	2 pillar & bannister, fixed etc. at Dr. Gailey's house						3	15	·

Hope Foundry was close to the railway station and the canal wharf. It was later the site of Churnet Valley Engineering.

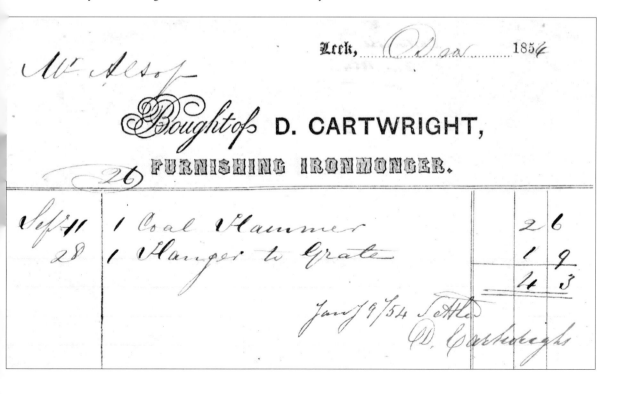

GUN SIDE,

Near Leek, *March 27th* 18*902*

To the Executors of the late John Brealey Esq

DR. TO T. W. CARTER, *Suk*

FARMER, &c.

	£	s	d
For Shooting on Gun Side Farm			
From March 25th 1901 to March 25th 1902	20	0	0
To eight *thring* of Oats at 2/- *per thive*		16	0
	20	16	0

Settled May 28th 1902
Li John Carter With Shacks

£20 for a year's shooting on the area of moorland owned by T.W. Carter at Gun Side is shown on this account.

Leek, *Dec* 185*4*

Mr Alsop

Bought of D. CARTWRIGHT,

FURNISHING IRONMONGER.

Sep 11	1 Coal Hammer	2	6
28	1 Hanger to Grate	1	9
		4	3

Jany 9/54 Settled
D. Cartwright

4rh   Leek, *Xpmas* 18*79*

Mr *H, Goldstren   Rork*

Bought of Daniel Cartwright,

FURNISHING IRONMONGER, SEED MERCHANT.

AGRICULTURAL IMPLEMENT WAREHOUSE.

5 per cent. charged on over due Accounts.

	£	s	d
To Account Rendered *for 1876 & 77*	9	14	3

---

*The Late Mr F. Cru*so   Leek   *Sep. 9* 18*52*

BOT. OF D. CARTWRIGHT,

General Furnishing Ironmonger,

& NAIL MANUFACTURER.

Cutler, Locksmith and Bell Hanger.

Dealer in Hops, Seeds, Oils, Paints & Colours.

				s	d
	1	Pr Finger Plates		8	6
21	1	Fender		6	.
		Jany 5/55		14	6
		Settled			
		D. Cartwright			

150 *Mrs. Elizabeth Flint* Leek, *Upon as* 188*1*

H. Chattinor Esq

BOUGHT OF DANIEL CARTWRIGHT,

FURNISHING AND GENERAL BUILDERS' IRONMONGER,

SEEDSMAN,

TIN-PLATE WORKER AND COPPERSMITH,

AGRICULTURAL IMPLEMENT WAREHOUSE,

Wheeler and Wilson's, Singer's, the Challenge, and other makes of Sewing Machines.

5 per cent. charged on all Overdue Accounts.

		£	s	d
Sept 3	1 · 3 in Pump for Damood	9	"	"
	Men Preparing Top Cleaning			
	out Well Fixing Stage, Beam			
	ready for Pump 136 hours	4	11	8
	Men 4 & Work fixing New Pump	1	12	·
	& Getting foot Air from Well			
	Candles		1	6
	Mason Work 26 hours		15	2
Nov 14	Hire of Pump Fork Spoon & Tackle		7	6
		£ 16	6	10

Daniel Cartwright, based in Sheepmarket, was a very inventive, small scale engineer. His invention of a small grinding mill won an award at the Great Exhibition of 1851, at the Crystal Palace.

22

Show Room & Warehouse, Globe Yard.

LEEK *June* 188.3

M⟨r⟩ *Bradshaw*

Bought of Daniel Cartwright,

FURNISHING & GENERAL BUILDERS' IRONMONGER,

Seedsman, Tin=Plate Worker & Coppersmith,

AGRICULTURAL IMPLEMENTS.

Wheeler and Wilson's, Singer's the Challenge, and other makes of Sewing Machines.
5 per cent. charged on all Overdue Accounts.

Jan 26	1 Rim lock ⁴/² Rep g locks ⁷/⁻	6	9
Apl 14	1 Oyster Knife	1	2
May 14	1 Chisel ¹/² 2 Spoon ⁶	1	8
" 24	1 Candle lantern	1	10
Jun 17	1 lb: Tray	5	·
	June 18/83	16	5
	Settled		

BRIGHT, HAPPY & CHEERFUL HOMES.

STEPHENSON BROS. SPECIALITIES

UNRIVALLED FOR THEIR PURITY & BRILLIANCE.

FURNITURE CREAM.		METAL PASTE.
PLATE POWDER.		METAL POLISHING FLUID
PEERLESS CARPET & CLOTH SOAP.		& KNIFE POWDER.

POLISHING – A PLEASURE!

Oct 7 1897

M⟨r⟩ *S Wood Horton*

BOUGHT of THE EXORS. OF Daniel Cartwright,

Furnishing Ironmonger and Seedsman,

3, SHEEP MARKET, LEEK, (*Staffs.*)

May 5.	1 Doz Ploughshares		

GENERAL PRINTING OFFICE.

Leek, *June* 1880.

Mr Goldstraw

Dr. to William Cartwright,

PRINTER, BOOKBINDER, STATIONER, &c.

ACCOUNTS RENDERED QUARTERLY.   INTEREST CHARGED ON OVERDUE ACCOUNTS.

Residence: 4. Queen Street.

50 Funeral Invitations		3
4 Pks Envelopes		1 3
100 Memory Cards folded		" "
50 do do		15 6
		19 9

Rec'd on a/c 10/ Aug. 4th 1881.

W Cartwright

Rec'd Balance Nov 9th/81.

W Cartwright.

Early 20th century view of St Edward Street with Sheep market leading off.
William Cartwright's printing works was also in Sheep Market.

CHALLINORS & SHAW,
SOLICITORS.

TELEGRAMS:
"CHALLINORS. LEEK".
TELEPHONE Nº 4.

Leek

Staffordshire.

20ᵗʰ October 1909

Dear Sir,

Our Bill delivered in 1904
of £3:2:6 re the Lease of the Shop
to the Co operative stores shell remains
unpaid and we must ask for this
matter to be now cleared. After previous
Correspondence with you you said you
would see the Cooperative Society's Manager
and endeavour to get him to pay half, but
this matter is between the owners and them
and the former Shopes discharge
our costs. Yours truly

Challinors & Shaw

Mr W Sandeman
Harpers Gate
Horton
Leek.

1896
mason work done
11/6/1904 Bill delivered
applied for every year
since.

RUSSELL STREET, LEEK.

Coal ordered by the Vicar

Mrs Brealey   *of Leek*

for the Alms Houses

Bought of THOMAS CHEETHAM,
COAL MERCHANT.

186_6_		Coals.	Tons.	Cwt.	Qrs.	Price.	£	s.	d.
January 18			8	„	„	12/6	5	„	„

Settled
5th Febry 1866
Thos Cheetham

CUSTARD STREET, LEEK   *Dec 17*   186_0_

Mr Revd G E Deacon

BOUGHT OF GEORGE CHELL,
LINEN AND WOOLLEN
DRAPER, SILK MERCER, HABERDASHER, HOSIER, ETC.

Funerals completely Furnished and every Article of Family Mourning.

66	Grey Worsted	14½		3.19.9
20	Calico	5		8.4
20	Lining	4		6.8
	Cotton &c			1.6
	Recd Payment			4.16.3

This address became 5 Stanley Street.

DERBY STREET, *Leek, Mids 1861*

*M*rs *Cruso*

Bought of George Chell,

Linen & Woollen Draper, Silk Mercer,

HABERDASHER, HOSIER, &c.

J. Upton, Birm.

Funerals completely Furnished & every Article of Family Mourning.

21 Jun	5¾/2	Bro Merino	15	3.11.10½
23 "	20	Calico	4	6.8
	20	Bro Lining	2½	4.2
		Cotton & Buttons		1.6
1 Feb	9	Bro Merino	15	11.3
			£	4.15.5½

Almshouse Charity

Telegraphic Address:
VALLEN. LEEK.

CHURNET VALLEY ENGINEERING Co.

HOPE FOUNDRY, LEEK,

May 27th 19

FOUNDERS IN ALL
METALS & ALLOYS.

Electrical.
Mechanical.
Heating and
General Engineers.
Millwrights &c.

BANKERS.
PARRS LTD LEEK.

CHURNET VALLEY ENGINEERING Co., Hope Foundry, Leek. This small foundry of general engineers and millwrights was situated off Newcastle Road, near to the basin of the Leek Canal. Being situated near to the Gas Works one of their specialities was the manufacture of steam separators and split collars for gas and water mains. The firm also made castings to customers' specifications.

CHURNET VALLEY ENGINEERING Co., Ltd.,

ENGINEERS AND IRONFOUNDERS,

CHURNET FOUNDRY,

LEEK, STAFFS.

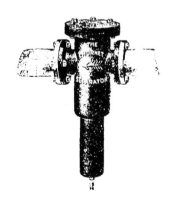

Telegrams: "CHURNET FOUNDRY, LEEK."
Telephone No. 101, LEEK.

MAKERS OF HIGH-CLASS CASTINGS to Customers' Own Patterns ; or we will make Patterns at a small extra charge to Drawings or Sketches.

Columns	Frames & Stands
Pipes (Standard or Specials)	Runners
	Loom Ends
Manholes	Loom Arms
Gulley Grids	Swing Levers
Gratings	Spindle Heads
Plates	Roses
Surface Boxes	Spur Wheels
Stop Tap Boxes	Bevel Wheels
Lamp Columns	Catch Wheels
Fire Bars	Loom Weights
Brick Kiln Castings	Cheeks
Hangers and Brackets	Pedestals
Pulleys	Etc., Etc.

Specialities :—

Small Electrical Castings in Special Brand of Scotch Pig-Iron.

CHURNET STEAM SEPARATOR & DRYER,

for Extracting Grease and Water from Exhaust or Live Steam.

Dry Steam is 50% more efficient than Wet Steam.

Our Separator is 20% more efficient than any other on the market.

There are no loose parts to get out of order.

LISTS & FULL PARTICULARS ON APPLICATION.

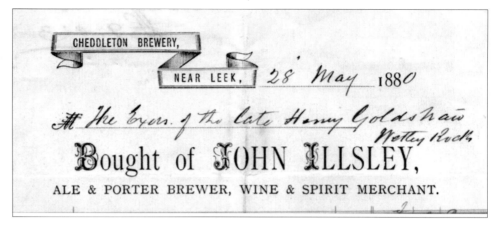

Cheddleton Brewery, Cheddleton Paper Mills and the Cheddleton Mental Asylum, provided
Cheddleton (picture opposite) many employment opportunities at the end of the 19th century.

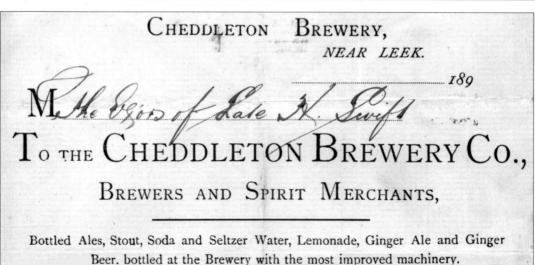

Cheddleton Paper Mills near Leek March 1st 1871

Memorandum from Samuel Goldstraw

Dr Sir   To Mr Challinor Esqr

Cheadle Collieries,
Cheadle, Jany 1st 1880

FOLIO No. 206   (Staffordshire)

Mr Henry Goldstraw W. Rocks

To ROBERT PLANT, Dr.

Terms Monthly.

The Cheadle coalfield with collieries in Cheadle, Foxfield, Kingsley and Coalpitford near Cheddleton
was still an important source of coal at the end of the 19th century.

CHURNET VALLEY RAILWAY,

FROM

MANCHESTER, *via* MACCLESFIELD, TO DERBY.

Capital, £1,000,000; in 50,000 Shares of £20 each. Deposit, £2 per Share.

Provisional Committee.

THOMAS HOULDSWORTH, Esq., M.P., Manchester.
EDMUND WRIGHT, Esq., Manchester.
THOMAS CRITCHLEY, Esq., Manchester.
GEORGE PEEL, Esq., Manchester.
ROBERT C. SHARP, Esq., Bramhall Hall, near Stockport.
WILLIAM C. BROCKLEHURST, Esq., Hurdsfield House, Macclesfield.
THOMAS NORBURY, Esq., Macclesfield.
THOMAS I. WATTS, Esq., Macclesfield.
THOMAS BRODRICK, Esq., Macclesfield.
RUPERT INGLEBY, Esq., Cheadle.
SAMUEL EVANS, Esq., Darley Abbey, Derby.

JAMES OAKES, Esq., Riddings House, Derbyshire.
HENRY COX, Esq., Parkfield, Derby.
DOUGLAS FOX, Esq., Derby.
SAMUEL BEAN, Esq., Nottingham.
WILLIAM HANNAY, Esq., Nottingham.
HENRY YOULE, Esq., Nottingham.
THOMAS EDWARD DICEY, Esq., Claybrook Hall, Leicestershire.
JOHN CARTWRIGHT, Esq., Loughborough.
JOSEPH CRIPPS, Esq., Leicester.
THOMAS MACAULAY, Esq., Leicester.
WILLIAM EVANS HUTCHINSON, Esq., Leicester.

With power to add to their number.

Engineer.
GEORGE WATSON BUCK, Esq.

Secretary.
EDWARD HALL, Esq., Macclesfield.

Bankers.

Messrs. WILLIAMS, DEACON, & CO., London.
THE MANCHESTER & SALFORD BANK, Manchester.
Messrs. BROCKLEHURSTS & CO., Macclesfield.

Messrs. EVANS & CO., Derby.
Messrs. J. & J. C. WRIGHT & CO., Nottingham.
PARES' LEICESTERSHIRE BANKING COMPANY, Leicester.

HEATH HOUSE,
CHEDDLETON, LEEK.

11 To the Executers of the Late Stephen Shenton 188

Bought of THOMAS CLARKSON,
BUILDER, CONTRACTOR
Brick and Pipe Manufacturer and Stone Merchant.

1896				
Jany 11	Joiner Putten Shelves in Cubart & Pane in Winder at Mrs Debers Cottage 4h		2	4
	12 foot of 1in Red Dale Boards to Do		3	11
	1 Pane of Glass Putter & Nales to Do	11	1	6

Agent for "K" BOOTS AND SHOES.

8, SHEEP MARKET, LEEK, *Sept 3¾* 19 12

A. H. Shaw Esq. *for Exs A Taylor*

Bought of John Cleland & Sons,

(Late H. KEATES),

BOOT MAKERS.

Shooting, Fishing, Walking, Hunting and Coachmen's Top Boots made on the premises.

A staff of the most skilful workmen in the district to do repairs, and nothing but the best material used.

Travelling Trunks, Railway Portmanteaux, Travelling Bags, Ladies' Fancy Satchels, Rug Straps, Purses Hat Cases, Cloth, Canvas and Leather Gaiters, Farmers' Strong Leggings, Fancy Leggings in great variety.

1912	To a/c Rend	1	9	9
Jul 5	Gent Shoe Sole Heel		4	—
30	Gent White Boot		12	6
Aug 13	" Shoe Heel & Stitch		1	1
21	" Boot Sole Heel		4	—
28	" Shoe Sole		3	—
	Shoe —			2
29	Patent Court Shoe		10	6
				4
	£	3	5	4

No. 3781

Sept 17 1912

Received of

Mess². *Chalmers & Shaw*

£ *3 . 5 . 4* & S.

FOR

JOHN CLELAND & SONS.

With Compliments and thanks.

Your further Orders will be esteemed.

Quarterly.

Established 1873.

Telephone No. 30 National.
Telegrams: "Clemesha, Leek."

CLEMESHA BROS. LTD.,

SILK, BRAID, AND BINDING MANUFACTURERS,

LEEK,

STAFFORDSHIRE.

July 22nd., 1910.

Mr. Gwynne,

    Leek.

Dear Mr. Gwynne,

    We have received the enclosed.   Shall we write them again

or is it best for you to take the matter up now?

      Yours faithfully,

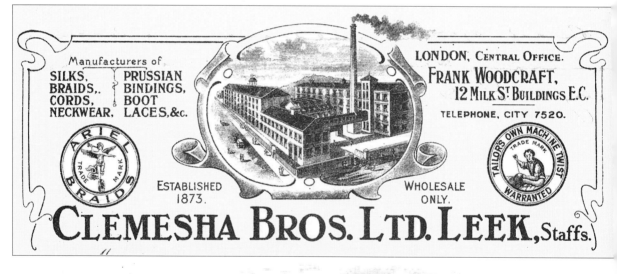

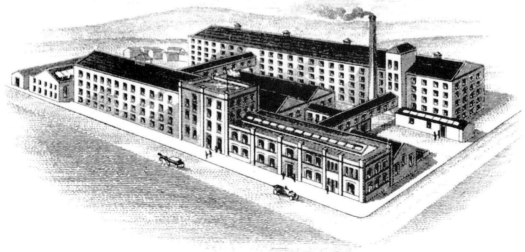

TELEGRAMS: "CLEMESHA, LEEK."
TELEPHONE: 30 LEEK.

WHOLESALE ONLY.

CODES:-
A.B.C. 4TH 5TH & 6TH 5 LETTER.
MARCONI INTERNATIONAL
WESTERN UNION, 5 LETTER

CLEMESHA BROS. & BIRCH LTD.,

ARIEL & NEW STREET MILLS, LEEK, STAFFS, ENGLAND.

Established 1873.

MANUFACTURERS OF

SILKS, BRAIDS, CORDS, KNITTED GOODS,
PRUSSIAN BINDINGS, BOOT LACES, &c.

LONDON:-
12 MILK STREET BUILDINGS.

OUR REF 4.   YOUR REF

Nov. 6th. 1924.

J. Wardle Esq.,
    Messrs. Challinor & Shaw,
        L E E K.

Dear Mr. Wardle,

            We shall be glad to know
if you have yet received a remittance from
the Strand Wholesale Clothing Co., 239,
Oxford Road, Manchester ?

            Please press for immediate
payment of the attached account:-

Mr. J. Katz,
    7, Newman Street,
        LONDON. W.1.   £10 - 7 - 0d.

CLEMESHA BROS. & BIRCH Ltd., New Street, Leek

John Clemesha, the founder of the firm, was born in Preston in December 1849. After working for some time in the woollen industry, he came to Leek in 1873, taking the tenancy of the 'shade' above three cottages at the bottom of Ashbourne Road, near the White Lion. He dealt in sewing silks, buttons and braids. He was joined by his brother William on April 8th 1874, and moved into larger premises in Wellington Street, trading as Clemesha Brothers, employing a spooler, a winder and an errand boy. After about four years the firm moved to Shoobridge Street. Business continued to increase, and after about four years they were employing a dozen people, at which time it became necessary to move to London Mills. Charles Birch joined the firm in 1901, becoming a director in 1902. The firm acquired the silk mills in New Street from Alsop, Downs and Spilsbury in 1907. Braid sheds and dyeworks were erected, as the firm expanded in the knitting industry. At its height, Clemesha Bros. & Birch Ltd. had over 500 employees. The New Street factory was destroyed by fire in January 1964. The firm was later taken over by British Trimmings Ltd., operating from Clemesha's other factory on Ball Haye Road.

158/

LEEK, *Dec 31*   186*5*

M. Challinor by

BOUGHT OF WILLIAM CLEMESHA,

(LATE R. NALL.)

Bookseller, Stationer, Printer, Engraver, Lithographer, and Bookbinder.

NEWSPAPER AND ADVERTISING AGENT.

Agent for "**The Staffordshire Advertiser.**"

⁂ The London and Manchester Daily Papers and all Magazines received by early trains, and delivered as speedily as possible.

Depot for the Religious Tract Society, and the British and Foreign Bible Society.

1865				
July 13	6 Sheets White Tissue	"	"	3
― 24	Repairing Shakspeare 6 & 4 Sheets Tracing Paper	"	1	10
Nov 5	2 Copies Notes & Queries	"	"	8
Dec 9	1 Put off 3 Vols	"	9	"
	1 The Black Panther	"	4	6
	Churchmans Penny Mage July to Dec	"	"	6
	Penny Post ―――――― do ――	"	"	6
	Boys Own Magazine ―― do ――	"	3	"
	Sunday Magazine ―――― do ――	"	3	6
	Bradshaws Guide Oct Nov & Dec	"	"	9
	Childrens Friend	"	"	8
	Staffordshire Advertiser July to Dec	"	10	"
	1 Swimming & Skating	"	"	6

Shirley's Buildings, St. Edward Street.

Leek, *Dec 31st*   188*8*

Mr H S Russell

Bought of CLEMESHA & CLOWES,

⇒⁕ LETTERPRESS ⁕ AND ⁕ LITHOGRAPHIC ⁕ PRINTERS, ⁕ ENGRAVERS, ⁕⇐

BOOKBINDERS, AND ACCOUNT BOOK MANUFACTURERS.

Billheads,
MEMO NOTES,
CIRCULARS.
CLUB RULES,
PAMPHLETS,
HANDBILLS
Posters,
And every descrip-
tion of Commercial
and General Work
executed with care
and economy.

646

1888			3
Nov 29	100 Visiting Cards from plate		4

Besides being a printer, Clemesha also supplied books and periodicals. This invoice appears to represent six months trading with Mr William Challinor. It shows a wide range of books, newspapers and periodicals - an indication of the interests of this well-respected Leek solicitor and his family.

Leek, *June 30th 1869.*

Mr Alsops Exors.

Bought of WILLIAM CLEMESHA,
MACHINE PRINTER,
BOOKSELLER, STATIONER, ENGRAVER, LITHOGRAPHER, AND BOOKBINDER.

NEWSPAPER AND ADVERTISING AGENT.

✱✱✱ The London and Manchester Daily Papers and all Magazines received by early trains, and delivered as speedily as possible.

Agent for "The Staffordshire Advertiser."

Apr. 22	Advt. J. Alsop	1 ce	Gazette	2	2	·
		2 ce	Daily News	2	15	·
		2 ce	Standard	3	·	·
		3 ce	S. A.	1	11	6
		3 ce	Sentinel	1	10	‡
1 London Gazette. 2 Daily News 2 Standards			@	·	2	7 ·
3 Advertisers. & 3 Sentinels			£	11	1	‡

Leek, *December 7. 1870*

11, STANLEY STREET,

Mr G. S. Fox

Bought of WILLIAM CLEMESHA,
STATIONER, ENGRAVER,
LETTERPRESS & LITHOGRAPHIC PRINTER, BOOKBINDER, &c.

✱✱✱ The London and Manchester Daily Papers and all Magazines received by early trains, and delivered as speedily as possible.

1869

WILLIAM CLEMESHA, 11 Stanley Street, Leek William Clemesha bought the printing business of George Nall & Son in 1865, and continued to operate from 11 Stanley Street, where he pioneered the hand-powered flatbed machine in Leek. This was capable of producing 500 copies per hour, and was a great step forward, for prior to this all printing had been done by the platen process. The business moved to St. Edward Street, where it remained until sometime after 1880.

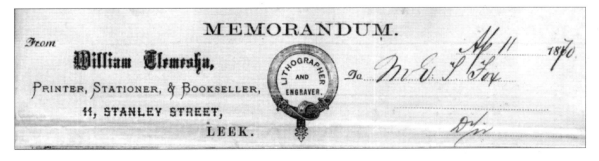

MEMORANDUM.

From
William Clemesha,
PRINTER, STATIONER, & BOOKSELLER,
11, STANLEY STREET,
LEEK.

Ap 11 1870

Dr M. G. S. Fox

LITHOGRAPHER AND ENGRAVER.

BASFORD, NEAR LEEK,

①   *Midsummer*   1901

Mess.rs Ash and Scarratt

To JAMES CLOWES & SONS,

BUILDERS, WHEELWRIGHTS, BLACKSMITHS, &c.

Colts Moor Farm Bradnop.

1900		£	s	d		£	s	d
October 27	Four Field Gates Oak Heads & Heal Larch Bars.	2	14	.				
	Two Coats Paint each and painting		10	.				
	3-6-3½ × 3 Oak 3-6-3×2 Oak 7-6-3½×2 R² Deal		2	6½				
	5-3-11×1 Red Deal ½ lb Cut Nails 1½ lb Paint		2	1				
	7-0-6×5- 7-0-6×5- 7-0-6×6 Oak Posts		17	11½				
	1 lb Paint 21½ lbs Lead 4/6		5					
	12 Hours Man @ 7/- Making Wicket Gate							
	planeing & painting Posts & two coats		7	3				
	5 Hooks, 8 Thimbles, 3 Sets chain fastness,							
			16					

BASFORD,

Near Leek, *July 9th* 1918

PROPRIETORS:
SAMUEL CLOWES
JOSEPH CLOWES

The x.ors of The Late Mrs Bold

DR. TO

JAMES CLOWES & SONS,

BUILDERS, etc.

Cheddleton Station. N.S.R.

1918		£	s	d
June 21	To English Oak Coffin lined and Polished with brass furniture Complete	5	14	4
	To Two Coaches from Leek To Cheddleton Church	2	15	0
	To 2 doz Funeral Cards		9	0
	To Burial Fees at Cheddleton Church		14	0

FOUNTAIN STREET BOX WORKS,

FOUNTAIN STREET,

LEEK, _____ 192

Wages paid to
Mrs Bevan.

Dr. to L. CLOWES.

She commenced work July 7/1925

week ending (Thursdays)
July 9   25½ hours   15   1

Clowes and Leech had a small
factory in Shoobridge Street.

Memorandum.

FROM

CLOWES & LEECH,

Silk Manufacturers,

LEEK
Staffordshire.

Apr 7   18 94

To Guymer Esq

Leek

Dr Sir,
I did not know that I could give notice
except on the due dates; thanks I accept the
notice as from Mch 12th
Yours very truly
W Leech

TALBOT STREET FURNISHING WAREHOUSE.

W. H. CLOWES,

PRACTICAL ∴ CABINET ∴ MAKER,

Upholsterer & Undertaker,

15, TALBOT ST, LEEK.

BRITANNIA SILK MILL

Russell and Clowes,

Silk Manufacturers,

LEEK. *Staffordshire*

Britannia Silk Mill was at the top of West Street. It later became Goodwin and Tatton. It was destroyed by fire during the Second World War.

Dr Richard Cooper was in Derby Street. The practice was later that of Dr Somerville, which moved to St Edward Street. The Fountain Street Medical Centre are their direct successors.

THE CHEAPEST & BEST PLACE

— TO GO TO FOR —

MEMORIAL ∻ CARDS

— OF ALL KINDS, —

And General Mourning Stationery,

— IS —

RICHARD CLOWES,'

ST. EDWARD STREET, LEEK.

✦✦✦✦✦✦✦✦✦✦✦✦✦✦✦✦✦✦

BOOKBINDING, MACHINE RULING,

— AND —

PATTERN ∻ CARD ∻ MAKING

OF EVERY DESCRIPTION, AT

CLOWES & Co.,

"Ye Caxton"

STEAM PRINTING WORKS,

LONDON MILLS, LEEK.

Professional letter headings usually only included the minimum of information - in complete contrast to those of manufacturers and traders.

Leek, 1866

William Phillips, Esqr.

To Cooper & Goodman, Surgeons, Dr.

Professional Attendance in January 1867 — March, April, May, June, July, August & to Sepr 6th 1865 — Medicine &c   £ s d
26. 8. 6

To Richd Cooper — Dr
Professional Attendance from Sepr 13 to Dec 31st 1866 — Medicine &c   12. 15. 0

£ 39. 3. 6

Ye Olde Coffee Tavern

CATTLE MARKET, LEEK,

Proprietor: A WARD.

HOT

DINNERS

DAILY.

PLAIN

AND

FANCY

TEAS.

PARTIES CATERED FOR.   ACCOMMODATION FOR CYCLISTS.

The Smithfield Commercial Restaurant-popularly known as the "Coffee Tavern" was founded by the Temperance movement. It was unlicensed - no alcoholic beverages - but it provided hot drinks and snacks.

The Coffee Tavern is seen here below, on the right, as the band marches down Ashbourne Road.

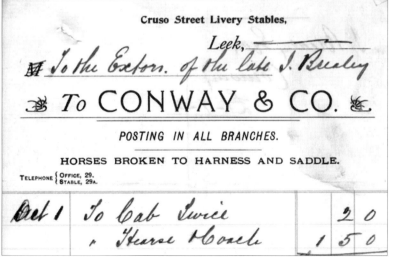

Cruso Street Livery Stables,

Leek,

To the Exetors. of the late J. Beasley

To CONWAY & CO.

POSTING IN ALL BRANCHES.

HORSES BROKEN TO HARNESS AND SADDLE.

TELEPHONE { OFFICE, 29.
{ STABLE, 29A.

Oct 1	To Cab Twice	2	0
	„ Hearse & Coach	1 5	0

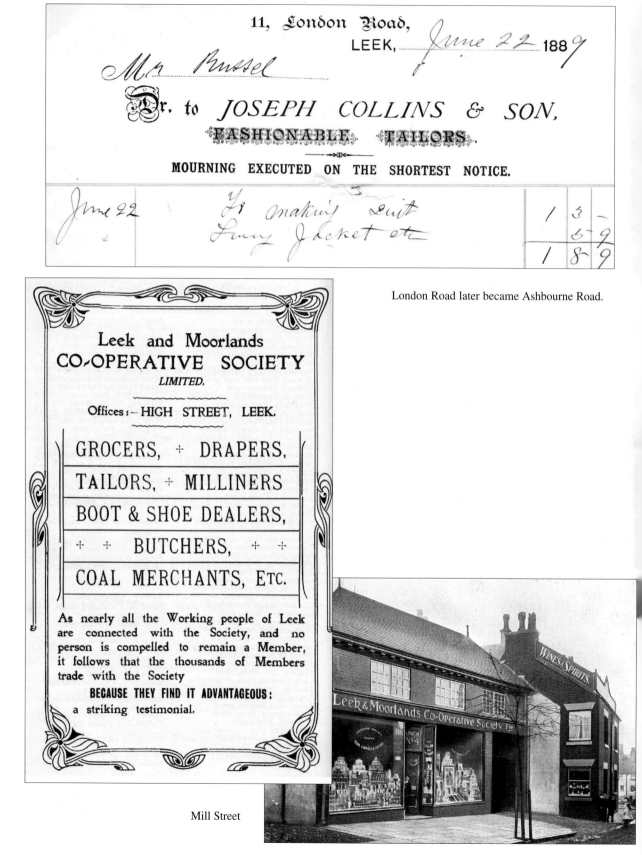

11, London Road,
LEEK, *June 22* 1889

Mr *Russel*

Dr. to JOSEPH COLLINS & SON,
FASHIONABLE TAILORS.

MOURNING EXECUTED ON THE SHORTEST NOTICE.

June 22	To making suit		1	3	-
	Linen Jacket etc			6	9
			1	8	9

London Road later became Ashbourne Road.

Leek and Moorlands
CO-OPERATIVE SOCIETY
LIMITED.

Offices:—HIGH STREET, LEEK.

GROCERS, + DRAPERS,

TAILORS, + MILLINERS

BOOT & SHOE DEALERS,

+ + BUTCHERS, + +

COAL MERCHANTS, ETC.

As nearly all the Working people of Leek
are connected with the Society, and no
person is compelled to remain a Member,
it follows that the thousands of Members
trade with the Society
BECAUSE THEY FIND IT ADVANTAGEOUS:
a striking testimonial.

Mill Street

SOME LEEK COOPERATIVE SOCIETY BRANCHES

Osborne Street

St. Edward Street

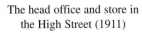

Milk Street

The head office and store in
the High Street (1911)

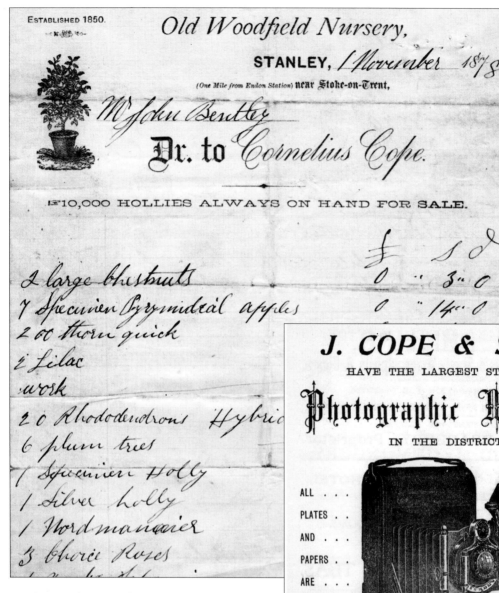

Established 1850.

Old Woodfield Nursery,

STANLEY, *1 November 1878*

(One Mile from Endon Station) near Stoke-on-Trent,

M*r* John Bentley

Dr. to Cornelius Cope.

☞ 10,000 HOLLIES ALWAYS ON HAND FOR SALE.

	£	s	d
2 large chestnuts	0	3	0
7 Specimen Pyramidal apples	0	14	0
2 00 thorn quick			
2 Lilac			
work			
20 Rhododendrons Hybrid			
6 plum trees			
1 Specimen Holly			
1 Silver Holly			
1 Nordmanianier			
3 choice Roses			

J. COPE & SONS

HAVE THE LARGEST STOCK OF

Photographic Materials

IN THE DISTRICT.

ALL . . .		❋
PLATES . .		
AND . . .		WE . . . .
PAPERS . .		RECEIVE . .
ARE . . .		SUPPLIES. .
GUARANTEED		DAILY . . .
PERFECTLY .		
FRESH. . . .		❋

DEVELOPING AND OTHER SOLUTIONS

correctly made to any formula at LONDON PRICES.

ANY DESCRIPTION OF CAMERA SUPPLIED AT MAKERS' PRICES.

Cawdry Drug & Photographic Stores,

CATTLE MARKET, LEEK.

Developing, Printing & Enlarging undertaken for Amateurs.

Raymond Cope, successor to J. Cope, was a dispensing chemist at the bottom of Fountain Street, by the 'Cattle Market', until the late 1970s when it sold out to what is now Lloyds chemists.

EXHIBITION PRIZE MEDAL ! !

ELIJAH COPE,

CARVER,   GILDER,   FRET-CUTTER,

ANTIQUE AND MODERN PICTURE FRAME MANUFACTURER,

46, LONDON ROAD, LEEK.

PICTURES CLEANED AND REGILT.

OLD PICTURES BOUGHT OR TAKEN IN EXCHANGE.

Every description of Picture Frames executed on the shortest notice. Best Price given for Old Books, Old Coins, Waste Paper, and Antique Furniture.   All orders promptly attended to.

This Elijah Cope was also a local poet of some repute who self published several works.

The "COZ" Corn Cure.

SAFE.   **SPEEDY.**   **SURE.**

Never Dries Up.   ::   POST-FREE 1/-

Sole Proprietor of Johnson & Sons' Celebrated Infants' Mixture.

Over Eighty Years' reputation and success.

Healthy Children and happy Mothers wherever used.   Post-Free 1/-

Cousins, at 13 Derby Street. It was originally Hartley's (p. 243) and later became Edward Jones who eventually sold out to Boots chemists.

Street.

Leek,   *Sep 29* **1917.**

Messrs Goldstraw + Son. Dyers

Shrobridge St

Bought of   **G. H. Cousins, M.P.S.**

(LATE HARTLEY),

Dispensing Chemist & Optician.

Proprietor of Johnson's Celebrated Infants' Mixture.   Hartley's Tussaline for Coughs. The "Coz" Remedies. Surgical appliances, dressings and Invalid requisites kept in stock.

1917		d
June 15 1 lb Tartan Emetic	5	9

ATS, CAPS, SHIRTS, TIES, FRONTS,

Collars, Cardigan Jackets, Gloves, Braces,

Un anything yo want, now's yer toime, roll up to

CRAZE'S, Sheep Market,

LEEK, STAFFS., ENGLAND.

Mr Craze liked to give his adverts a touch of humour with quirky comments in 'dialect'.

Shoobridge Street,

Leek, _____ 189

M

From I. Creighton,

BOBBIN ∴ MANUFACTURER.

	£	s	d
Debts owing to Mr Creighton	123	13	7
Debts owing by Mr Creighton	69	4	7
Balance £	54	9	0
Money in Stores	44	16	3½
Cheque for Dog	6	6	0
Money in Mr Creighton's Pocket	3	0	0
Club Money about	20	0	0
£	128	11	3½

Furniture

39 : 18 : 0

72 . 74. 76 ...

Grove St.

Wm Floor Sons

20.

Taxes ... 4/-

By Land tax ... 2 4/3

Isaac Creighton was listed as a bobbin turner at 4 Cromwell Terrace and Shoobridge Street in Kelly's 1888 Directory, and continued to be listed until 1907. From 1912 William Creighton is operating the same business from 10 Westwood Terrace and Shoobridge Street, and later, as Creighton & Co., Sneyd Street.

STANLEY STONE QUARRY,

Ivy House **STANLEY,** *Dec 7th* 1881
STOKE-ON-TRENT.

Memorandum,

From **Thomas E. H. Cooper,**

Endon, **June** 1892
Stoke-on-Trent.

Mr John Mountford

To WILLIAM CRITCHLOW,

JOINER, BUILDER, AND UNDERTAKER.

Dealer in Paints, English and Foreign Timber, &c.

1892		£	s	d
June	2 new field gate with oak head & heel, & hung complete	1	12	6

TALBOT STREET, (Works, Leonard Street),
LEEK *Sep. 14th* 1908

Mrs Jackson

To R. A. CROMBIE,

Joiner, Cabinet Maker, Upholsterer, and Complete House Furnisher.

Furniture of all kinds made to order. Funerals conducted on the most reasonable terms,

6 Bottles of Beer @ 6d each		3	0
1 " " Port		2	0
1 " " Whiskey Special		4	0
1 " " Sherry		2	0
1 pair of Stockings			6½
		11	6½
1 Cloth rug. Debt.		8	6

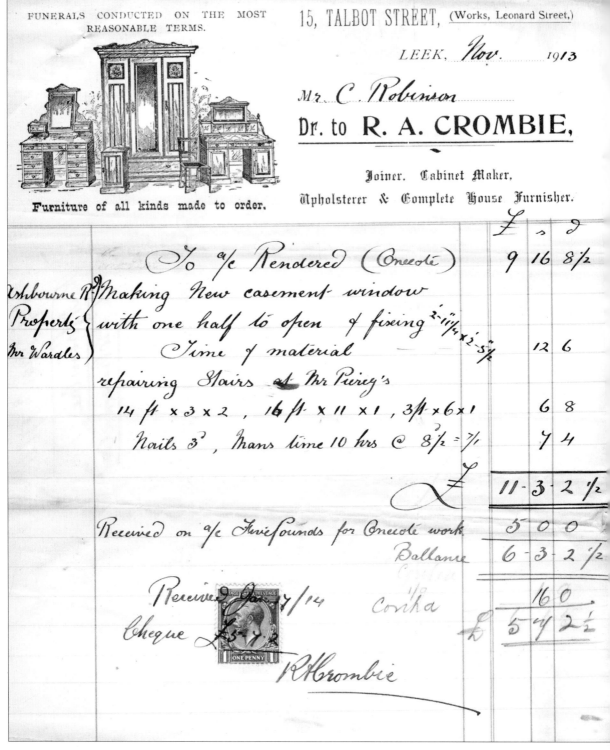

FUNERALS CONDUCTED ON THE MOST
REASONABLE TERMS.

Furniture of all kinds made to order.

15, TALBOT STREET, (Works, Leonard Street,)

LEEK, *Nov.* 1913

Mr. *C. Robinson*

Dr. to R. A. CROMBIE,

Joiner. Cabinet Maker,
Upholsterer & Complete House Furnisher.

	£	s	d
To a/c Rendered (Onecote)	9	16	8½
Ashbourne R./ Making New casement window with one half to open & fixing 2-11¼ × 2-5½		12	6
Property Mr Wardles / Time & material repairing Stairs at Mr Piercy's			
14 ft × 3 × 2 , 16 ft × 11 × 1 , 3 ft × 6 × 1		6	8
Nails 3ᵈ, Mans time 10 hrs @ 8½ = 7/1		7	4
£	11	3	2½
Received on a/c Fivepounds for Onecote work	5	0	0
Ballance	6	3	2½
Conta		16	0
£	5	4	2½

Received Nov 7/14
Cheque £5/4/2

R A Crombie

ONE PENNY

R.A. CROMBIE, Talbot Street, Leek. The workshop was in Leonard Street, was also a undertaker, house
furnisher and furniture maker. The firm later moved to Grosvenor Street, where they remained until the 1960s.

8, BROOKLANDS ASHBOURNE ROAD,

LEEK,   *Oct* 1913

To Executor of

Mr Robinson

Dr. to Mrs. Cumberbatch,

COSTUMIER.

22nd	Making Costume		17. 6
	9 " " "		16. 4
23	" "		14. 10
	Serge	4.	6. 3
	Silk		12. 9
	" "		11. 8
	" "		9. 4
	Buttons		2. 8
	Glacede		4. 6
	Canvas & petishem		1. 5½
	Serge	1.	9. 5
	Material		8. 7
		£10.	15. 2½
	Paid 12		4. 5½
	1913		
	M.A. Cumberbatch	10.	19. 8
	with thanks		

VERNON DANIELS,

CAB & OMNIBUS PROPRIETOR,

ROE BUCK YARD, LEEK.

POSTING

IN ALL ITS BRANCHES.

FIRST-CLASS

Wedding & Party Carriages

On the shortest notice, at moderate prices.

HEARSES & MOURNING COACHES.

During the 1920s a new kind of trader emerged - the radio, or "wireless" dealer. Walter Day was a forerunner in this field, a householders invested in this new media o information and entertainment. This is an early, hand-written credit sale agreement.

WALTER DAY,

WIRELESS SUPPLIES.

SNEYD STREET,

LEEK,
STAFFS.

Feb: 11th 1926

I the undersigned agree to pay this 11th day of February 1926 the total sum of Seven pounds fifteen shillings & seven pence to Walter Day for wireless goods supplied, by weekly payments of ten shillings following this date, of my signature, until the total sum of £7-15-7 has been paid by me, or immediately on the sale of the wireless set held by me which I value at nineteen pounds.

Witness my hand this 11 day of Feb. 1926

Witness ..... Day
Witness ..... A. Day.
23 Hugo St.

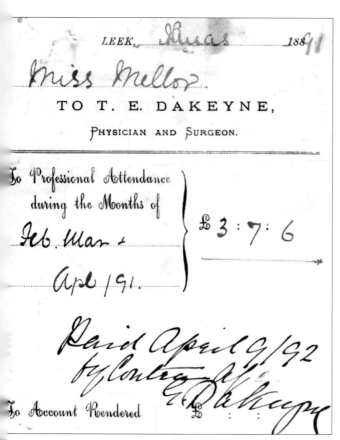

LEEK, *Xmas* 188*1*

Miss Mellor

TO T. E. DAKEYNE,

PHYSICIAN AND SURGEON.

To Professional Attendance
during the Months of
Feb Mar +
Apl /91.

£ 3 : 7 : 6

Paid April 9/92
by Contra ...
T. E. Dakeyne

To Account Rendered   £   :   :

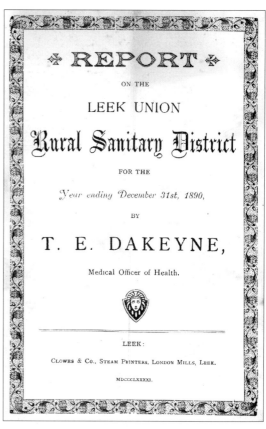

✠ REPORT ✠

ON THE

LEEK UNION

Rural Sanitary District

FOR THE

Year ending December 31st, 1890,

BY

T. E. DAKEYNE,

Medical Officer of Health.

LEEK:

CLOWES & CO., STEAM PRINTERS, LONDON MILLS, LEEK.

MDCCCLXXXXI.

Dr Dakeyne lived and practised on the corner of Bath Street with Stockwell Street. The premises remained a doctors' surgery until the mid-1980s (Dr Lawson/Elsdon, Drs Watson and successors). He followed Dr J.J Ritchie as Medical Officer of Health for Leek in 1893 and was in turn followed by Dr J Mountford Johnson in 1900. Fields House, High Street, is shown below in the early 20th century. It was also a doctors' - the names on the plates on the gate are Dr Frederick Ernest Fielden and Dr W.E. Davies - who had moved to King Street by 1912.

Memorandum Leek, *Aug 3. 1896*

From George Davenport & Co.
Hope Silk Mills, Leek,
Staffordshire.
and 36 Monkwell Street, London

To Messrs Challinor & Shaw
Leek
Mr Wm Newall

Dear Sir,

Re. Insurance on our Machinery for £.1000. We only hold the original Policy of the ~~London & Staffordshire~~ Insurance Company has any other been issued since and in which case do you hold it & has Mr Arkcoll had it

Yours Truly
for Geo Davenport &
EG.

> Hope Silk Mill was at the
> bottom of Mill Street.

TELEPHONE No. 65.
TELEGRAMS:-
"SWANNECKS, LEEK."
"ADAMS"

PRIZE MEDAL 1851.

ESTABLISHED 1828.

TRADE MARK REGISTERED.
TRADE MARK REGISTERED No 20050.
TRADE MARK REGISTERED.
TRADE MARK REGISTERED.

HOPE SILK MILL,
LEEK, *Jany 18 1909*
STAFFS:

Mr W Young C/o Mr C Watson Leek

BOUGHT OF GEO. DAVENPORT, ADAMS & CO.
SILK & BRAID MANUFACTURERS.

PLAIN & FANCY BRAIDS, DRESS TRIMMINGS & ORNAMENTS,
SEWING, MACHINE, LEGEE, KNITTING & EMBROIDERY SILKS,
MERCERISED MACHINE TWIST AND EMBROIDERIES.

TERMS:-   5% interest charged on overdue Accounts. No goods received back after one week from date of Invoice.

1/2 for Braid Spoiled as per enclosed.	17.	6	
To cleaning Machine		2	6

Posting and Livery Stables, Black Swan Hotel Yard,

SHEEP MARKET, LEEK, *HC* ____ 189 *5*

Messrs Challinor & Shaw

Dr. to HENRY DAVENPORT,

Baker and Corn Dealer.

TERMS CASH.

Dec 12	*Cab to Rushton & over*		*8*
	Paid Dec 13/95		
	W Davenport		

Telephone No. 18.   Telegrams: "DAVENPORT'S, LEEK."

Posting and Livery Stables, Black Swan Hotel,

Sheep Market and Field Street, _____ *July 8* _____ 190 *9*

Mr C. G. Gwynne

DR. TO W. & H. DAVENPORT,

HEARSES & MOURNING COACHES.

WEDDING AND PARTY CARRIAGES ON THE SHORTEST NOTICE.

TERMS :—CASH.

			£	
To dog cart & drive to				*10*
Warrington				
Pd drive				*2*
				12

TELEPHONE No. 18.   Telegrams : "DAVENPORT'S." LEEK.

Posting and Livery Stables, Black Swan Hotel.

Sheep Market and Field Street, Leek,   *Mar 30* 1912

M A. H. Shaw Esq

Dr. to **W. & H. DAVENPORT**

Hearses & Mourning Coaches.

Terms: CASH.   Wedding and Party Carriages on the Shortest Notice.

1912

Feb 16   Landaulette Ashcombe   10 6
                                   10 6
No. A. 424   Leek, *June 8* 1912   £ 1 1 0

W. & H. DAVENPORT,

Posting and Livery Stables, Black Swan Hotel,
SHEEP MARKET & FIELD STREET.

Received of *W. H. Shaw*

A succession of billheads across the Edwardian years for W. and H. Davenport marks the transition from the 19th to the 20th century, with stately hearses and funeral carriages as reminders of the Victorian way of mourning. Below: A funeral approaches St Edward's Church.

A SELECTION OF HORSE DRAWN
TRANSPORT FROM THE LEEK AREA
AT THE TURN OF THE CENTURY.

Right: The Earl of Shrewsbury's coach
leaving the Red Lion.

Below: A large vehicle at the top of
Stockwell Street.

Bottom: A carriage outside
Swythamley Hall.

Above: A family cart or gig outside the Moss Rose, Buxton Road.
Below: A gentleman's gig outside the Red Lion in the Market Place.

TELEPHONE No 18.

TELEGRAMS: "DAVENPORTS, LEEK."

Posting and Livery Stables, Black Swan Hotel,
SHEEP MARKET, LEEK, April 3 190 6

Mr Robinson

Dr. to W. & H. DAVENPORT,

Hearses & Mourning Coaches,

WEDDING AND PARTY CARRIAGES,

ON THE SHORTEST NOTICE. TERMS: CASH.

Mar 26	Gig to Waterfall & Waterhouses	10	.
	Cab to Nab Hill	1	.
		. 11	.

Recd April 3-06
E. Davenport
With Thanks

TELEPHONE No. 18.

TELEGRAMS : " DAVENPORTS, LEEK."

Posting & Livery Stables, Black Swan Hotel,
SHEEP MARKET, LEEK, May 13 190 2

Messrs Heath & Lowe

Dr. to W. & H. DAVENPORT,

Hearses & Mourning Coaches,

Wedding & Party Carriages,

ON THE SHORTEST NOTICE. TERMS ; CASH.

1901				
June 2	To Hearse & Three Coaches to Cheddleton	3	10	0

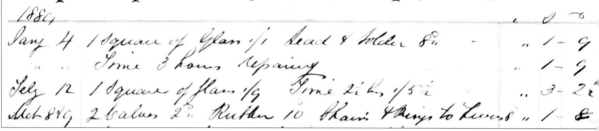

MARKET STREET, LEEK, *Mar* 188*7*

At Josh Challinor Esq (Wetton Compton School,)

To W. DAVENPORT,

Painter, Plumber, Glazier, Gas-Fitter, Paper Hanger, &c.

1880

Jany 4	*1 Square of Glass 1/ Lead & Solder 8d*		*1 - 9*
..	*Time 3 hours repairing*		*1 - 9*
Feby 12	*1 Square of Glass 1/9 Time 2 hrs 1/5½*		*3 - 2½*
Mch 8 & 9	*2 Calves 2d Putter 10 Chain & Rings to Levers*		*1 - 8*

Wardle & Davenport Ltd.

MANUFACTURERS & DYERS OF

PURE MACHINE & SEWING SILKS·
TAILORS'& LEGEE TWISTS·BOOT CLOSING
SILKS & TWISTS·SPUN SILKS & TWISTS·
CREWEL FILOSELLE & KNITTING SILKS·
TAPESTRY FLAT CHENILLE, PERI-LUSTA,
EMBROIDERY, KNITTINGS & CHENILLES·
BELT WEBS·PRUSSIAN BINDINGS·SILK
CUSHION & FURNITURE CORDS·LACING
& CORSET CORDS·SILK MOHAIR & COTTON
BOOT, SHOE & CORSET LACES, COSTUME
BRAIDS, RUSSIAS, &c.

TELEGRAMS, "SILK, LEEK."

LEEK,

24th Dec, 190*1*

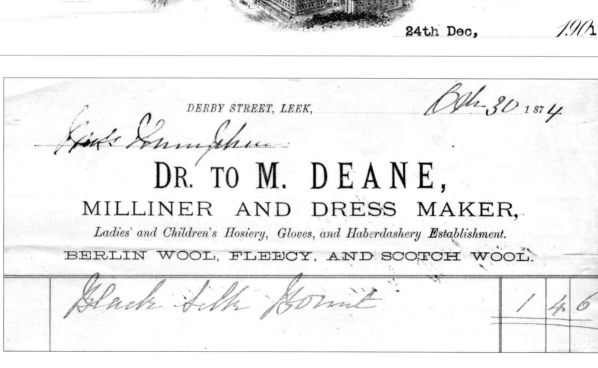

DERBY STREET, LEEK, *Oct 30* 187*4*

DR. TO M. DEANE,

MILLINER AND DRESS MAKER,

Ladies' and Children's Hosiery, Gloves, and Haberdashery Establishment.

BERLIN WOOL, FLEECY, AND SCOTCH WOOL.

Black Silk Bonnet	1	4 6

No. 3, DERBY STREET,

Leek, Midsummer 18 *69*

M *W Challinor Esqr*

Bought of THOMAS DEAKIN,

COOPER.

ALL KINDS OF DAIRY UTENSILS, TURNED HOLLOW-WARE GOODS, CASKS, &c.

TERMS—MIDSUMMER AND CHRISTMAS.

Feby 2	*2 Weed Brooms & Stails*	*3 . 8*
13	*9 new hoops on 2 Water tubs*	*10 . 8*
June 21	*Repairing 1 Stable Bucket & painting*	*2 . 6*
		16 . 10

ESTABLISHED 1825.

1 & 3, DERBY STREET,

Leek, 188*4*

Mrs Thos Plant

Bought of THOMAS DEAKIN,

COOPER.

All kinds of Dairy Utensils, Turned Hollow-ware Goods, Casks, Barrel & Oval Churns, &c.

TERMS:—QUARTERLY.

Jany 4	*1 Fir Clothes Box*	*11 . 0*

Settled August 18th /84

Thomas Deakin

Barrels and tubs were produced by this firm, trading in Derby Street since 1825. Subsequent proprietors all carried the nickname of "Tubthumper" Deakin.

If you fail to be elected as a Member of the

MUSTARD CLUB - -

You are still eligible to join my list of Customers who are out to secure

SEASONABLE CHRISTMAS GIFTS

Wm. DELANEY,
39, DERBY ST.

Manufacturers of

SEWING SILKS & TWISTS.
SILK & MILITARY BUTTONS.
SILK EYE-GLASS CORDS & WATCH GUARDS.
SILK & LINEN FISHING LINES.
SILK & COTTON WHIP CORDS.
HAIR CURLERS, &c.

TELEGRAMS: "DISHLEY, LEEK."

Established 1850.

H. Dishley & Co.,
Silk Manufacturers,

Leek, *Aug 24ᵗʰ 191?*
STAFFS.

M/s *Challinor & Shaw*   *Re Bates*

Gents

I wrote re a/c & offered to accept £15/- at once £20/- Say 20ᵗʰ post dated Cheque & balance Oct 1ˢᵗ I will ... he replies

H. Dishley's factory was in Novi Lane.

The District Bank (now NatWest) Derby St (Architects, Sugdens)

Manchester and Liverpool
DISTRICT BANK,
LIMITED,
LEEK.

ESTABLISHED 1829. LEEK BRANCH OPENED 1833.

Subscribed Capital £9,480,000. Paid-up Capital £1,896,000.
Reserve Fund £1,410,000.

HEAD OFFICE, SPRING GARDENS, MANCHESTER,
AND

214 Branches in Lancashire, Cheshire, Staffordshire,
Shropshire, Yorkshire, Derbyshire, Cumberland, Westmorland,
and North Wales.

HOURS OF BUSINESS:

MONDAYS	
TUESDAYS	FROM 10 TO 3.
THURSDAYS	
FRIDAYS	
...ESDAYS	FROM 10 TO 4.
...DAYS	FROM 9 TO 12.

EXCEPTIONS.

...day and Friday in August Bank Holiday
Week (Leek Holidays) From 9 to 11 a.m.

BANK HOLIDAYS.

| Good Friday. | Whit Monday. |
| Easter Monday. | The First Mon. in Aug. |

Christmas Day,
he next following week-days (26th or 27th of
December as the case may be).

NORMAN MASSÉ,
Manager.

Manchester and Liverpool
District Banking Company,
Derby Street, Leek.

—o—

Banking Hours from 10 to 3; Wednesdays 10 to 4;
Saturdays 10 to 1.
London Agents: Smith, Payne, & Smith.
A. R. WHYATT, Manager.

50, DERBY STREET,

LEEK, *21st March* 1892

To The Executors of Mrs Hannah Birch deceased

BOUGHT OF E. DONE,

BOOT AND SHOE MAKER.

REPAIRS PROMPTLY ATTENDED TO.

1892				9	0
Jany 21	To 1 pair of Boots				

Settled ...
E Done

A local carrier outside the Cock Inn, Derby Street.

J. DONE'S

BOOTS & SHOES

— ARE —

GOOD,

STYLISH

AND CHEAP.

DUKE OF YORK

LEEK.

A Popular Resort Of the CRICKET, . . FOOTBALL & CYCLING FRATERNITY. . . .

Musical Free-and-Easy every Evening.

PRIME ALES and STOUT, A1 WINES and SPIRITS and FINEST BRAND CIGARS.

FIRST-CLASS STABLING.   W. H. PEACH, PROPRIETOR.

This site is now the Derby Street office of the Leek United Building Society.

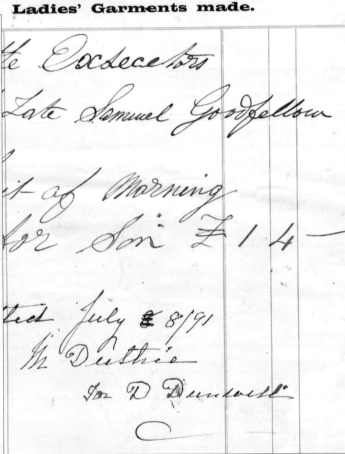

21, Church Street, Leek,

6 May 1891

M ....

Bought of D. DUNWELL.

TAILOR, WOOLLEN DRAPER, &c.

Ladies' Garments made.

...te Executors

...Late Samuel Goodfellow

...t of Morning

...for Son £ 1 4 —

...ted July 8/91

Th Duthie

for D Dunwell

W. A. DUTTON & CO.,

Sheep Market

MAGNIFICENT FURS
- and FUR SETS -

Gloves,
Silk and Art Silk
Underwear,
- Handkerchiefs, -
Silk & Art Silk Hose

W. A. DUTTON & Co.,

Sheep Market,
⊱ LEEK. ⊰

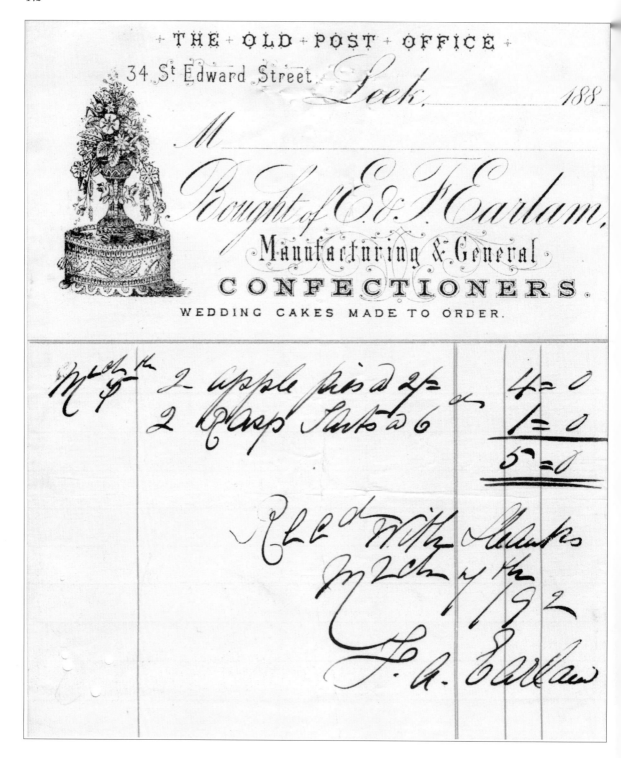

⸭ THE ⸭ OLD ⸭ POST ⸭ OFFICE ⸭
34 St Edward Street *Leek,* 188

M

Bought of E. & F. Earlam,
Manufacturing & General
CONFECTIONERS.
WEDDING CAKES MADE TO ORDER.

March 5th   2 Apple pies @ 2/=   4 = 0
             2 Rasp Tarts @ 6d   1 = 0
                                    5 = 0

Rec'd with Thanks
March 7th
19 2
F. A. Earlam

Spout Street, Leek,

1850

Mr I Robinson

To William Eaton,

TAILOR, WOOLLEN DRAPER, &c.

FAMILY MOURNING COMPLETED ON THE SHORTEST NOTICE.

(Accounts delivered at Midsummer and Christmas.)

		£	s.	d.
August 17th	To 1 Green Russell Cord Jacket	1	4	0
1851 April 30th	*Settled Eaton*			

SPOUT STREET, LEEK.

Mr James Allen Esqre

Bought of E. EATON & SON,

TAILORS AND WOOLLEN DRAPERS,

NECK-TIES, SHIRT COLLARS, AND GENTLEMEN'S SCARFS.

Family Mourning executed on the shortest notice.

1862				£	s.	d.
July 11	To 1 Super Mixture Livery Coat & Vest			3	0	0
"	1 Pair Drab Kersey Smalls & gaiter			1	12	0
"	1 Stable Suit			2	12	6
Decr 23	1 Super Drab Kersey ... & Cape			4	4	0
				£11	8	0

1865
18th
J Eaton Settled with thanks

ONE PENNY

Spout Street, Leek.

William Challinor Esqre

Bought of E. EATON & SON,
TAILORS AND WOOLLEN DRAPERS.

DEALERS IN HATS & CAPS, GENTLEMEN'S SCARFS, NECK-TIES, & SHIRT COLLARS.

Family Mourning executed on the shortest notice.

1865

Jany 7	Supr Black Frock Coat frm	4	1	6
	Melton Trowser Marm 4		19	0
March 11	2 Black Vests at m	1	8	0
18	Repairg Frock Coat		2	0
	" Top Coat		1	9
May 13	" Trowser		1	3
June 1	Supr Black Coat	1	8	0
	" Trowser frm	1	6	6
16	Making Frock Coat & Trimmings		16	0
	2½ Silk at 5/-		12	6
	Making Trowsers & Trimmings		6	6
July 8	Making Frock Suit & Trimmgs		18	6
	Black Trowser		19	6
	Supr Black Vest		14	0
15	Making Trowsers & Trimmgs		6	6
August 4	Repg Trowsers		2	0
Sepr 16	Rep Coat & New linings		2	3
	1 Alp at 2/6		2	6
	Rep Coat & New lings		2	3
	1 Alpaca at 2/6		2	6
30	Remaking 2 Jackets at 6/-		12	0
Oct	Repairg Trowser		1	3

St. Edward Street, Leek.

—*Mr. Goodwin and Whitley Rock.*

Bought of E. EATON & SON,

TAILORS & WOOLLEN DRAPERS.

SILK AND FELT HATS, CAPS, SCARVES, SHIRTS, COLLARS, UMBRELLAS,
MACKINTOSHES, HOSIERY, &C.

MOURNING EXECUTED ON THE SHORTEST NOTICE.

AGENT TO THE LIVERPOOL, LONDON, & GLOBE ASSURANCE COMPANY.

1881			
Jany 3.	Sup Blck Suit	4.. 4.. 0	
	Shird 4/- Hat 12/6	16.. 6	
		£ 5.. 0.. 6	

St. Edward Street, Leek, 6 Nov. 1893.

The Executors of the late Mrs. E.M. Prince

ПО E. EATON & SON,

✷ TAILORS ✷ AND ✷ WOOLLEN ✷ DRAPERS, ✷

Ladies' Habit, Jacket, and Ulster Makers.

SILK & FELT HATS, CAPS, TIES, SHIRTS, COLLARS, UMBRELLAS, MACINTOSHES, HOSIERY, &c.

MOURNING EXECUTED ON THE SHORTEST NOTICE.

AGENTS TO THE LIVERPOOL, LONDON & GLOBE INSURANCE COMPANY.

1893						
Sep 30	Black Doeskin Trousers	Devan Trough		1	4	6
" "	do Worsted Coat	Trough		2	6	6
				3	11	..

3441

Received ...
By Cheque ...
December ...
John Eaton

E. EATON & SON.

DERBY STREET,
L E E K, _____ 18

Mr Critchlow

Bought of W. A. EATON,
WHOLESALE AND RETAIL CONFECTIONER,
Fancy Bread and Biscuit Establishment.

1861		£	s	d
April 15th	To 15 lbs Funeral Biscuits at 1/4 per lb	1	0	0
"	2 lbs Finger Biscuits at 1/4		2	8
	50 Funeral Cards & Envelopes		6	0
"	10 Loaves of Bread at 6½		5	5
	6 lbs Sugar at 5½		2	9
	1 lb Lump Sugar			6½
	6 oz Tobacco		1	6
	¼ Mustard			5
	£	1	19	3½

Settled same time W. A. Eaton

41, DERBY STREET,

LEEK, _____ 183

Mr The Exors of the late Miss Mellor

Bought of **W. A. EATON,**

Confectioner, ∗ Grocer ∗ and ∗ Provision ∗ Dealer.

DEALER IN ALL KINDS OF FANCY BISCUITS.

1891	Bt Fd		1	19	10
Nov. 27	Tea 5½ Coffee 5				10½
	Rice 3 Sugar 7½				10½
	Marmalade 6½				6½
	Currants 5 Raisins 5				10
	Treacle 6 Soft Soap 4				10
	Flour 5½ Soap 7			1	0½
	Custard Powder 3				3
	Jellys 4½ Bread 7½			1	0
Dec. 11	Tea 5½ Coffee 10			1	3½
	Sugar 7½ Treacle 1/-			1	7½
	Soap 3 Flour 5½				8½
	Bread 10 Rice 3			1	1
	Marmalade 6½				6½
	Swiss Milk 1/-			1	0
18	Currants 1/7½			1	7½
	Raisins 1/0½ Sugar 6			1	6½
	Nutmeg 1				1
	Mixed Peel 1/2			1	2
			£	2	16	9

The Moorlands Press,

Leek, Sepr. 1. 1912.

Roland Taylor. Esq.

Dr. to W. H. Eaton,

Artistic Printer, Lithographer, Bookseller,

Manufacturing Stationer, &c.

1910	a/c Rendered		5	6
Oct 26 1912	Binding & interleaving hitherto	1 - 0		
May 24	Eng. plate & pty 50 cards from do	4 6		
		5. 6		

Recd. Sept. 17. 1912

W H Eaton

Agent for Oxford University Press.
 „ Cambridge Warehouse.
 „ S.P.C.K.
 „ Religious Tract Society.

The Leek Printing Offices and Stationery Warehouse.

Leek, Decr. 1897

Mr Marsh   Stockwell St.

Bought of William H. Eaton,

Printer, Lithographer, Bookseller, Account Book Maker, Manufacturing Stationer, &c.

Engraving, Die Sinking and Relief Stamping.   Artists' Materials.   Cricket and Lawn Tennis Goods.

Sepr.	9	Ream toned demy.	9	6
		500 a/c Heads	2	6
		1 Ream Dble demy	10	0
		100 sheets Royal sto.		9
		50 sheets Yellow & Crown		9
		1 Ream Dble demy toned	10	0

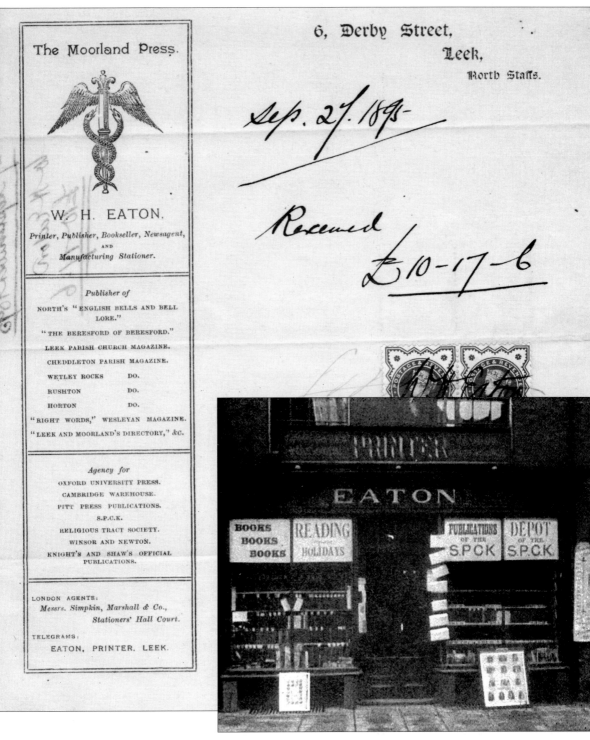

The Moorland Press.

W. H. EATON,

Printer, Publisher, Bookseller, Newsagent,
AND
Manufacturing Stationer.

Publisher of

NORTH'S "ENGLISH BELLS AND BELL
LORE."

"THE BERESFORD OF BERESFORD."

LEEK PARISH CHURCH MAGAZINE.

CHEDDLETON PARISH MAGAZINE.

WETLEY ROCKS   DO.

RUSHTON   DO.

HORTON   DO.

"RIGHT WORDS," WESLEYAN MAGAZINE.

"LEEK AND MOORLAND'S DIRECTORY," &c.

Agency for

OXFORD UNIVERSITY PRESS.

CAMBRIDGE WAREHOUSE.

PITT PRESS PUBLICATIONS.

S.P.C.K.

RELIGIOUS TRACT SOCIETY.

WINSOR AND NEWTON.

KNIGHT'S AND SHAW'S OFFICIAL
PUBLICATIONS.

LONDON AGENTS:
Messrs. Simpkin, Marshall & Co.,
Stationers' Hall Court.

TELEGRAMS:
EATON, PRINTER, LEEK.

6, Derby Street,
Leek,
North Staffs.

Sep. 27. 1895

Received
£10-17-6

WILLIAM H. EATON, The Moorland Press, 6 Derby Street, Leek A traditional jobbing printer, William Henry Eaton took over the premises formerly occupied by Thomas Mark. He built up a reputation meeting any demand for printing at short notice. His comprehensive stocks of commercial stationery provided a good service for the needs of local businesses. Amongst the many books and booklets published by The Moorlands Press was the first edition of W.H. Nithsdale's *In the Highlands of Staffordshire* in 1906. W.H. Eaton was also an accomplished musician, being the organist at Leek Parish Church. Under different ownership, The Moorlands Press continued to trade until the 1960s.

W. H. Eaton,

MACHINE!   **PRINTING!**

The Moorland Press,
DERBY STREET,
Leek.

A Choice Selection of
ATTRACTIVELY BOUND BOOKS
SUITABLE FOR PRESENTS,
W. H. EATON, THE MOORLANDS PRESS, LEEK.

---

a/123

FAR MORE SEEMLY WERE IT FOR THEE
TO HAVE THY STUDY FULL OF BOOKS
THAN THY PURSES FULL OF MONEY.
Lyly's Euphues.

Accounts Quarterly.

Depot S.P.C.K.
„   Religious Tract Society.
Agent for Oxford University Press.
„   Cambridge Warehouse.
„   Ordnance Survey.

The Moorlands Press and Leek Stationery Warehouse.

Leek Chamber of Commerce.

Leek,   March 31 1900

Bought of William H. Eaton,
Artistic Printer, Lithographer, Bookseller, Account Book Maker,
Manufacturing Stationer, &c., &c.

Engraving, Die Sinking & Relief Stamping.   Artists' Materials.   Cricket, Golf & Lawn Tennis Goods.

GENERAL DRAPERY ESTABLISHMENT,

23, Market Place, LEEK, *13 Mch* 187 *8*.

Bought of **H. EDDOWES,**

GENERAL MERCER, DRAPER, &c.,

FAMILY MOURNING.   FUNERALS COMPLETELY FURNISHED.

TERMS CASH.

Served by	Examined by

8 Holland 1/—	8	0
Remt Cord		10
	8	10

Paid W E

Memorandum. 18

From

H. EDDOWES,

GENERAL MERCER, DRAPER, &c.

23, MARKET PLACE,

LEEK.

To

Dec 20 / 80

Re from the Exors of the late Henry Goldstraw fifteen pounds on a/c

H. Eddowes

23, Market Place, LEEK, July 1st 1880

The Exors of the late Mr Goldstraw

Dr to H. Eddowes, Biddulph Rocks

General Mercer, Draper, Hosier, Haberdasher, &c.

Family Mourning. Funerals completely furnished.

		£	s	d
Jany 2nd	1 Blk Satin 3/6. 2¼ Ribbon 8		5	0
	1 Wing 6½. 1 doz Linen Hdkfs 8/6		9	0½
	69½ Blk Persian Cord 1/2½	4	4	0
	24 — — — 1/0½	1	5	0
	23 — Cashmere 2/2	2	9	10
	10 — — 3/3	1	12	6
	15 — Persian Cord 1/6	1	2	6
x	Pins 2. 2 Toilet Covers 1/4. 1/4½		5	7
x	2 do 1/2. 1 Cloth Table Cover 12/6		14	10
	1 Blk Skirt 10/6. 4/9. 2 do 3/4½	1	2	0
	7 prs Ladies Fch Kid Gloves 2/11	1	0	5
	3 — — — 2/9		8	3
	14 — — — — 1/11½	1	7	5
	11 — Gents — — 3/6	1	18	6
	1 15/6 Crape 3/6. 5 Silicia 4½		8	8
	8 do 7½. 8¼ Crape 2/8. 5½ do 4/6	2	11	9
	36 Braid 1. Postage 4/9. 6 Buttons 8		11	9
	3 doz Buttons 9½. 1 pr Hose 1/11. 2 do 2/6		9	3½
	1 Scarf 1/10½. 2 do 1/6.		4	10½
6	10¾ Muslin 5½. 6 Lining 7½		8	8
	8 Alpacca 6½. 1/4 lb Cord 1/2. Cotton 7½		5	3
	12 Blk Cashmere 2/2	1	6	0
14	1 Gloves 1/11½. 2 Calico 4. 4 Muslin 3½		3	9½
	8 Cord 1/0½. 11¼ Domett 7½		15	4½
21st	4 Lining 7½. 1/2 Buttons 9½		2	11
x 26	1 Umbrella 6/11		6	11
		£26	0	1½

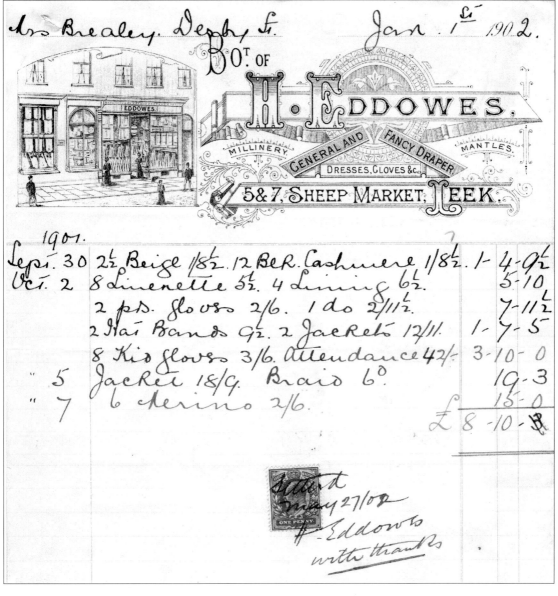

Mrs Brealey. Derby St.   Jan. 1st 1902.

BOT. OF

H. EDDOWES,

MILLINERY.   GENERAL AND   FANCY DRAPER   MANTLES.
              DRESSES, GLOVES &c.

5 & 7, SHEEP MARKET, LEEK.

1901.

Sept. 30	2½ Beige 1/8½. 12 BeR. Cashmere 1/8½.		1	4	9½
Oct. 2	8 Linenette 5½. 4 Lining 6½.			5	10
	2 pᵈˢ. Gloves 2/6. 1 do 2/11½.			7	11½
	2 Hat Bands 9½. 2 Jackets 12/11.		1	7	5
	8 Kid Gloves 3/6. Attendance 42/-		3	10	0
" 5	Jacket 18/9. Braid 6ᵈ.			19	3
" 7	6 Merino 2/6.			15	0
		£	8	10	8

May 27/02
H. Eddowes
with thanks

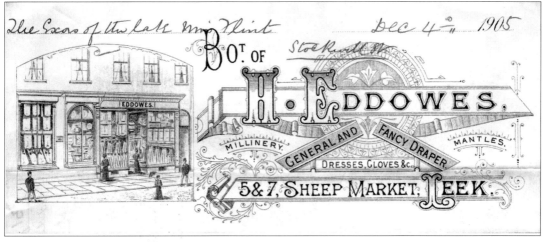

The Exors of the late Mrs Flint   Dec 4th 1905

BOT. OF   Stockwell St.

H. EDDOWES,

MILLINERY.   GENERAL AND   FANCY DRAPER   MANTLES.
              DRESSES, GLOVES &c.

5 & 7, SHEEP MARKET, LEEK.

5 & 7 SHEEP MARKET, LEEK,

Sept 23rd 191/

Mrs Knowles

Bought of H. EDDOWES,

GENERAL DRAPER, MERCER, &C.

Dresses, Gloves, Hosiery, Coats, Costumes, Corsets, &c.

HOUSEHOLD DRAPERY OF EVERY DESCRIPTION.

Family Mourning a Speciality.

1 Waterproof Sheet			10"0

Telephone: 45. ESTABLISHED 1874. Telegrams: EDDOWES. LEEK.

BLOUSES. GLOVES. Corsets etc.

H. EDDOWES.

DRAPER. COSTUMIER, & LADIES OUTFITTER.

Household LINENS. Dresses. Hosiery etc.

5 & 7. Sheep Market. LEEK.

Feby 15th 1922

Mrs Brealey + Son.

Ash Almshouse Charity

To 7 Tweed Dresses, as per Estimate		£ 9 10 0	

13, Stockwell Street,
LEEK, *June* 1874

Miss Henry

Dr. to J. EDGE,

DRESS AND MANTLE MAKER,
STAYS, TRIMMINGS, HOISERY, GLOVES AND HABERDASHERY.
FAMILY MOURNING ON THE SHORTEST NOTICE.

1874
June   To 1 White Peigue Jacket   £ 12 0

MARKET PLACE. *Leek Xxxs* 1867

Mr W. Challinor Esq

Bought of L. Ellerton,

MOURNING ON THE
SHORTEST NOTICE.

Clothier and Outfitter.
HATTER, HOSIER, GLOVER & SHIRT MAKER.

1867 June 15th 1 Light Over Coat 4 Sis   £ 1 17 0

Settled Jan: 7/1/68
L. Ellerton

FREDERICK ELKES,

BAKER, CONFECTIONER AND GROCER.

Rich Bride, Maderia, Sultana and
Baden Cakes in Stock or to order on the shortest notice.

Superior Currant & Seed Bread, Buns & Pastry fresh daily.

ESTIMATES GIVEN FOR SCHOOL TREATS &c.

TINNED GOODS OF THE BEST BRAND.

Agent for Tower Tea.

11, RUSSELL STREET, LEEK.

Elkes 1892

LEEK DRAPERY AND MILLINERY WAREHOUSE,

4, Derby Street, Leek,

..................................189

M..................................

Bought of H. ELLERTON,

WHOLESALE AND RETAIL

Draper, Silk Mercer, Hosier, &c

Blankets, Sheets, Counterpanes, &c. Dresses, Skirts, Ulsters, Jackets, Bonnets, Hats, Flowers, Feathers, &c.

FAMILY MOURNING.

Ser^d. by *Ex^d. by*

4½ Foule 1/2½		5	5¼
2½ Silkette 1/5		1	0½
1½ Lining 4½			7
3 Trimmg 3			9

24

4, Derby Street, Leek, June 6th 1911

M Exors of the late Mr G. N. Gould

Bought of H. ELLERTON,

GENERAL & FANCY DRAPER.

Millinery, Mantles, Dresses, Gloves, Umbrellas, &c.

1911				
Feb 10	3½ Ribbon 7½ 6½ Calico 5½,		5	2½
	2 Cotton 1½ 3 Collars 4½		1	4½
" 15	1½ Ribbon 7½ 1 Toilet Cover 1/6½ 4 Diaper	7½	5	0
" 18	2 Hose 1/4½		2	9
Mch 7	1½ Ribbon 2½, Wool 6½, Thread 2, Needles 1		1	1½
	Cotton 4½, Tape 1½ Buttons 1/3½		1	9½
	4 Dimity 7½ 1 Coat 16/11		19	5
" 20	1 Overall 2/2, 13 Calico 4 1 Gloves 9½		3	5½
Apl 13	3 Muslin 7½		1	10½
May 10	1 Blouse 8/11, Pins 1 1¼ F Net 1/0½		10	3
	3 Hdkfs 3 1½ Ribbon 2½		1	1

Leek Millinery & Drapery Warehouse,

4, DERBY STREET, LEEK,

April 20th 1928.

Miss Bull, Derby Street.

H. ELLERTON,

DRAPER, MILLINER, HOSIER, ETC.

Family Mourning.

9 Serviettes 1/4½, 2 Gloves 2/6,	17	4½	
½ Casement 1/6½, 1 Blouse 8/11,	9	8½	
1 Coat 32/6, 29/6,	3	2	0
6½ Net 10½d, 1 Skirt 15/11,	1	1	7½
1 Jumper 8/11, 1 Hat 9/11,	18	10	
6 Tea cloths 8½d, 1 Hose 1/11½,	6	2½	
1 Scarf.	7	6	

Etches had a shop in Sheep Market in 1835.

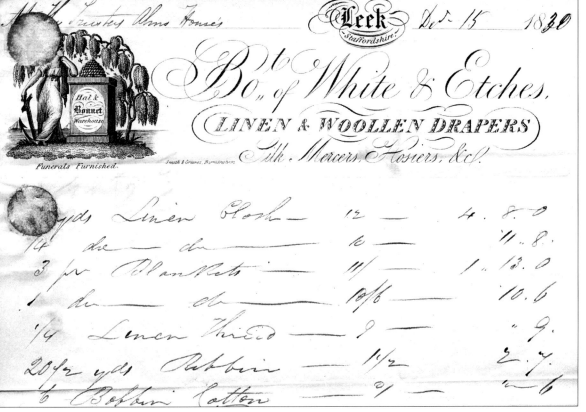

EVANS & SON,

High-class Tailors

24 & 25, Market Place,

LEEK.

Gentlemen waited upon. | Distance no object.

41 & 45, Ballhaye Road,

Leek, Aug 1st 1895

Mr Thomas Robinson

Bought of SAMUEL EYRE,

COAL ✢ MERCHANT.

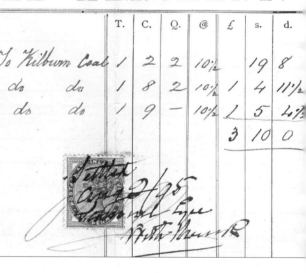

	T.	C.	Q.	@	£	s.	d.
To Kilburn Coal	1	2	2	10½		19	8
do do	1	8	2	10½	1	4	11½
do do	1	9	—	10½	1	5	4½
					3	10	0

AN EXCELLENT SELECTION
at most Reasonable Prices.

PORTS—
Fine Old Port 2/6
Douralto Rich Ruby 3/-
Fine Matured, Douro, Rich Tawny ... 4/-
Kopke's "Old World" 5/-
Finest Old White 4/-

SHERRIES—
Old Golden 3/6
East India 6/6

MADEIRA—
Crown 4/-

TARRAGONA—
Superior 3/-

CLARETS—
Chateau Loudenne 3/-
St. Julian 1916 ... ... 5/-

BURGUNDIES (Australian)—
'Harvest,' 'Keystone,' 'Rubicon.'
'Blancona, 4/6

AUSTRALIAN WINES—
'Wrangoo,' Rich Ruby 3/-
'Ophir' Rich 3/3

———ALSO———

Sauternes, Graves, Chablis, Hocks, Moselles,
——— Saumur and Champagnes. ———

Liqueurs, Brandies, Rums, Gins and all
——— Proprietory Whiskies. ———

PLEASE ASK FOR COMPLETE PRICE LIST.

S. F. EVE,

(LATE GEORGE WALKER)

Walker's Brewery was in
Broad Street.

CYCLES, MOTORS and all Accessories.

LEWIS EVERETT.   5, COMPTON, LEEK, Staffs.

Mʳ Brealey ✓   Feby 8 1907

Dear Sir,

I suppose I may understand that you will send me word when you have information respecting the house No 8 Compton.

And greatly oblige.

Yours truly

L Everett.

Everett's Cycle Store was on the corner of Pickwood Road and Brook Street.

8, STOCKWELL STREET,

Leek......*Feb 5*......188 8

Mr Smith

Bought of JOHN FALLON & CO.,

Fish, Fruit, Game and Poultry Salesman,

OYSTER MERCHANTS, &c.

1887				
Dec	to a/c rendered	4	16	9
22	apples/7 russetts/3 kippers/6	1	4	
24	oysters 14	1	6	
27	goods/7½ 29th oysters 1/3	1	10½	
30	oysters 2/ Shrimps/8	2	8	
"	Haddack 1/ apples/4	1	4	
31	nutts /6 finnies/4½		10½	
1888 January 4	carrotts 1/6 17th oysters/	2	6	
18	grapes 1/ 26th oysters 1/ score 2/6	3	6	
28	russetts/6 Shrimps/8 Hadock/8	1	10	
Feb 7	oysters 2/6 Sole 2/	4	6	
10	Haddacks/6 oysters 1/3	1	9	
15	finnies/10 kippers /6	1	4	
22	oysters 2/6 finnies/4	2	10	
22	kippers /6 apples 1/4	1	10	
28	oysters 2/6 finnies /4½	2	10½	
28	kippers/6 Sole 1/2	1	8	
March 3	apples 1/4 russells/6	1	10	
3	filberts 1/ oysters/ 2/6	3	6	
		£ 6	16	3

8, STOCKWELL STREET,

Leek, *April 19* 1888

Mr Smith

Bought of **JOHN FALLON & CO.,**

Fish, Fruit, Game and Poultry Salesman,

OYSTER MERCHANTS, &c.

March				£	s	d
	a/c renderd			6	16	3
10	oysters 1 score				2	6
19	oysters 1 score				2	6
23	do 1 do				2	6
23	Shrimps					6
"	plaice fileted					7½
"	funnies 1 ¾ lbs					5
April				7	5	3
10	Sole 1 lbs 1/4				1	4
"	funnies					5
"	Sole 1/4 1/4				1	8
14	oysters 1 score				2	6
"	Rhubarb 2 Bls					6
"	orenges					1
			£	7	12	8

Sir / Your earley atention
to the above will
oblige as I am in wants of
Money Very Bad Just now

8, Stockwell Street,

Leek, *Oct 30* 189*3*

Mrs Prin

Bought of

J. FALLON & Co.,

Fish, Game & Oyster Merchants.

Wholesale & Retail Dealers in English & Foreign Fruits.

Wedding Bouquets, Sprays, Buttonholes, Cut Flowers Funeral Wreaths, &c. to order.

June 10	Strawbs 2 tt		1	4
16	Strawbs 2 tt		1	
17	Oranges 6			6
July 13	2g Plums 1 tt			6
14	mushrooms 1 tt		1	2
25	green grapes 1 tt			6
Sept 19	Pears			4
23	Pears 6		1	
			6	4

Paid debt
13/93

Annie Fallon

John Fallon owned several shops at different addresses.
The original Stockwell Street shop was located below the old fire station, and established in 1884.

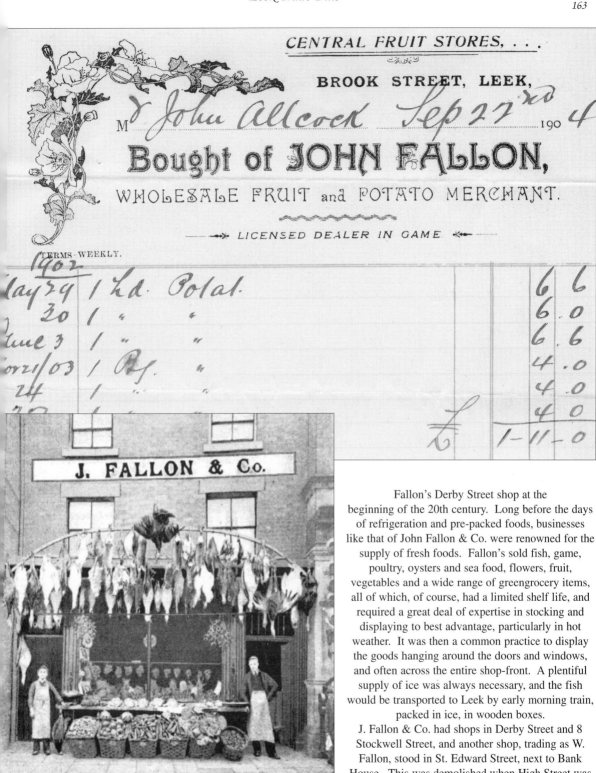

CENTRAL FRUIT STORES, . . .

BROOK STREET, LEEK,

M⎺ *John Allcock* *Sep 22ᵗᵈ* 190 4

Bought of JOHN FALLON,

WHOLESALE FRUIT and POTATO MERCHANT.

⟶ LICENSED DEALER IN GAME. ⟵

TERMS WEEKLY.

1902

May 29	1 Ld. Potat.			6	6
30	1 " "			6	0
June 3	1 " "			6	6
or 21/03	1 Bag "			4	0
24	1 " "			4	0
				4	0
		£	1	11	0

J. FALLON & Co.

Fallon's Derby Street shop at the beginning of the 20th century. Long before the days of refrigeration and pre-packed foods, businesses like that of John Fallon & Co. were renowned for the supply of fresh foods. Fallon's sold fish, game, poultry, oysters and sea food, flowers, fruit, vegetables and a wide range of greengrocery items, all of which, of course, had a limited shelf life, and required a great deal of expertise in stocking and displaying to best advantage, particularly in hot weather. It was then a common practice to display the goods hanging around the doors and windows, and often across the entire shop-front. A plentiful supply of ice was always necessary, and the fish would be transported to Leek by early morning train, packed in ice, in wooden boxes.

J. Fallon & Co. had shops in Derby Street and 8 Stockwell Street, and another shop, trading as W. Fallon, stood in St. Edward Street, next to Bank House. This was demolished when High Street was constructed about 1900.

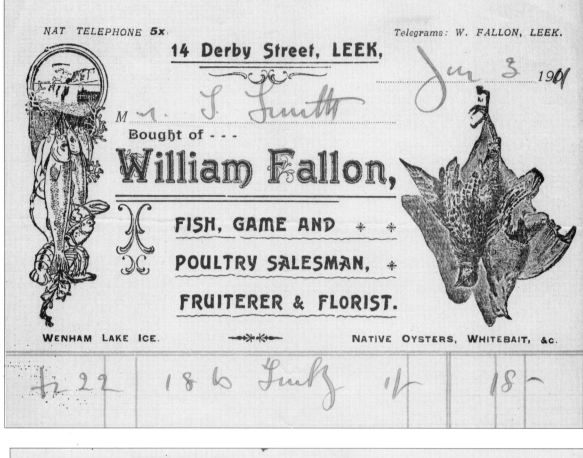

NAT TELEPHONE **5x**.

Telegrams: *W. FALLON, LEEK.*

14 Derby Street, LEEK,

Jan 3 190*1*

M*r. S. Smith*

Bought of - - -

William Fallon,

FISH, GAME AND   *   *
POULTRY SALESMAN,   *
FRUITERER & FLORIST.

WENHAM LAKE ICE.   **NATIVE OYSTERS, WHITEBAIT, &c.**

£ 22	18 6 *Smith*		1	18 —

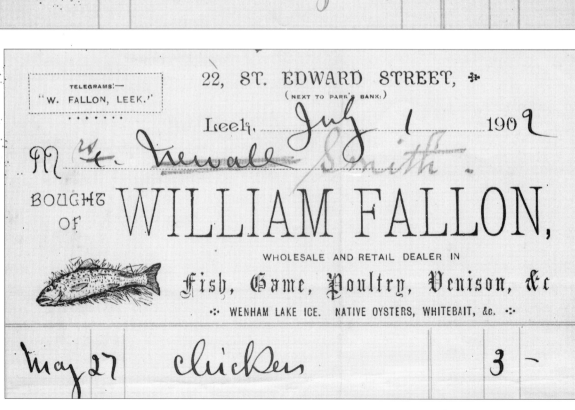

TELEGRAMS:—
"W. FALLON, LEEK."

22, ST. EDWARD STREET, ✤

(NEXT TO PARR'S BANK.)

Leek, *July 1* 190*2*

M*r. Newall Smith*

BOUGHT
OF

WILLIAM FALLON,

WHOLESALE AND RETAIL DEALER IN

Fish, Game, Poultry, Venison, &c

✧ WENHAM LAKE ICE.   NATIVE OYSTERS, WHITEBAIT, &c. ✧

May 27	*chickens*		3 —

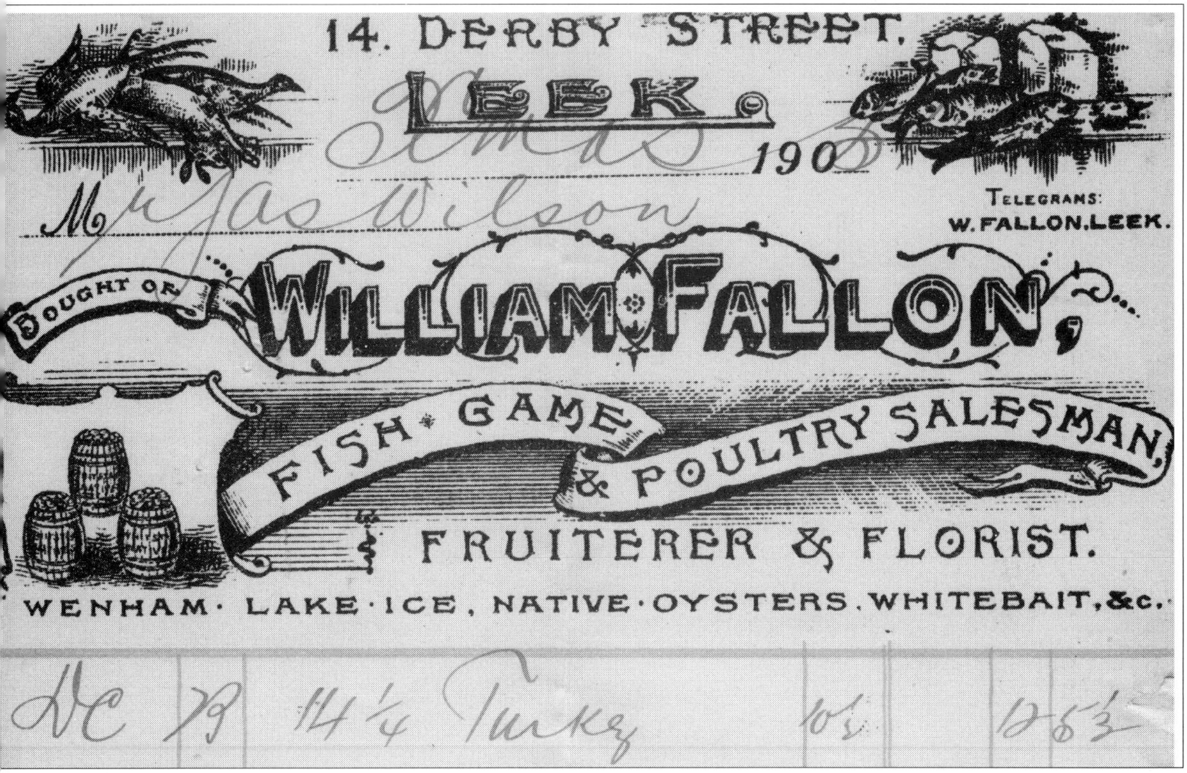
14. DERBY STREET.
LEEK.
190
Mr Jas Wilson
TELEGRAMS:
W. FALLON, LEEK.
BOUGHT OF
WILLIAM FALLON,
FISH • GAME
& POULTRY SALESMAN,
FRUITERER & FLORIST.
WENHAM · LAKE · ICE, NATIVE · OYSTERS, WHITEBAIT, &c.
Dec 23 14¼ Turkey 10½ 12 5½

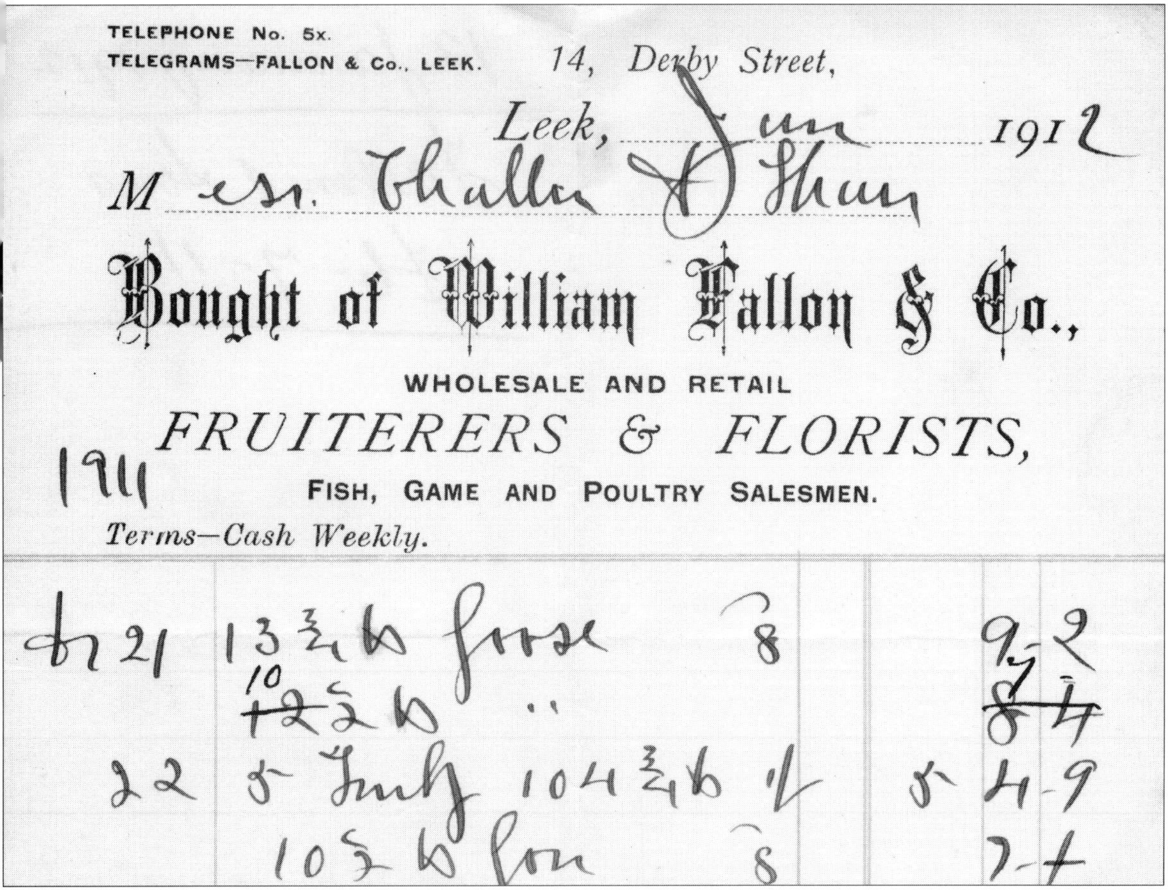
TELEPHONE No. 5x.
TELEGRAMS—FALLON & Co., LEEK.
14, Derby Street,
Leek, Jan 1912
Messrs
Bought of William Fallon & Co.,
WHOLESALE AND RETAIL
FRUITERERS & FLORISTS,
1911
FISH, GAME AND POULTRY SALESMEN.
Terms—Cash Weekly.
Dec 21 13¾ lb Goose 8 9 2
22 5 Turky 104¾ lb 1/- 5 4 9
10½ lb Goose 8 7 -

F. S. FELTHOUSE

(Late T. Lockett),

LONDON HOUSE,

SHEEP MARKET, LEEK.

General and Fancy Draper

MILLINERY & BLOUSES
a Speciality.

OPPOSITE PAGE: Mills in Leek from Park Road

INTERNATIONAL EXHIBITION, PHILADELPHIA, 1876.

PRIZE MEDAL FOR SEWING SILKS OF EXCELLENT QUALITY AND BRILLIANT COLORS.

LEEK, Staffordshire, *Oct. 27th 1885*

and 12, King St. Cheapside, LONDON, *E.C.*

Memorandum From Sheldon & Fenton,

SILK MANUFACTURERS.

To Messrs Challinors & Co. Leek.

INTERNATIONAL EXHIBITION, PHILADELPHIA 1876.

PRIZE MEDAL FOR SEWING SILKS OF EXCELLENT QUALITY AND BRILLIANT COLORS.

LEEK, Staffordshire. *May 30th 1895*

and Fountain Court, 2 Aldermanbury, LONDON, *E.C.*

Memorandum From Sheldon & Fenton,

SILK MANUFACTURERS.

To Messrs Challinor Shaw.

ALL GOLF SUPPLIES IN STOCK.   TUITION BY APPOINTMENT

GOLF CLUBS
MADE
TO ORDER.

DR. TO
Walter B. Fenton,
PROFESSIONAL AND
CLUB MAKER,

REPAIRS
AND
MAINTENANCE.

LEEK GOLF CLUB, BIG BIRCHALL, LEEK, STAFFS.

Mr. Wardle   31st August   193 8

July 30	6 Warwick Balls		9	-

Received payment
with thanks
W. B. Fenton
10th Sept 1938

W. B. FENTON,

Professional Golfer

LEEK GOLF CLUB,

LEEK, STAFFS.

BAGS • BALLS • SHOES • CLOTHING • GOLF SUNDRIES

Mr. G. Wardle,
Compton House,
LEEK.   1st July, 1940.

Mar 26	1 Chipper	16.	6
26	1 New Grip	2.	0
26	Mashie Regriped	2.	0
		£ 1. 0.	6d

LEEK, ———————— 184 7.

M̲r̲. *John Leech Esqr*

To R. Fergyson, Auctioneer, Appraiser, &c,

Agent for the Sale of

INDIA AND BURTON ALE AND PORTER.

Furniture Agent for Messrs, Farley and Mills, Cabinet Manufacturers, 3, Featherstone Street, London.

		£	s	d
une 29th	To Attending Sale of Hay grass at the white Lion bridge end the property of the late Mrs Fowler of Highfield	1	1	0
1848 Feby 18th	Attending Sale at the White Lion Bridge end Hay & Corn Stacks at Highfield	1	1	0
	£	2	2	0

1848 May 8th Settled

Robt Fergyson

R. Fergyson was in business in the 1820s, chiefly as an auctioneer, valuer and furniture broker, trading from 21 Market Place and later also at 29 Stockwell Street. It is interesting to note that Fergyson was also agent for the sale of ale and porter. Fergyson and Son later became shipping agents, able to issue tickets for all the major steamship companies, and agents for fire, life and accident insurance.

LEEK, *July 2nd* 18 *53*

Mess. *Chalinor Badnall & Chalinor*

To R. Fergyson, Auctioneer, Appraiser, &c.

AGENT FOR THE SALE OF
INDIA AND BURTON ALE AND PORTER.   FURNITURE BROKER.

Machine-dressed and Stove-dried White and Grey Goose Feathers always on hand.

1853		£	s	d
June	To Auctioneers fees with expences			
"	to the Sale &c of the Ball			
"	Haye Estate and attendance			
"	at the Red Lion Inn on			
"	the 16th instant offering the	16	16	0
"	Same by Auction in Lots			
"	When all the Lots were			
"	sold and realized upwards			
"	of £10,000.			

July 30th 1853

Settled Robt Fergyson

ESTABLISHED 1826.

Telegraphic
and Postal Address:
"FERGYSON,"
LEEK.

STOCKWELL STREET,

LEEK, *July 16th* 1900

Thos. Robinson Esq.

To FERGYSON & SON,

AUCTIONEERS, VALUERS,

ESTATE, INSURANCE AND SHIPPING AGENTS.

Sale at Grove Cottage Grove
St Leek July 14th 1900
re Mrs Martin decd.

	£	s	d
advertising sale in "Leek Times" & "Leek Post"		9	6
printing catalogues postors		14	6
posting bills in Leek & delivering to public houses		5	
Clerk writing at sale		5	
2 men assisting at sale		10	
Displaying two posters on platform at Leek Railway Station		5	
July 14. To our commn for attending selling goods by Auction also previously taking Inventory & preparing goods for sale 5% on £26:16:2	1	7	
Received.	£3	16	

Fredk Fergyson

T. FLANAGAN,

Fish, Fruit, and Poultry Salesman,

50, ASHBOURNE ROAD, LEEK.

FRESH SUPPLIES DAILY

1916

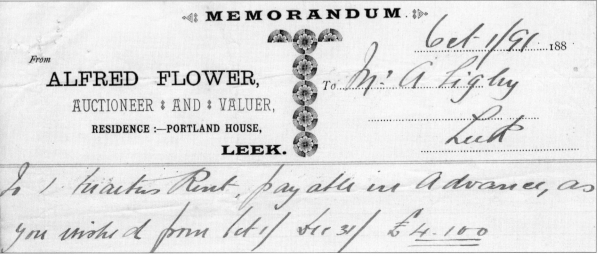

THE LIVERY STABLES, SHOOBRIDGE STREET,

Leek, *June 10 97* 189

Messrs Exers Leti John Hodgekiss

To A. FLOWER,

CAB PROPRIETOR.

POSTING IN ALL ITS BRANCHES.

HEARSE AND MOURNING COACHES A SPECIALITIE.

TERMS:—CASH.

June 10 Hearse & Pair &

3 Mourning Coaches

3 Pr Horses from

Rushy and to Stockton ..... 8 . .

Recd Alfred Flower

with thanks

June 30/97

MEMORANDUM

Oct 1/91 188

From

ALFRED FLOWER,

AUCTIONEER & AND & VALUER,

RESIDENCE :—PORTLAND HOUSE,

LEEK.

To Mr A Tigley

Leek

To 1 Quarter Rent, pay all in Advance, as you wished from Oct 1/ Dec 31/ £4.10.0

Joseph Flower purchased the old Town Hall, which stood at the bottom of the Market Place, in 1872 and used some of the masonry to build Portland House in Rosebank Street, where Alfred Flower was living in 1891.

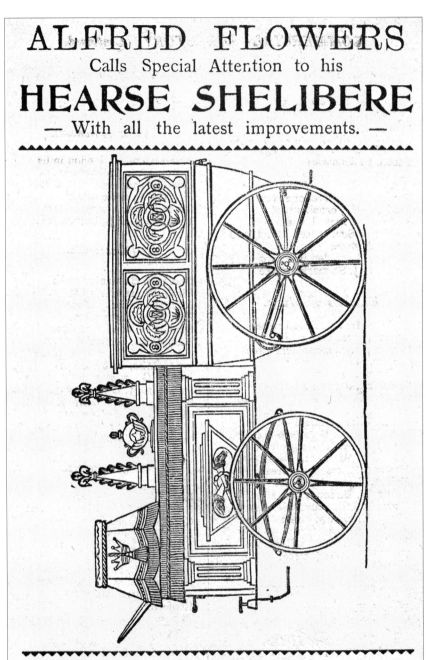

ALFRED FLOWERS
Calls Special Attention to his
HEARSE SHELIBERE
— With all the latest improvements. —

SHOOBRIDGE ST. LIVERY STABLES, LEEK.

Alfred Flower is first shown as a cab proprietor in Queen Street in Kelly's
1892 Directory. By 1904 he was operating from his livery stables in
Shoobridge Street, where he remained for many years.

THE LIVERY STABLES, SHOOBRIDGE STREET,

Leek, *May* 193

M *Colonel W. F. Challinor*

TO . .

A. FLOWER,

CARRIAGE PROPRIETOR.

HEARSE AND MOURNING COACHES ON
THE SHORTEST NOTICE.

Terms: CASH.   Wedding and Party Carriages.   Posting in all its Branches.

Dear Sir,

I had a letter from your agents at Leek this week, re allowance for Land taken off, the amount stated 8/6 a year, in my opinion it is very little, any way may I say that I think you could allow me "more" taking into consideration that I have the most exposed piece to contend with in the future also the trespass & especially being the Corner Junction Rd., where all the trespassing takes place, and where they deposit all refuse, and thrown into top field, the trouble which I have is more than you are aware of, may I suggest to you also your agent that I think would be fair & reasonable say which is only small 15/- which I then should be satisfied, thanking you for your consideration, between yourself & Mrs Brealy & for your agents, Trusting to receive a most favourably reply

Kindest regards.

Folio......*1*......

Offices and Coal Depot; Leek Station.

Mrs *Trustees f S Birch*

BOUGHT OF CHARLES FOGG,

COAL MERCHANT.

Residence: 42, BRUNSWICK STREET.

5 Per Cent. charged on Overdue Accounts.

190*0*	COALS.	Tons. cwt. qrs.	Price per Ton	£	s.	d.
May 26	6 Ash Iron Boxes		4/9	1	8	6

*Examined, correct
but should have been
demanded here this £/6*

per M.

*Paid With
thanks C Fogg
June 18 1912*

42, Brunswick Street,

LEEK, *Dec 31* 19*13*

Mrs Cotton

Dr. to C. W. FOGG,

PLUMBER, PAINTER & GLAZIER,
Gas and Hot Water Pipe Fitter, &c.

Jl	3½ ell Solder		9 4
	1 Washer 2 Clips		
	time 2 Hours	1 6
	To Painting and		
	Cleaning out Spouts		
	and glazing		
	Seven Houses		
	as per Contract	4 2 6
		£ 4 5 1

18*th* April 1914

Examined the above it is
done satisfactory according to
Contract. G.C.

[signature]

Apr 21 1914

60, ST. EDWARD STREET,

LEEK, *October* 188*8*

Mrs Mackey

BOUGHT OF JOHN C. FOGG,

Printer, · Stationer, · Bookbinder, · and · Lithographer,

NEWSPAPER AND ADVERTISING AGENT.

Oct 21	50 Memory Cards Holding Silver & Black		8	0
	Envelopes to ditto		1	0
24	1 doz additional 4/- Envelopes 3		2	3
			11	3

Received Oct 24/88
With thanks
John C Fogg.

55

PRINTING AND STATIONERY WAREHOUSE,

LEEK, *November* 1892

Messrs Challinors & Shaw

ACCOUNTS DUE WHEN FURNISHED.

Dr. to JOHN C. FOGG,

PRINTER, LITHOGRAPHER, ACCOUNT BOOK MANUFACTURER,

Engraving, Die Sinking and Relief Stamping.

August	29	1000 Demy Bills Massage Stockwell St	1	5	0
	150 Demy Folio Particulars 3pp + Endorse			
	Plans pasted in	2	2	0
	End	= 3	7	0

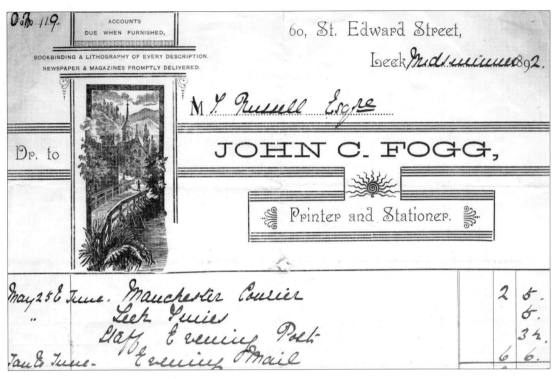

Printers usually excelled themselves in designing their own letterheads, and John C. Fogg was no exception.
This heading incorporates an illustration which looks very impressive, but has no bearing on printing or Leek!
This selection of Fogg's headings demonstrates the versatility of design.

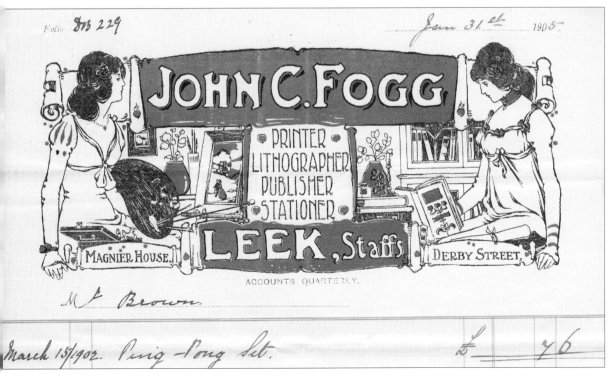

JOHN C. FOGG, Magnier House, Derby Street. In order to advertise the best features of their craft, most printers
had elaborate printed stationery. John C. Fogg is no exception, and, with these elegant young ladies,
has introduced a Pre-Raphaelite style to his heading.

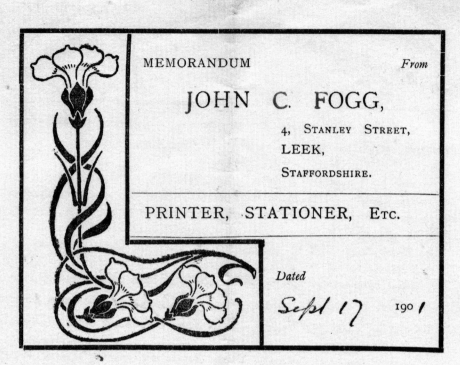

MEMORANDUM *From*

JOHN C. FOGG,

4, STANLEY STREET,
LEEK,
STAFFORDSHIRE.

PRINTER, STATIONER, ETC.

Dated

Sept 17   190 1

Mr Robinson

Dear Sir

In reply to my letter
re "Dane Cottage" "Sale" charges
in the Macclesfield Courier
I have received the enclosed

Yours truly
John C. Fogg

Froghall & Barrow Lime, Cement, & Plaster Depot.

BRIDGE STREET. **UTTOXETER** 188

Mr Salt Blacksmith Sudbury

To **PETER FORD**, & SONS, **Dr.**

Sculptor, Mason & Builder,

MONUMENTS, TOMBS, HEADSTONES, TABLETS, COPING, HEADS & SILLS.

STEPS, LANDINGS, GRINDSTONES, SINKSTONES, PAVING & CURBING, CHIMNEY-PIECES, HEARTHS, &c.

DEALER IN BRICKS, TILES, QUARRIES, ALL KINDS OF PAVING BRICKS, GARDEN BORDER TILES & COPING BRICKS, FIRE BRICKS, CHIMNEY TOPS, FLUE COVERS, GLAZED SANITARY PIPES, FIELD DRAIN PIPES, &c. &c.

MANUFACTURER OF LARGE GRINDSTONES FOR EDGE TOOL WORKS. PROPRIETOR of the ALTON & STANTON STONE QUARRIES.

and Lessee of Alabaster Mines, Fauld, near Sudbury, N.S.Ry

GEO. A. FOX,

(C. GREEN, Manager),

MOTOR ENGINEER,

Cycle & Motor Cycle Dealer & Repairer.

ALL KINDS OF MOTOR AND CYCLE ACCESSORIES.

CARS FOR HIRE.

SPECIALITY:—Complete Overhaul of any make of Car.

21, Market Place, Leek.

There were many small quarries in the area supplying gritstone and limestone, local to the building needs. Fine sandstone for quality stonework often came from the Alton/Hollington area.

Nurseries in the Wetley Rocks area have supplied the district's gardens for a long time.

Memorandum

FROM

George Tipping Fox.
The Nurseries,
Wetley Rocks,

To

near Leek. *June 3rd 1872*

To W. Challinor Esq

STEPHENSON'S *Non-Smear* **FLOOR POLISH** AND **FURNITURE CREAM**

STEPHENSON'S *Non-Smear* POLISH

Dec 31st 1941

Mr C. Wardle Esq.

Bought of **A. FOSTER**   Phone 415

Ironmongery, Glass, China and Household Stores

Rugs, Mats and Matting   Pyrex   Tables and Mangles   **24 Market Place, LEEK**

July 30	2 Mop Heads				2	6
	3 Dish Cloths				2	4½
Aug 6	3 Saucers 6 3 Plates 6				1	0
" 20	2 Pie Dishes				1	6
Nov 4	4 Mop Heads				6	0
" 17	2 Hand Brushes				7	0
	2 Scrub " 1/- 1/3				2	3
Dec 24	2 Hearth Bru...					

Dec.d ...

A. Fos...

STEPHENSONS' FLOOR POLISH

Linoleum, Oil Cloth,
Brown Boots, Polished
& Varnished Woodwork,
Motor Cars, Harness, &c.

Mess.. Challinors & Shaw   *Aug 9 1914*

Bought of **A. FOSTER,**

Iron, Tinplate and Copper Worker, Hardware Dealer,

5 Church Street, LEEK.

H. FOSTER,

TINMAN AND COPPERSMITH,

23, MARKET STREET, LEEK,

Having enlarged his business premises is now prepared
to undertake every description of

TIN & COPPER WORK,

Good Material used by experienced workmen,
and all orders expeditiously executed.

Workshop :-5, SILK STREET.

21, Market Place, Leek,

March 9th 1900 189

M⁓ *Clowes*

Bought of **Freeman, Hardy & Willis,**
LTD.,

Terms—CASH.   **Boot and Shoe Manufacturers.**

	£	s	d
7o 1 ½ Girls Boots		4	3

Paid with thanks
W. Mulkin

ESTABLISHED 1879.   Telegrams: "GALE," Leek.

59, St. Edward Street,

LEEK,_____190

(AND "SENTINEL" BUILDINGS, HANLEY.)

Mr. J. W. Lee

...Dr. to... **S. GALE,**

TAILOR AND OUTFITTER.

Folio... 355

June 17/04				
2 Coloured Shirts			7	10
½ doz Collars			3	3
2 Cuff links			1	6

Telegrams: "Gale, Clothier, Leek."   Feby 25   1914

Mr Robinson Decd,

Dr. to S. GALE,

Clothier and Outfitter,

59, St. Edward Street, Leek.

Established 1879.

June 7/13 Wool shirt			6	11
Blue trousers			17	6
		£ P	4	5

15, Church Street,

Leek, *Jan 29th 1875*

M *Rev. E. Deacon & other Trustees of the*
Leek Alms Houses.

Bought of H. & S. GARNER,
MILLINERS AND MANTLE MAKERS.

RIBBONS, FLOWERS, GLOVES, HOSIERY, TIES, COLLARS, AND TRIMMINGS, FLEECY AND
SCOTCH WOOLS OF ALL KINDS ALWAYS ON HAND.   CHILDREN'S CLOTHING, &Cʰ

Jan 2nd 53 yds Wincey 1/3	√3	6	3
6 " Lining 4½	√	2	3
15½ " Calico 5	√	6	5½
Cotton, Cord, Buttons &c.		1	8
Making 7 Dresses at 2/9 each		19	3
	£4	15	10½

Feby 25 Paid Wm Garner

1, CLERK'S BANK, LEEK.
S. GARNER,
DRAPER.

Ribbons, Flowers, Gloves, Hosiery, Ties, Collars,
Trimmings, Fleecy and Scotch Wools. Children's
Clothing &c.

Hand and Machine made Underclothing in Stock and to order.

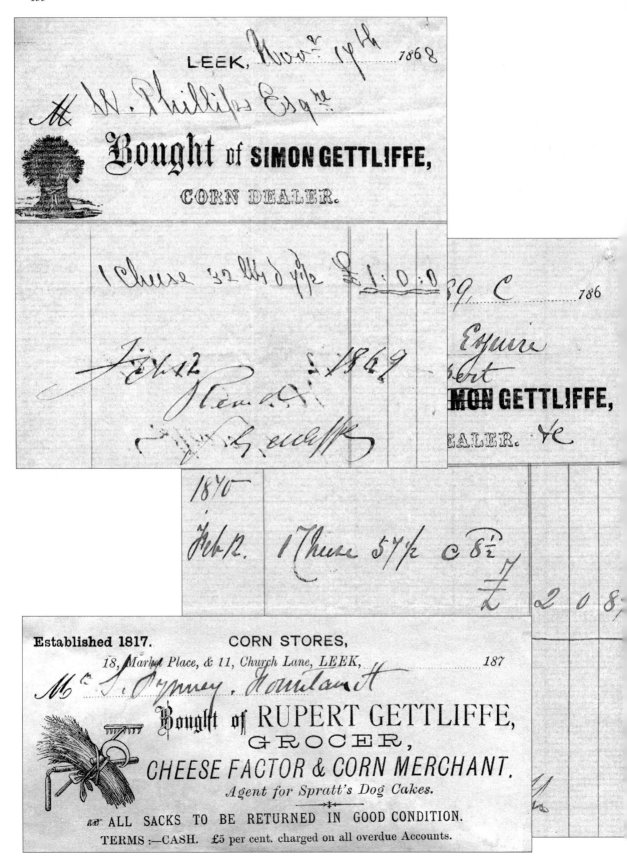

LEEK, *Nov.r 19th* 1868

M.r W. Phillips Esq.re

Bought of SIMON GETTLIFFE,
CORN DEALER.

1 Cheese 32 lb d 7½ £1:0:0

Feb 12 1869

189. C   786

Esquire

...bert

...MON GETTLIFFE,
...EALER.   4e

1870

Feb 12. 1 Cheese 57½ @ 8½

      2 0 8

Established 1817.   CORN STORES,
18, Market Place, & 11, Church Lane, LEEK,   187

M.rs S. Pymney, Hornlandt

Bought of RUPERT GETTLIFFE,
GROCER,
CHEESE FACTOR & CORN MERCHANT.
Agent for Spratt's Dog Cakes.

☞ ALL SACKS TO BE RETURNED IN GOOD CONDITION.
TERMS :—CASH. £5 per cent. charged on all overdue Accounts.

If you are not at present drinking
BLACK & GREEN'S TEA, then do so, and we feel
confident you will be better pleased than with
any other Tea. This, at any rate, is the experience of thousands of our customers. The test
is worth making.

New Road, LONGNOR,

Buxton, *Feb.* 19/3

M *Exor. of Late*

Bought of *Joseph Bircham*

ISAAC GEE,

Family Grocer and Corn Merchant.

BLACK & GREEN'S TEA..

It is Delicious

Prices: 1/4, 1/6, 1/8 1/10, 2/-, 2/4

"THE GEORGE,"

Family & Commercial Hotel,

LEEK, STAFFORDSHIRE.

JOHN HY. PLATT,

OMNIBUS MEETS ALL TRAINS.   PROPRIETOR.

Ed Challinor Esq 1899

1863 2 Bots Why. 16 0

Use of Sale Room 0 10 0

"The Geo[rge]

Family & Commercial Hotel,

ST. EDWARD ST. & CHURCH ST.,

J. H. PLATT, Proprietor.

AGENT FOR :—Allsopp's Celebrated Pale and Burton Ales, Nicholson's
Gin. John Jameson's, Sir John Power's and Roe's and Dunville's
Irish Whiskeys. Buchanan's, Mountain Dew, Rhoderick Dhu, Uam
Var, Teacher's Highland Cream, John Dewar and Sons' Gold Medal
Special Old Highland Whiskey, and Glenlivet Scotch Whiskeys.

Hennessey's and Martell's Brandies. Finest Jamaica Rum, Ports,
Sherries, Clarets, Champagnes, Hocks, Moselles and Burgundies of
the best known Brands.

HILL EVANS & Co.'s BRITISH WINES.

A Choice Selection of Havana and Mexican Cigars.

JOHN HENRY PLATT, GEORGE HOTEL, LEEK.

The George Hotel
LEEK.

THE RECOGNISED FAMILY, COMMERCIAL AND MOTORISTS' HOTEL.

Entirely free from Brewers or Spirit Merchants.

FIFTEEN BEDROOMS.
Stabling for 20 horses.

EXCELLENT   MOTOR   ACCOMMODATION.

This Hotel is most conveniently situated for all the neighbouring resorts.—RUDYARD LAKE, DANES BRIDGE, THE ROACHES, &c.

Complete Tariff on application to the Proprietor,

JAMES HAWORTH.

The fact that two important turnpike roads passed through Leek meant that coaching inns and post houses were to be found in abundance along those routes. Typical of its kind, but one of many, **THE GEORGE HOTEL** stood at the intersection of two such roads, at the junction of St. Edward Street and Church Street. It had a high reputation, and was said to offer the best stabling and accommodation between Manchester and Derby.

20, COMPTON,

LEEK, *May 17* 19*13*

Messrs *Challinors & Shaw.*

Dr. to ERNEST GIDDINGS,

(Late S. Giddings),

CHIMNEY SWEEP.

	s	d
For Sweeping Chimney and flues	13	9
E Giddings		
Settled		

James E. Gibson,

FAMILY GROCER.

IMPORTER OF **DANISH BACON,**

PLAIN & SMOKED.

TEA & COFFEE SPECIALIST,

ORDERS delivered Town and Country.

71, DERBY STREET, LEEK.

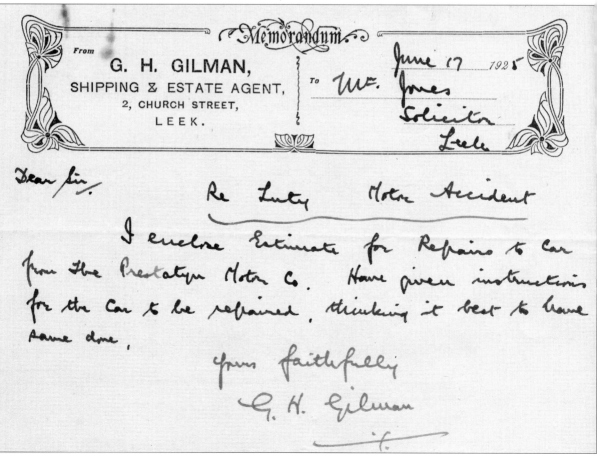

Memorandum.

From

G. H. GILMAN,

Accountant & Estate Agent,

4, CHURCH STREET,

LEEK.

June 9 1906

To Messrs Challinors & Sha

Solicitors

Leek

Dear Sirs,   Re Heath & Lowe

Some few weeks ago I wrote asking how the above estate was going on having several claims against it of which you have had notice of. I must ask for same as my clients are very anxious to know what has been done.

Memorandum

From

G. H. GILMAN,

SHIPPING & ESTATE AGENT,

2, CHURCH STREET,

LEEK.

To Mr. Jones

June 17 1925

Solicitor

Leek

Dear Sir,

Re Lutey   Motor Accident

I enclose Estimate for Repairs to Car from the Prestatyn Motor Co. Have given instructions for the Car to be repaired, thinking it best to have same done,

Yours faithfully

G. H. Gilman

G. H. GILMAN,

Accountant & Estate Agent,

4, CHURCH STREET, LEEK.

AGENT FOR THE ORIENT PACIFIC ROYAL MAIL,
SHAW, SAVILL & ALBION COMPANY, and
CANADIAN PACIFIC RAILWAY COMPANY.

FIRE AND LIFE OFFICES :—SUN, LAW UNION AND CROWN.

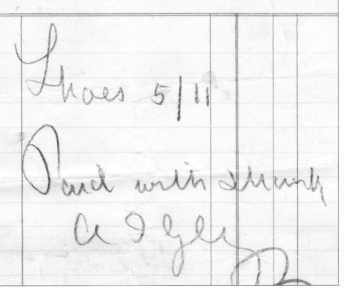

55, St. Edward Street
Leek,_____ 192

M.......................................

Dr. to **A. J. GLEGG**

HIGH-CLASS MILLINERY

LADIES', GENT'S AND CHILDREN'S BOOTS, SHOES AND SLIPPERS

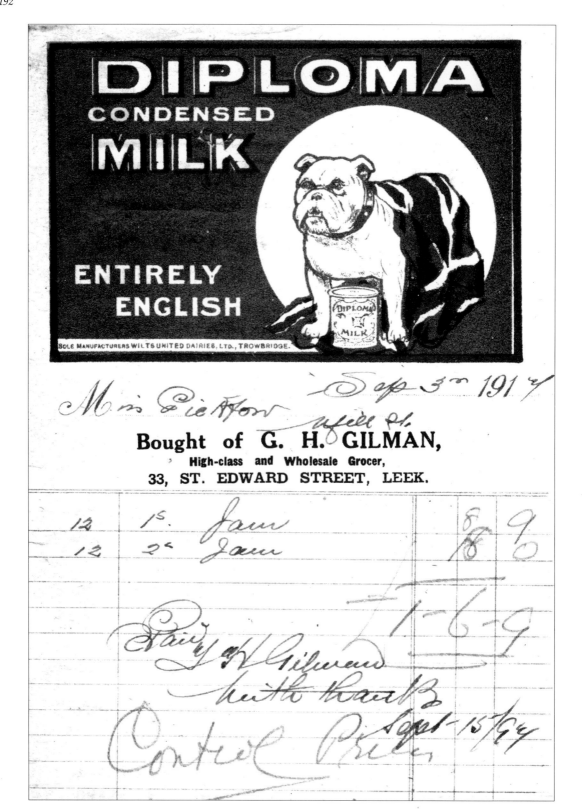

DIPLOMA
CONDENSED
MILK

ENTIRELY
ENGLISH

SOLE MANUFACTURERS WILTS UNITED DAIRIES, LTD., TROWBRIDGE.

Miss Pickford

Sep 3rd 1917

Ufill St.

Bought of G. H. GILMAN,
High-class and Wholesale Grocer,
33, ST. EDWARD STREET, LEEK.

12	1s.	Jam		8	9
12	2d	Jam		8	0
			1	6	9

Paid G H Gilman
with thanks
Control Prices *Sept 15/17*

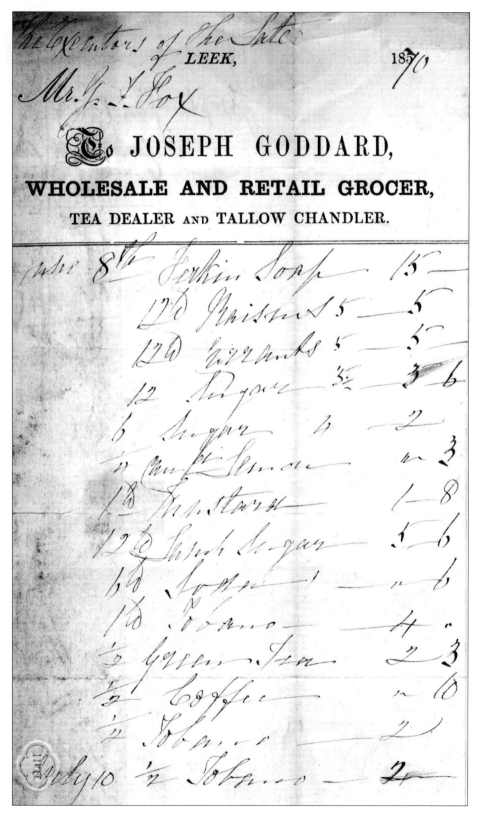

Joseph Goddard was at 27 St Edward Street.

PRIME BEEF, MUTTON, VEAL & LAMB.

CORNED BEEF & PICKLED TONGUES.

ESTABLISHED 1857.

26 & 27, MARKET PLACE,

Leek. (Staffs.) *Aug: - 1902*

M J W. Sney & Son.

Bought of S. Godwin.

(LATE WARRINGTON.)

PORK & GENERAL BUTCHER.

MEAT SENT TO ALL PARTS OF THE TOWN & DISTRICT DAILY.   FRESH PORK SAUSAGES DAILY.
FOUR PRIZE MEDALS AWARDED FOR ENGLISH HAMS & BACON.

To a/c Rend June 30/02 £47 . 4 . 3½

The name of Godwin has long been associated with the butchery trade in Leek,
trading from various address at different times

MEMORANDUM

From — *To the Exors of the Late*
HENRY GOLDSTRAW.
STONE MERCHANT, &c.,
WETLEY ROCKS,
LEEK.
STAFFORDSHIRE.

Jan'ry 16th 1880

To — *Bucknall Railway*

576   *To 7 Stones left by Watson & Smith*   £. s. d.
   " Deducted from my A/ct and used   2. 16. 0
   by Railway men

2

TELEPHONE No. 3Y2.

**23, DERBY STREET,
LEEK.**

EYE SIGHT TESTED FREE.

BOUGHT OF **W. W. GOLDSTRAW,**

GOLDSMITH & JEWELLER,

CERTIFIED OPTICIAN.

PERSONAL ATTENTION GIVEN TO REPAIRS OF ALL KINDS.

Clocks Wound and Repaired by Yearly Contract.

Messrs Challinors & Shaw   *Jan 1 1909.*

1908	To A/c Rendered	10	6
Aug 7	" Clock in front office Cleaned & &c	3	6
28	" Barometer Rep'd, new weight and		
	new mercury	4	6
Dec 25	" Winding Clocks for one year	10	6
	Rec'd with thanks £ 1. 9. 0		
	Dec 31/09		
	W H Goldstraw		

17, PARLIAMENT ROW, HANLEY,

AND

23, DERBY STREET, LEEK.

Aug. 13ᵗʰ 188*8*

Mr Hudson

DR TO W. W. GOLDSTRAW,

WATCH MAKER, JEWELLER, OPTICIAN, &C.

1888. June 9		£	s	d
	To Marble, French clock (Presentation to Mr Harrison)	5	15	0
	New Barometer (do)	1	10	0
		7	5	0
	Silver Inscription plate & inscription engraved. Given Gratis Also discount — 5/-		5	0

Watches,
Clocks,
Jewellery,
Plate,
Spectacles,
and
Eye Glasses.

220

23, DERBY STREET, LEEK,

AND AT 17, PARLIAMENT ROW, HANLEY.

Sep   1901

Mrs Brealey Derby St.

Dr. to W. W. GOLDSTRAW,

Watch-maker, Jeweller, and Certified Optician.

Repairs of ALL kinds to Watches, Clocks, Jewellery, Spectacles, Chiming Clocks, Musical Boxes, &c., &c. promptly attended to.

1901		£	s	d
Apr 3	To clock cleaned & new gut		3	6
Oct 7	Clock, new Mainspring, only charge		4	0
			7	6

Recd with Thanks
May 27/02
Frank Goldstraw

THE OPTICIAN.

W. F. GOLDSTRAW,

F.S.M.C

Eye-sight Specialist and Jeweller,

23, Derby St., Leek.

GREENWICH TIME DAILY BY WIRELESS.

Telephone No. 3 Y 2.

EYESIGHT
TESTED FREE.

23, DERBY STREET,

LEEK, *Sep.* 1912

M A H Shaw Esq for Mr R. Taylor

Bought of **W. W. GOLDSTRAW,**

GOLDSMITH AND JEWELLER.

CERTIFIED OPTICIAN.

Personal attention given to Repairs of all kinds.   Clocks Wound and Repaired by Yearly Contract.

To a/c Rendered to June 30/12 | £ | · | 9 | 6

23 DERBY STREET   **1437**
LEEK *Sep* 17 1912
RECEIVED *with thanks the sum of*
£ — : 9 : 6
On behalf of
W. W. GOLDSTRAW

From *A H Shaw Esq for*

W. F. GOLDSTRAW,

QUALIFIED OPTICIAN.

REGISTERED FOR SIGHT TESTING UNDER
THE NATIONAL HEALTH INSURANCE ACT.

Bring your Optical Letter to
23, Derby Street,

LEEK.

WILLIAM GOLDSTRAW,

Baker, Confectioner, & Provision Dealer,

38, RUSSELL STREET, LEEK.

N.B.—Funerals and Parties supplied with promptitude and on
the most reasonable terms.

A CHOICE ASSORTMENT OF

PRESERVES & MARMALADES

Always on hand, equal to Home-made.

No 13.   19/3

HōVIS
Trade Mark

BREAD
is EXCELLENT for
Children of all :
ages ; It makes
and keeps them
sound—physically
and intellectually !

M⁣ʳ⁣ C Robinson
BOUGHT OF (Deceased)

Alfred Goldstraw,

BAKER AND FLOUR DEALER,

2 South Bank Street,

.·. Leek.

Shops, Schools and Parties supplied.
Snow Flake Self-Raising Flour.

1913.		s	d
June. 13	To Goods. 2/0½	2	0½
23	Flour 10 (14) Goods 5/4½	6	2½
19.	Goods 1/11 (25) Flour 5	2	4
30.	Goods 2/5½	2	5½
Aug 1st	Goods 2/1 (2) Goods 4/11	7	0
5	Butter 4 (6) Goods 2/8½	2	8½
7	Eggs 8 (13) Goods 4/2	4	10
14	C Roman 6½ (18) Flour 10	1	4½
29	Flour 10 Tea 6 Cocoa 7½	1	11½
Sept 19	Salmon 11 (24) Salmon 11	1	10
Oct 11	Goods 4/4	4	4
15	Flour 6		6
18	Cake 3		3

Settled from
Contra acct   £ 1 . 17 . 10
E Goldstraw Nov. 13. 1913

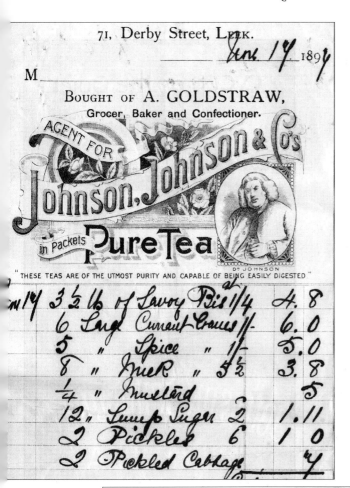

71, Derby Street, Leek.

Jᵘⁿᵉ 17 1894

M

BOUGHT OF A. GOLDSTRAW,
Grocer, Baker and Confectioner.

AGENT FOR

Johnson, Johnson & Co's

in Packets **Pure Tea**

Dʳ JOHNSON

"THESE TEAS ARE OF THE UTMOST PURITY AND CAPABLE OF BEING EASILY DIGESTED"

14	3½ lb of Savoy Bis	1/4	4.	8
6	Large Currant Cranes	/-	6.	0
5	" Spice "	/-	5.	0
8	" Duck "	5½	3.	8
¼	" Mustard			5
12	" Lump Sugar 2		1.	11
2	Pickles 6		1	0
2	Pickled Cabbage			4

California Mill is seen in the
photograph on page 167.

Memorandum Sep. 16ᵗʰ 1892.

From **G & J. GOLDSTRAW,**
CALIFORNIA DYEWORKS.
LEEK,
STAFFORDSHIRE.

To Mʳ G H Gadd
Leek.

Dear Sir

I beg to enclose my cheque.
Of or £35 which with £15 you owe
me according to the agreement
made at Macclesfield before I
would undertake to buy Goldstraws
business. makes £50 the amount.
of rent due on June 31ˢᵗ not June 24

Yours. Keep 4

34 St. Edward Street, LEEK,

Mar 14ᵗʰ 1931

Mr Sant

Bot of E. Goodfellow

Pastry-Cook and Confectioner.

20 Teas Supplied	2/3	£2	5 0

MARSH VIEW,

Rushton, Feb 28 1912

MACCLESFIELD.

Mr Bettany

Dr. to JAMES GOODFELLOW, Jun.

COAL MERCHANT, &C.

TERMS MONTHLY.   INTEREST CHARGED ON OVERDUE A/CS.

Date	Description	Tons cwts. qrs.	at	£	s.	d.
	To Groceries, Coal etc up to Dec 1910			3	9	6
Sep 2/11	Cash				10	0
				2	19	6
Oct 23/11	"				3	0
~~Jan 30/12~~	"			2	16	6
Jan 30/12					5	0
				2	11	6
Sep 9/11		2.1	10½		2	0
Oct 18 "		2 1	11		2	1

Many loads of coal made their way to Leek along the Leek branch of the Caldon Canal.

COAL DEPOT, LEEK WHARF

And 9, Westwood Terrace.

The
M Trustees of St Edward's School

Bought of NATHAN GOODFELLOW,
Coal Merchant.

189 4	Class	T.	C.	Q.	Price.	£	s.	d.
	Clerk's Bank							
Oct 4	Coals	1	1	0			15	9
26	„	1	2	0			16	6
Nov 22	„	1	2	2			16	10½
23	Carting 1 Ld Coke						1	6
						£ 2	10	7½
	add other						2	1	6
Janry 17 1895						£	4	12	1

Most local coal merchants had their depots at Leek Station, and coal waggons can be seen
in this picture of Leek sidings.

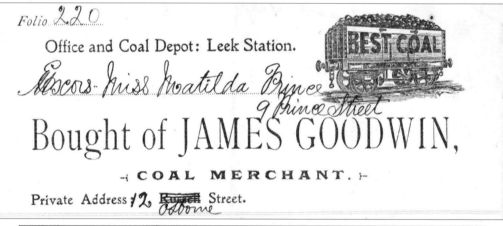

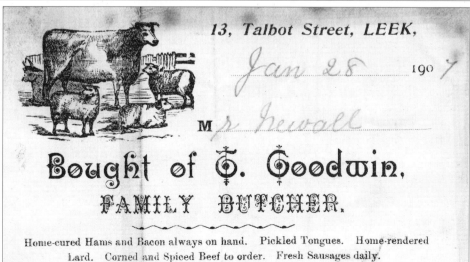

LONGNOR.

"CREWE & HARPUR" ARMS
(FULLY LICENSED).

Board and Residence, Luncheons, Teas.

FISHING OBTAINABLE.

MRS. M. G. GOULD.

⊱ 2, ⁜ BALL ⁜ HAYE ⁜ ROAD, ⁜ ⊰

Leek, *Octᵈ 1* 1892

STAFFORDSHIRE.

Mr G. H. Plant, trading as Messrs. G & J Goldstraw

To G. H. GOULD, Dr.

MEMORANDUM.

Telegraphic Address:—
GEORGE GOULD, LEEK.

Copy

From **G. H. GOULD,**
2, BALL HAYE ROAD,
LEEK,
STAFFORDSHIRE.

April 15 1892

To *J. Shaw, Esqʳ*
Messrs Challinors & Shaw,
Leek

Dear Sir,

Mr. G. H. Plant and his clerk Mr. Nixon have just been to my office and read to me from a paper as follows:—

"Tender to Mr Gould in notes & gold £24 for dividend on £95-18-11 the difference between £161-3-11 amount Work expenses for which he distrained and £65-5-0 the amount tendered to you for ½ years rent and expenses of distraint."

Plant then put a note and gold on the counter and asked me if I would accept it. I replied "I don't understand what you have read and cannot accept it without knowing what it is for

Stephen Goodwin's address at this time was 70 St. Edward Street.

STEPHEN GOODWIN & TATTON (1904), LIMITED.

Issue of First Mortgage Debentures of £100 each, bearing interest at £4½ per cent. per annum, all ranking pari passu, and numbered 1 to 90 inclusive.

No. *81*   DEBENTURE.   £100

Goodwin and Tatton's mill in West Street.

THOMAS GRACE, Broad Street, Leek. In the 1870s, the address of this firm was Canal Street; this then became Broad Street when a number of Leek street names were changed. A major contract won by Thomas Grace was the building of the Leek Technical Schools, next to the Nicholson Institute, in 1900.

Canal Street,

LEEK, _Aug 13_ 188 0

Mr Bacnal

DR. TO THOMAS GRACE,

BUILDER AND CONTRACTOR.

DEALER IN ALL KINDS OF BUILDING MATERIALS.

		£		
1879				
Nov 1	Bricklayer 1½ days	5/10	8	9
	Labour 1½ days	3/.	4	6
	30 Common Bricks		1	0
	2 pecks of Cement	1/.	2	0
	1 Peck of Plaster	9		9
	1 barrow of mortar	1/.	1	0
	repairing Grate. Pointing &			
1880	at Dr. Fowler's —			

1589

TELEPHONE No. 56.

LEEK, Xmas 1916

STONE YARD,
SAW MILLS,
AND
JOINERY WORKS,
BROAD
STREET.

Mr. Arthur Meakin, Osborne St.

Dr. to THOMAS GRACE,

BUILDER AND CONTRACTOR,

JOINER, BUILDERS' MERCHANT, &c.

DEALER IN ENGLISH AND FOREIGN TIMBER.

1916				
Oct 27.	Bricklayer 25 Hrs 11d. Labourer 25 Hrs 8d. Man 7 Hrs 8d	2	4	3
	36 Roof tile 2/6. 80. 6" Red Quarries 1d ea.		9	2
	3½ Barrows Mortar 1/2 6 peck cement 1/-		10	1
	1 6" Iron grid 8d. 3 Blue Bricks 1. 100. 1 qr 3 Air Brick 1/6		2	5
	1 6" Snap & iron grid 5/6. 1 4" pipe 1/-.		6	6
	1 4" Knuckle 1/6. 1 4" Bend 1/6.		3	0
	Repairing at the Late Mr C. Robinson's prop. Parker St.			
Nov. 24	Joiners 36 Hrs 11d	1	13	0

816 D.

STONE YARD, SAW MILLS, & JOINERY WORKS,
BROAD STREET, LEEK, Aug 30th 1901

Messrs Ash & Scarratt

DR. TO THOMAS GRACE,

BUILDER, CONTRACTOR, JOINER, &c.

DEALER IN ALL KINDS OF BUILDING MATERIALS, ENGLISH AND FOREIGN TIMBER.

1901					
June 30	650 Quarries 6/6 100. 3 Barrows Mortar	½	2	5	9
	1 peck Cement ½. 6 4" pipes	9½d		5	11
	Fetched by J Brassington Cartledge Bradnop		"	"	"
	£		2	11	8
				1	2

Settled with thanks Allowed

Steam Saw Mills, Broad Street,

LEEK, ...189

M...

DR. TO THOMAS GRACE,

ENGLISH AND FOREIGN TIMBER MERCHANT.

Shafts, Spokes, Naves, Felloes, Beds, Coffin Suits, and Carriage Builders' and Wheelwrights' Requisites.

			£	s	d
	Brought forward		4	5	0
1896 June 27th	16'-6" sup 1½" Ash	5¼d		7	2½
	11'-4" sup 1¼" Ash	4¼d		4	0
	13'-9" sup 1¾" Ash	6d		6	10½
	14'-6" sup 1" Elm	2½d		3	0
	21'-8" sup 1" Larch	2¾d		4	11
	18'-4" sup ¾" Larch	2d		3	0½
	1 pine Board 13'-0" x 12" x ¾"	2½d		2	8½
	3 Deal Boards 16'-0" x 11" x 1". 48 feet	2½d		10	0
	7 Deal Boards 13'-0" x 11" x ¾". 91 feet	2d		15	2
	4 Deal Boards 12'-0" x 11" x ¾". 48 feet	2d		8	0

Grace's Yard was in Broad Street on the right of this picture.

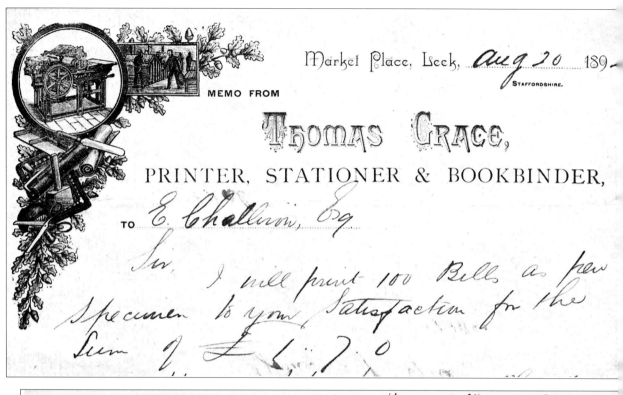

Market Place, Leek, *Aug 30* 189—

STAFFORDSHIRE.

MEMO FROM

Thomas Grace,

PRINTER, STATIONER & BOOKBINDER,

TO *E. Challinor, Esq*

Sir,

I will print 100 Bills as per Specimen to your Satisfaction for the Sum of £1.7.0

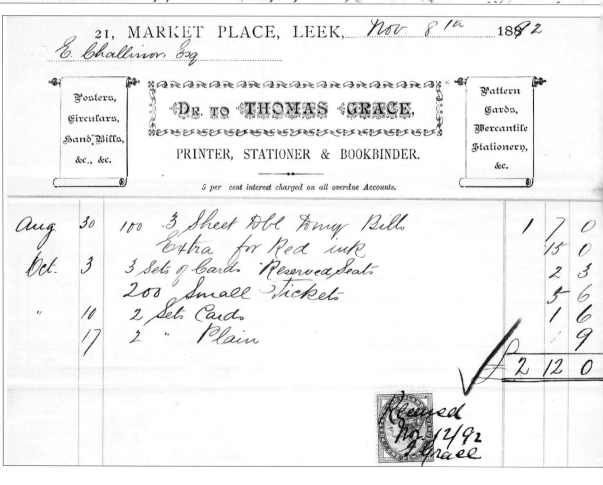

21, MARKET PLACE, LEEK, *Nov 8th* 1892

E. Challinor Esq

Posters, Circulars, Hand Bills, &c., &c.

Dr. to Thomas Grace,

PRINTER, STATIONER & BOOKBINDER.

Pattern Cards, Mercantile Stationery, &c.

5 per cent interest charged on all overdue Accounts.

				£	s	d
Aug.	30	100	3 Sheet Dbl Demy Bills	1	7	0
			Extra for Red ink		15	0
Oct.	3	3 Sets of Cards "Reserved Seats		2	3
		200	Small Tickets		5	6
"	10	2 Sets Cards		1	6
	17	2 " Plain			9
				2	12	0

Received No. 12/92 T Grace

This business is now in Derby Street.

E. GRAINGER,
67, HAYWOOD STREET,
. LEEK

China, Glass and Hardware Dealer.

Splendid variety of China Tea Sets to select from

years experience in a Manufacturer's
in a position to give best possible value

GRAND THEATRE
AND
PICTURE HOUSE

XMAS DAY ONLY.
At 7-30 p.m.

A LADY of QUALITY

Featuring Milton Sills, Virginia Valli & Earle Fox.

For the FIRST TIME in LEEK.
This Special Picture will be shewn at both the
GRAND THEATRE and PICTURE HOUSE.

We aim at presenting to the people of Leek and District the Latest and Best in Pictures and Music.

Tel.-LEEK **167**   Manager-JAMES PILKINGTON.

SMITHFIELD CARRIAGE WORKS, HAYWOOD STREET,

LEEK, *Nov 18th* 1893

Mr G Ratcliffe

DR. TO A. GREEN AND CO.,

CARRIAGE BUILDERS.

REPAIRS OF EVERY DESCRIPTION PROMPTLY ATTENDED TO.

July 7th To following repairs to Broken Dog Cart

1 Pair New Lancewood Shafts
5 New steps
resetting springs & Straightening Axle
straightening Scroll irons
which carry springs
New Seat Back
painting & Varnishing
all Iron work had to come
off To be made true fitting you
as agreed £8 . 0 . 0

SMITHFIELD CARRIAGE WORKS, HAYWOOD STREET,

LEEK, *June 27* 1893

Mr R. W. Brunt

~~DR.~~ TO A. GREEN AND CO.,

CARRIAGE BUILDERS.

REPAIRS OF EVERY DESCRIPTION PROMPTLY ATTENDED TO.

Dear Sir It will cost £8 = 0 = 0 the very lowest I can
do it (The Dog Cart) for, it could be made
a £10 = 0 = 0 Job, it will be as much work as
making a New Trap almost, as all the Iron
work will have to come off, so badly bent
& broken

Yours Faithfully
A. Green & Co

Messrs Challinor pro. **LONDON ROAD,**

Mr Thos Brealey for the Hall House Farm Cheddleton

Leck, October 188O

Dr. to GREEN and HALL,

JOINERS, BUILDERS, FUNERAL UNDERTAKERS,
&c.

		£	s	d
October Mostro	To Work as per Contract	98	0	0
	To Closet door & hinges		5	0
	3 large panes to bed room Window		3	6
	Cement for ditto			6
	2½ Days Carpenter to repairing gates hanging Closet door repairing bed room floors & fixing partition &c		13	9
	one dorma Window Glass &c		14	3
	30 ft of 6×1 flooring boards		2	6
	Nails & Wood for gates		2	1

London Road was the old name of Ashbourne Road.

41 × 45 Wood

~~27, BATH~~ **STREET, LEEK,** June 22ᵈᵉ 1878

Late Mrs Massey' Executors

Dr. to Green, & Hall,

BUILDERS, &c.

	£	s	d
To Oak Coffin Polished, Lined, best furniture, Shroud, Pall, Attendance, Invitations and postage	4	4	0
Dinner as per Bill at Ipstone	1	5	11
Sexton for Taking down palisades Making grave & refixing Palisades	1	0	0
	6	9	11

Messrs. Challinor prd.

LONDON ROAD,
Leek, _____ October 188 0

Mr Thos Brealey for the Hall House Farm Cheddleton

Dr. to GREEN and HALL,
JOINERS, BUILDERS, FUNERAL UNDERTAKERS,
&c.

		£	s	d
October	To Work as per Contract	98	0	0
Bought	To Closet door & hinges		5	0
	3 large panes to bed room Window		3	6
	Cement for ditto			6
	2½ Days Carpenter to repairing gates hanging Closet door repairing bed room floors & fixing partition &c		13	9
	one dorma Window Glass &c		14	3
	30ft of 6×1 flooring boards		2	6
	Nails & wood for gates		2	6
	4 setts of Window blind rollers &c		8	0
	3 panes to Stairs case Window		3	0
	1 T hinge for Stairs foot door			5
	28½ Yds of O. G 4½ spouts at 1/6	2	2	9
	3 outlets		4	6
	2 of 2" swannecks		4	0
	2 of 2 shoes 1/8 1 of 3" ditto 1/0		2	8
	1 of 3 shoes 1/0 1 of 3" swanneck 2/6		3	6
	1 of 3" fall pipe 2/6		2	6
	2 of 6ft fall 2"		4	0
	White washing all through £ 1	1	10	0
	£	105	10	4

Oct 30 88

pr Green

pro Green & Hall

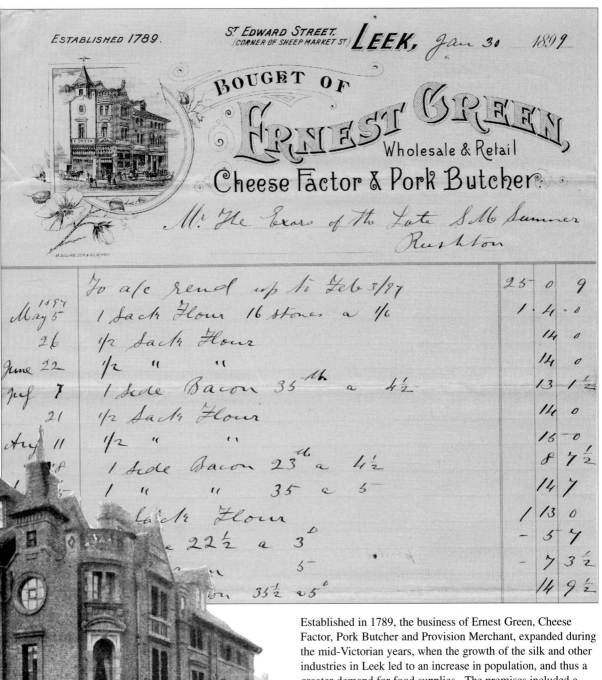

ESTABLISHED 1789.

Sᵀ EDWARD STREET.
(CORNER OF SHEEP MARKET Sᵀ) **LEEK**, *Jan 30* 1899

BOUGHT OF

ERNEST GREEN,

Wholesale & Retail

Cheese Factor & Pork Butcher

Mr The Exors of the Late S M Sumner
Rushton

		£	s	d
	To a/c rend up to Feb 3/97	25	0	9
May 5 1897	1 Sack Flour 16 stones a 1/6	1	4	0
26	½ Sack Flour		14	0
June 22	½ " "		14	0
July 7	1 Side Bacon 35ᵗʰ a 4½		13	1½
21	½ Sack Flour		14	0
Aug 11	½ " "		16	0
18	1 Side Bacon 23ᵗʰ a 4½		8	7½
	1 " " 35 a 5		14	7
	Sack Flour	1	13	0
	22½ a 3ᵈ		5	7
	5		7	3½
	35½ a 5ᵈ		14	9½

Established in 1789, the business of Ernest Green, Cheese
Factor, Pork Butcher and Provision Merchant, expanded during
the mid-Victorian years, when the growth of the silk and other
industries in Leek led to an increase in population, and thus a
greater demand for food supplies. The premises included a
large warehouse for the wholesale distribution of cheese
throughout the country, and extensive cellars for the curing of
hams on the large stone stillages. The business enjoyed a high
reputation for the quality of its cheeses. Shirley Buildings on
the corner of Sheepmarket and St. Edward Street is shown
here. They moved to the large Edwardian shop opposite, on
the corner of High Street, built when the street was constructed
about 1901 (See billhead on the next page). This well-
preserved property was occupied by Pickford's Grocers until
very recently, and is at present an antiques shop.

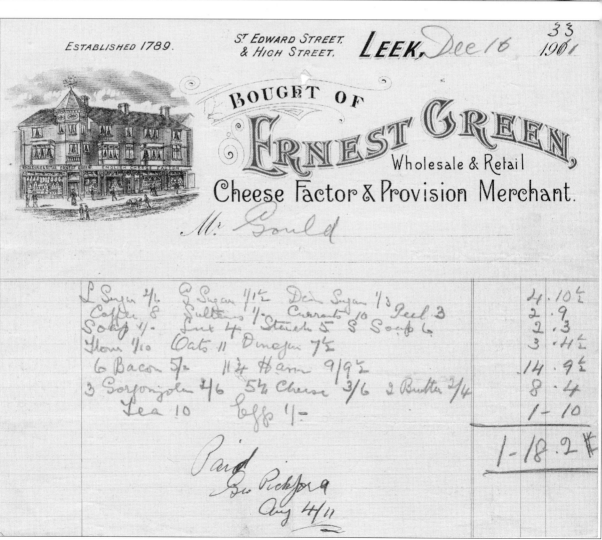

TELEGRAPHIC ADDRESS: "GREEN, LEEK" 49 St Edward Street.

The Exors of the Late S. M. Sumner Leek, Jan 30 1899
Rushton

Bought of Ernest Green,
Wholesale Cheese Factor

Terms Nett Cash

Accounts over 28 days will be charged 5% interest.

		£	s	d
	1 Milk Float as agreed	17	0	0
Nov 13/97	Paid Hamlyn & Co; Bill for Grains } St Annes Sq Manchester }	15	17	0
		32	17	0
		35	15	8

ESTABLISHED 1789.   ST EDWARD STREET. & HIGH STREET,   LEEK, Dec 16   33 / 1901

BOUGHT OF ERNEST GREEN,
Wholesale & Retail
Cheese Factor & Provision Merchant.

Mr Gould

	£	s	d
L Sugar 2/6 G Sugar 4/1½ Dem Sugar 1/3 Peel 3	4	10½	
Coffee 8 Sultanas 1/- Currants 10	2	9	
Soap 4/- Lux 4/ Starch 5 Soap 6	2	3	
Flour 1/10 Oats 11 Vinegar 7½	3	4½	
6 Bacon 5/- 11¾ Ham 9/9½	14	9½	
3 Gorgonzola 2/6 5½ Cheese 3/6 2 Butter 3/4	8	4	
Tea 10 Eggs 1/-	1	10	
	1 - 18 - 2		

Paid
Geo Pickford
Aug 4/11

ESTABLISHED 1765.

DEALER IN
PLASTERERS' LATHS,
CEMENT, TILES,
ENGLISH & FOREIGN
TIMBER.

TELEGRAMS
Green, Waterhouses,

ACCOUNTS HALF-YEARLY.

Waterhouses, *March 16th* 1914
Near Ashbourne.

M^r B Young Esq

Memo. from **SAMUEL GREEN,**

Joiner, Builder, & Funeral Undertaker.

Railway Station :—WATERHOUSES, via LEEK, N.S.R.

Dear Sir

Re Bottom of Cauldon Farm
My price for new concrete water pit of 6" concrete
10 yds wide & 4ft 6" deep. 100 yds of 3" socket
pipe from building to old water pit. & spouting 4"
wood to building as requested. will be Twenty pounds
17/-
Trusting the same will meet with
your approval & Remain
Yours Truly
Saml Green

Prospect and Heath House Nurseries,

Cheddleton, near Leek, ... 187

To Trustees of the late Mrs George Allen

Bought of WILLIAM GROSVENOR,

NURSERYMAN AND SEED MERCHANT.

1876				
Feby 4	4.000 Strong Mountain Ash	4 to 6 feet at 40/ 1000	£ s d	
			8 0 0	

Paid

delivered at Feltbouse Wood

BROOK STREET,

LEEK, *Xmas* 190 *7*

Mess Chelline & Shen

Bought of J. GROVE,

COMPLETE HOUSE FURNISHER.

Picture Framing in all its Branches.

5 per cent Interest charged on Overdue Accounts.

			£	s	d
May 22d	1 Leather Cushion for Office			2	6
	10 Yds of Sash Cord			1	3
	Mans time 5 hours putting				
8	Sash Cords in Windows	7		2	11
				6	8

LEEK, *Decr* 1854

Mr Richd Smith

BOUGHT OF E. GWYNNE,

WHOLESALE AND RETAIL

LINEN & WOOLLEN DRAPER, HATTER, HOSIER & GLOVER,

IMPORTER OF IRISH LINENS, &c.

EVERY ARTICLE FOR FAMILY MOURNING.

PURIFIED GOOSE FEATHERS.

			£	s	d
May 16	12 1/4 Shirting 3/8		2	4	0
17	2 Window Hold 9			1	6
	Elastic Hat bands			1	6
21	1 Rich Silk Hdkf			6	6
June 29	5 3/4 Oil Cloth 3/			15	0
30	Balloon			2	6

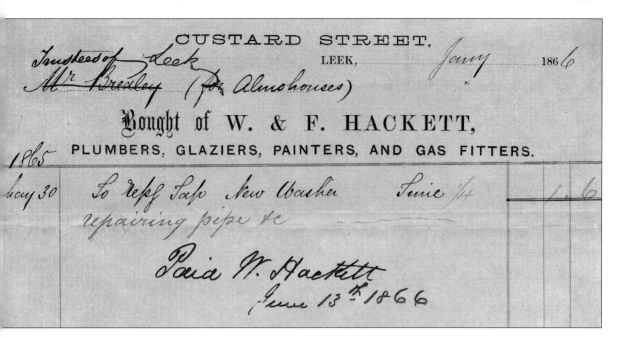

CUSTARD STREET,

Trustees of Leek

Mr Bradley (for Almshouses)

LEEK, _____ Jany _____ 1866

Bought of **W. & F. HACKETT,**

PLUMBERS, GLAZIERS, PAINTERS, AND GAS FITTERS.

1865

May 30	To Reps Tap New Washer repairing pipe &c	Twine /4		1. 6

Paid W. Hackett
June 13th 1866

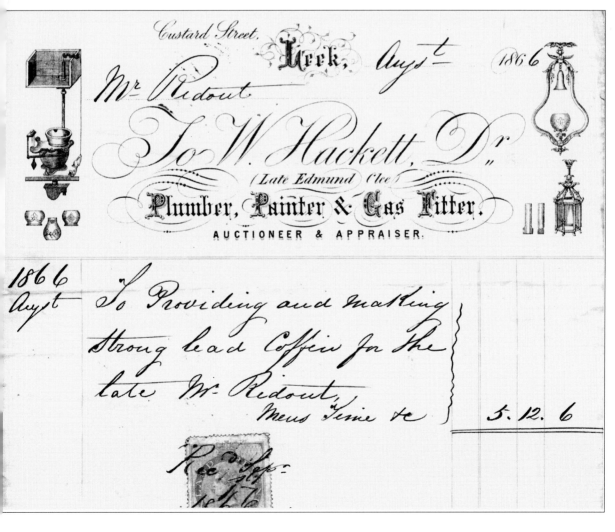

Custard Street,

LEEK, Augt _____ 1866

Mr Ridout

To W. Hackett, Dr.

(Late Edmund Clee)

Plumber, Painter & Gas Fitter.

AUCTIONEER & APPRAISER.

1866
Augt

To Providing and making
strong lead Coffin for the
late Mr Ridout,
Mens Time &c 5. 12. 6

Rec'd Sep.
1866

Phone 423

59, ST. EDWARD STREET,

LEEK *Dec 12* 1930

mr Sakyni

Bought of E. R. HAIGH,

Florist, Seedsman, etc.

WREATHS, CROSSES, BOUQUETS, and ALL FLORAL
DESIGNS on the shortest notice

Wreath		12	6

RECEIVED WITH THANKS
£ 12 6
p.p. E. R. HAIGH.
Date 13/ 12 30

FOR
High Class & Ready Made

Clothing,

AT THE LOWEST POSSIBLE PRICES.

In all the latest Materials, Fashion, Fit and
Finish to your liking. Wedding and Mourning
Suit made to order on the shortest notice.
Ladies' & Gentlemen's Waterproof over Gar-
ments secured to order.

E. HALL,

Practical Tailor and General Clothier.

THE OLD ESTABLISHMENT,

59, ST. EDWARD STREET, LEEK.

£19.

BUXTON ROAD, & COAL DEPOT, LEEK STATION.

Messrs Challinors & Shaw. Derby St.

Bought of HENRY HALL & SON,
(Late R. & M. A. Hall)
Coal Merchants.

19|2.	Coals.	Tons.	Cwt.	Qrs.	Price	£	s.	d.
April 30	Coke.	2	18	0	8.	1	15	4
May 6.	S L Coal	8	6	0	1/1	8	19	10.
	Cartage for Coke.						4	0.
						£10	19	2

Paid *Shaw* 14th 1912 *H Hall*

COAL DEPOT, LEEK STATION.
Buxton Road and Park Terrace, Ashbourne Road,

M Exors of the late Mrs J. Maryman Northam Place.

Bought of Henry Hall & Son,
(Late R. & M. A. Hall),
COAL MERCHANTS.

192 9	COALS	Tons	Cwts.	Qrs.	Price	£	s.	d.
Jan 23	H G Coal	1	3	2	2/5	2	16	9

Memorandum.   Jany 16th 1888

From

H. HALL,

JOINER, BUILDER, &c.,

LONDON ROAD,

RESIDENCE:
41, WOOD STREET,   **LEEK.**

To Messrs. Challinor & Co

Gentlemen   The Bedroom Ceiling at Mr Gibsons Overhouse Burslem — requires partly taken off and replastering at estimated cost of — 15/0 Gable Wall — requires to be partly took down and made good + Window fastened and painted — at a probable cost of Three or Four pounds —

LONDON · ROAD,

→ LEEK,   Sept 29th 1904

(RESIDENCE: 41, WOOD STREET.)

Mr Mottershead for The Trustees for Richd Turnock

Dr. to HERBERT HALL,

JOINER, BUILDER, FUNERAL UNDERTAKER, &c.

1904

			£	s	D
July 25th	Carpt time to repry in Victoria St Hanging Sashes fixing locks and door handles and taking down wood spouting 22 Hours			15	1
	1 plate lock 9"			2	8
	1 Rim latch & handle			1	4
	1 pr Handles —				7
	29 yds Sash cord —			2	4
			£1	2	0

Settled Oct 3d /0

For
Really
Delightful
XMAS
FARE

Phone
279.

Place your orders at once with

JAMES HALL, CAWDRY BUILDINGS, LEEK.

LEEK WHARF.

Mr W Phillips Esquire

Bought of JOSEPH HALL.

186_9_	COALS.	Tons	Cwt.	Qrs.	PRICE.	£	s.	d.
January 5th	Coals	1	1	0				
14th	"	"	19	"				
23rd	"	1	3	0				
Feby 2nd	"	1	2	0				

LEEK WHARF,

Trustees of Plum Howes

Bought of R. & M. A. HALL.

187*5*	Coals.	Tons.	Cwt.	Qrs.	Price.	£	s.	d.
Jan 9th	Coals	4	4	„	20/10	4	4	6

67, BUXTON ROAD, & COAL DEPOT, LEEK STATION.

Messrs Challinors & Shaw. Derby St.

Bought of R. & M. A. HALL,
Coal Merchants.

190*8*	Coals.	Tons.	Cwt.	Qrs.	Price	£	s.	d.
Sept. 9	Nth Coals	1	3	3	1/0½	1	4	9
„ 25	Nth Cobbles	1	0	3	11½		19	10
						£2	4	7

Received with thanks
10 Novr 1908
Henry Hall
for R & M A Hall

17 Canal St

~~37 ALSOP STREET,~~

Leek, Jan 21st 1880

Mr W. Goldst____

BOUGHT OF THOMAS HALL,

Tea Dealer, Family Grocer,

PROVISION MERCHANT, and TOBACCONST.

	To Old a/c	2	1	6
Sept 27	by Cash J. Hall	5		0
Nov 10	by Cash J. Hall	6		0
24	by Cash J. Hall	5		0
Dec 8	by Cash J. Hall	10		0
	Left on		15	6
Oct 1	1 lb Coff		1	6
"	6 lb Suger Lump		2	0
"	1 doz Dry Soap			9
12	½ lb Coff			9
"	6 " Suger J		1	6
"	3 " Suger Lump		1	0
"	4 " Candles		2	0
"	½ G Vinegar			10
22	1 lb V. Raisens			4
"	1 " Currents			4
"	¼ " Peel			3
27	6 " Suger Lump		2	1½
"	6 " Suger Jh		1	9
"	3 " Soap			10½
"	1 doz Dy Soap			9
"	1 doz Blacking		3	3½
"	2 lb Candles		1	0
Nov 15	1 lb Coff		1	6
"	6 " Suger Jh		1	9
		1	16	9 ½

17, CANAL STREET, *Leek, April 14 1896*

To the Executors of the Late Mrs
H. Ridout

Bot. of Thomas Hall,
Wholesale & General Grocer,
TEA DEALER & ITALIAN WAREHOUSEMAN.
PRESERVED MEATS IN TINS IN GREAT VARIETY, BEST BRANDS.

PEEK FREAN & Co's & JACOB'S CELEBRATED BISCUITS.
Pickles.
SAUCES,
JELLIES, JAMS,
SARDINES.
MARMALADE.
POTTED MEATS,
DESSERT FRUITS.
SPICES.
Cocoa, Chocolate &c &c

		£	s	d
Brot Fard		3	6	1.½
8 Weeks & 3 days. 5 each Week				
of Breakfasts Dinners &				
Tapoca Pudings & Milk				
Viz 43 days @ 1/6 per day		3	4	6
	£	6	10	7.½

Canal Street was the old name for Broad Street..

SPRINGFIELD COTTAGE, ABBOTT'S LANE,
LEEK, 2 5   1914

Mr Dishley for Mr Yarnets' Devises Kiln Lane

Dr. to T. HALL,
BRICKLAYER AND GENERAL REPAIRER.
ESTIMATES FREE.

			s	d
Bricklayer 1½ hour		1		
Labourer 3 "		1	7	½
6in trap 4/6 cement 6d		5		
		7	7	½

32, LIVINGSTONE STREET,

LEEK *Sat 22/8/* 1908

M*rs* *To the Trustees of the late S Birch Repair to Property Buxton Rd Ordered by Mr G Cotton*

DR. TO T. HALL,

BRICKLAYER AND GENERAL REPAIRER.

	£	s	d
Time 24 Hours		18	0
Labourer 24 "		12	0
375 Quarries Red and Blue	1	2	6
6 Barrow of Mortar		6	0
6 Peck of Cement		6	0
100 6 Bricks		4	0
24 Firebricks		3	0
4 Peck of Plaster		3	4
2 Barrow of Sand			6
25 Tiles		1	0
1 Kitchen Boiler and Drilling Same		4	6
1 Furness Door and Bottom		4	0
1 Grate Back		2	6
1 Joiner Time 12 Hours		8	0
1 Piece of Timber for Window Sill		2	0
1 Lintel		1	0
1 Piece for Splicing Door Frame			8
8 Pieces of Glass		2	6
1 lb of Putty			4
1 lb of Nails			4
1 Angle Iron for Broken Tenent			6
	5	2	8

Settled With Thank
J. T. ...
Leek ... 08

MEMO. FROM

BUILDER AND CONTRACTOR, AND BUILDER'S MERCHANT.

Wm. HALL,
39, Grosvenor Street,
— LEEK.

Dealer in all kinds of Sanitary and Agricultural **DRAIN PIPES, BRICKS, TILES, CEMENT, and PLASTER.**

LEEK, *Apl* 190 4

Mr *Thos Robinson*

Bought of **William Hall,**

BUILDER AND CONTRACTOR.

Postal Address : 39, GROSVENOR STREET.　　　　　5% Charged on Overdue Accounts.

	£	s	d
To Work done at Poultary Market	1	15	0

J. Finney Void　　　　　　　　*Stockwell Street, Leek,*

Messrs Challinor & Co.

TO EDWARD HALLOWES,
Letter-Press, Lithographic, and Copperplate Printer,
BOOKSELLER, STATIONER & BOOKBINDER.

LEDGERS, JOURNALS, DAY AND CASH BOOKS, RULED AND BOUND TO ORDER ON THE SHORTEST NOTICE.
New Books, New Music, Periodicals, &c., procured twice a week.

1864		£	s	d
July 27	Printing 150 Crown Bills :– Sale of House Garden, &c. at Ladderedge	"	14	"
Aug. 5	Advertising Sale of the above House, &c. in the Staffordshire Sentinel (twice ..	"	11	"
" "	Advertising Ditto Ditto Ditto in the Staffordshire Advertiser	"	6	"
J. E. 519	Settled Mar. 23/65	£ 1	11	"

Edward Hallowes

The Exec.rs of the
late Miss M. Mellor,

14, STOCKWELL STREET,
➤✠LEEK, *March 5* 1892

To Edward Hallowes,

PRINTER, BOOKBINDER, BOOKSELLER, STATIONER, NEWSAGENT, &c.

1891					
Mar. 3,	Bottle of Ink 2d; One Pint of Ditto 4d	"	"	6
Apr. 25	2 Packets Envelopes & One Packet Paper	"	1	5
" 28	5 Child's First Steps to the Piano Forte	"	5	"
May 1	2 dozen Scripture Manuals	"	15	"
" 8	1 dozen Exercise Books 4d; Box of Stationery 1/-	"	5	"
" 23	The World's Lumber Room 2/6; 26th Ink, 2d	"	2	10
" 27	Horner's Stories 2d; 29, 8 Catechism of C. Things 8d	"	8	2
" 29	Eight Catechism of the Old Testament	"	8	"
" "	2 Horner's Stories 2d; 30th, 4 dozen Envelopes & Paper 2/8	"	2	10
June 12,	Barriers burned away 1/-; 26th, Envelopes & Ink 4d	"	1	4
" "	Blotting Paper 4d; Flap Paper 4d; Ruled Paper 7d	"	1	3
July 1,	Mem. Book 1d; Box of Pens 6d; Ditto 1/-	"	1	7
" "	Box of Pencils 5d; July 6, Envelopes 3d	"	"	8
" 11	Note Paper 6d; 27th 6 sheets Brown Paper 6d	"	1	"
Aug. 21,	Envelopes 3d; Sep. 7, Envelopes 2½; Sep. 14 Ink 4	"	"	9½
Sept. 16,	2 Gall's History 4d; 4 Horne's Geography 4	"	"	8
" 22	Star Reader 1/4; 23, 13 Books 1/1	"	2	5
" 24	2 Pinnock's Catechism 1/; 2 Testaments 8d	"	1	8
	Carried forward	3	0	1 ½

Edward Hallowes served his apprenticeship with George Nall. He was in business in his own right in 1860 as a letterpress printer and bookbinder. A splendid first-hand impression of his shop appeared in an article by 'The Small Boy in the Market Place' which appeared in 'Leek News' for December 1933.

M E Challinor Esq

NORTH STAFFS. CYCLE DEPOT, 10, SHEEP MARKET,
LEEK 20/5/1897

BOUGHT OF # C. G. HAMBLETON,

Cycles by all Leading Makers.
Repairs on the premises.   Cycles let on hire by the day, week, or month.
All Cycling Requisites.

	£	s	d
To balance of acct. rendered	7	0	6
1 Centaur Model B Roadster with Dover Gear Case, Dunlop Tyres &c. £30			
Dis 30 % = 9			
Nett	21	—	—
Extra for Self Sealing Air Chambers	1	1	—
	29	1	6
By allowance for Bicycle	10	—	—
	19	1	6
	—	5	6
	19	7	—

CYCLES! ACCESSORIES!

The best of everything.   The BEST Machines obtainable.

ALL THE GREAT MAKERS' MACHINES at Prices Lower than those of the City Warehouses.

The Best Machines at Medium Prices.

The Best and Most Reliable Cheap Machines.

The Best Selection of New Machines in the Midlands.

The Best Selection of Second-hand Machines

The Best and Largest Stock of Accessories.

The Best Shop for Repairs.

The Best Shop for Hiring.

"HUMBER"

To obtain the Best Possible Value, buy your Machines and Accessories from

C. G. Hambleton's North Staffordshire Cycle Depot,

This splendid advert illustrates comprehensively the twin aspects of Hambleton's business.

C. G. HAMBLE...

PIANOS

Pianos

AND

Organs

HANDSOME, RELIABLE DURABLE.

Sole Agent for John Broadwood & Sons' Celebrated Pianos,
AND ALL PRINCIPAL MAKERS.

Three years system applied to any instrument.   Best discounts for cash.   Skilled tuners sent to all parts of the country.   Old instruments taken in exchange.
LARGEST STOCK OF MUSIC IN THE MIDLANDS.   LONDON PARCELS ARRIVE DAILY

One of the chief attributes of the "Daydream" is — its marvellous smooth running.

10, Sheep Market,

Leek, *Oct 15/02* 189

Mr *Birch*

To **C. G. HAMBLETON,**

MANUFACTURER OF THE

"DAYDREAM" CYCLES

Oct 8/02	1 sheet Best blue backed emery cloth.		"	- 3
" 9	1 Ladys Brook's B 10. Saddle		=	8. 4

DAYDREAM CYCLES

In 3 Grades, Manufactured by

C. G. HAMBLETON,

SHEEP MARKET, LEEK,

ARE HONEST VALUE FOR MONEY.

N.B.—One of the chief attributes of the "Daydream" is its Marvellous Smooth Running.

INSPECTION INVITED.   CATALOGUES FREE.

New and Second-hand Bicycles of every description.
Fittings, Accessories, Repairs, Enamelling, Plating, &c.

NOTED WAREHOUSE FOR

MUSICAL INSTRUMENTS,

Sheet Music, and all Musical Requisites.

OUR STOCK INCLUDES

ALL THE LATEST NOVELTIES.

SEE

The SELF-PLAYING ORGAN, may be played by anyone without the
slightest knowledge of music, or in the ordinary way.

The "SOLO," or "MELODY" ORGAN, beautiful Solo effects
and great variety may be obtained on this Organ.

The SUPER-OCTAVE COUPLER ORGAN, a great improvement
on the ordinary coupler.

The KIMBALL UPRIGHT GRAND PIANO, an upright Piano
combining all the qualities of a Concert Grand in tone & touch.

The PATENT TRANSPOSING PIANO which gives a choice of
Six Keys to each note on the Piano.

The GRAMOPHONE, Talks, Sings, and Plays; the
Best Entertainer in the World.

The PENNY-IN-THE-SLOT GRAMOPHONE.

GRAMOPHONE RECORDS, a large selection in stock.

The PENNY-IN-THE-SLOT SYMPHONION and other Musical
Boxes, Organettes, Concertinas, Melodeons, Violins, &c., &c.

All kinds of MUSICAL INSTRUMENTS TUNED & REPAIRED ON THE PREMISES.
TUNERS SENT TO ALL PARTS.

C. G. HAMBLETON,

10, SHEEP MARKET, LEEK.

C.G. HAMBLETON, 10 Sheepmarket, Leek The unlikely combination of musical instruments and pedal cycles could be found at Hambleton's shop in Sheepmarket. A full range of instruments was stocked, from pianos, parlour organs and harmoniums to flutes, penny whistles and banjos. A piano tuning service was also available, and sheet music was sold. Something of an entrepreneur in the world of music, Mr. Hambleton arranged concerts in Leek, with famous artistes of the day. Hambleton's comprehensive stock of cycles encompassed all the leading makes, including the 'Daydream', the sales slogan of which stated *"One of the chief attributes of the 'Daydream' is its marvellous smooth running"*. As might be expected, Mr. Hambleton was himself a keen cyclist. An old guide book of 1908 states that the shop was *"the headquarters of the International Journal of Music for Bands and Orchestras, the department being in the hands of Mr. Dague R. Pryor, who has a fine orchestra under his baton at Rudyard during the season"*.

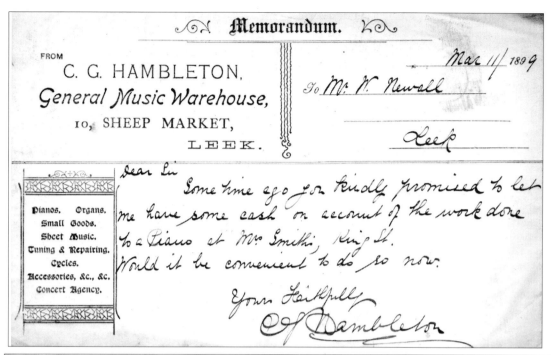

❧ Memorandum. ❧

FROM

C. G. HAMBLETON,

General Music Warehouse,

10, SHEEP MARKET,

LEEK.

Mac 11/ 189 9

To Mr W. Newall

Leek

Pianos. Organs.
Small Goods.
Sheet Music.
Tuning & Repairing.
Cycles.
Accessories, &c., &c.
Concert Agency.

Dear Sir
    Some time ago you kindly promised to let me have some cash on account of the work done to a Piano at Mr Smith's, King St.
Would it be convenient to do so now.

    Yours Faithfully
    C G Hambleton

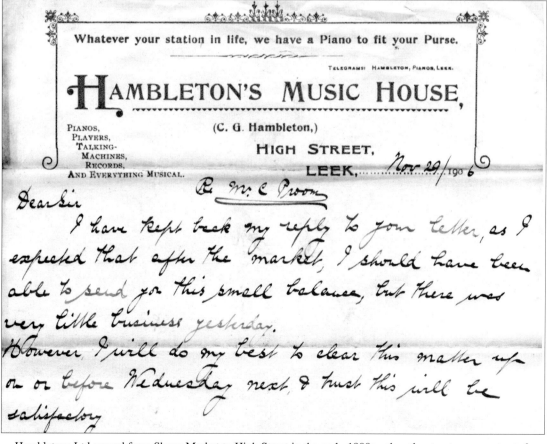

Whatever your station in life, we have a Piano to fit your Purse.

TELEGRAMS: HAMBLETON, PIANOS, LEEK.

HAMBLETON'S MUSIC HOUSE,

PIANOS,
PLAYERS,
TALKING-
MACHINES,
RECORDS,
AND EVERYTHING MUSICAL.

(C. G. Hambleton,)

HIGH STREET,

LEEK, Nov 29/ 190 6

Re Mr C Groom

Dear Sir
    I have kept back my reply to your letter, as I expected that after the market, I should have been able to send you this small balance, but there was very little business yesterday.
However, I will do my best to clear this matter up on or before Wednesday next, & trust this will be satisfactory

Hambletons Ltd moved from Sheep Market to High Street in the early 1900s, when the street was constructed. Here they had more commodious premises, with a large showroom, in the property adjoining the newly-built Grand Theatre and Hippodrome. The letters above, like many others in the collection, highlight the familiar cash flow problems of small retail business.

Hambletons Ltd.

the go-a-head concern that caters for the Musician's and Cyclist's every requisite, have very fine premises in High Street, Leek. In matters pertaining to their line of business, they are experts, and employ none but factory-trained hands in their tuning and repairing departments. Here, too, is the Headquarters of the International Journal of Music for Bands and Orchestras, the department being in the hands of Mr. Dague R. Pryor, who has a fine Orchestra under his baton at Rudyard, during the Season. This organization secured very high recommendation for their performance at the Leek Agricultural Show in September, 1907, and the Show Authorities did them the honor of awarding a special diploma, as a token of appreciation of the rich treat they had provided. We hear that Hambletons' are soon to erect a large Motor Garage.

High Street, LEEK.

MILLINERY ESTABLISHMENT.

MARKET STREET, LEEK.

Mrs A. Robinson

BOUGHT OF **M. & E. Hambleton,**

—— **MILLINERS** ——

Agents for Achille Serre, Ltd., Cleaners & Dyers.

Terms: CASH   Gloves, Veilings, etc.   Mourning Millinery.

	£ s d
Plush Hat 6/11	
Satin 2/-	
Feather 2/9	
Trim 10	12 6

18, STANLEY STREET, LEEK.

Mr Henry Goldshaw

To SAMUEL HAMBLETON,

MANUFACTURER OF AND DEALER IN

ALL KINDS OF CABINET FURNITURE,

Barometers, Thermometers, Clocks, Looking Glasses, Picture Frames, &c.,

Cotton and Wool Flocks, Feathers, Mattresses, Brass and Iron Bedsteads, Bedding and Hardware,

Washing, Wringing and Mangling Machines, etc.

WEDDING RINGS.   SEWING MACHINES.

** NOT RESPONSIBLE FOR CARRIER'S DAMAGES.

TERMS:—Interest at the rate of 5 per cent. per annum charged on over-due Accounts.

		£	s	d
22 May 1878	2 Bordered doormats a 3/6	0	7	0
4 Sept	Repairing mahogany sofa	1	6	6
19 March 1879	Cloth hearthrug	0	9	6
30 Sept	Repairing barometer	0	5	6
	Box frame for seaweed	0	4	0

52, Broad Street,

LEEK, *June 12* 1906

Mr. *Mitchell*

. TO .

S. Hambleton & Son,

MAKERS OF ALL KINDS OF
FURNITURE AND BEDDING.

Dealers in Bedsteads, Carpets, Pictures, Clocks, Wringing
Machines, Sewing Machines, Flocks, Feathers, and
every description of Furnishing Goods and
Materials.

1906			£	s	d
ag 80	1 - 4 X 4½ Caris sqr. 18 sqr yds a 3/9		3	7	6
31	5½ sqr yds linoleum a 1/9		0	9	7½
	mans time laying carpet & surrounding				
	Do. with lino 5 hr. a 8½d		0	3	6½
	Youths time Do. 1 hr a 5d		0	0	5
	2 boxes drugget pins a 1d		0	0	2
		£	4	1	3

Rec with thanks July 5/06
per pro S. Hambleton & Son

Leek, _____ 18 71

The late
Miss _____ Rider
Barnfields

To E. P. Hamilton,

SURGEON, &c.

1871

To Medicine and attendance for _____ Miss Rider

in the Month of _____ March _____ £ 2 .. 3 .. 6

Settled
E. P. Hamilton
May 5th /71

5/4/71

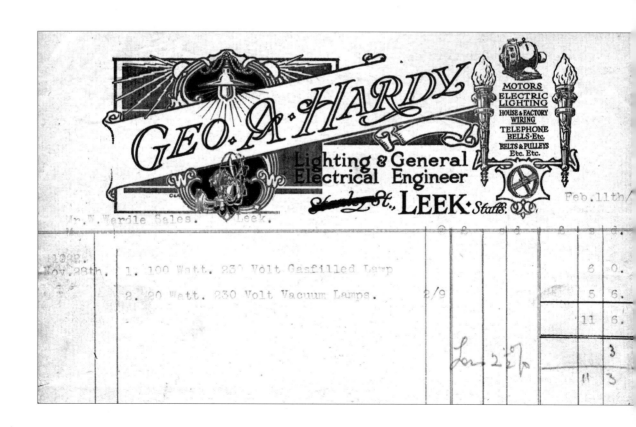

GEO. A. HARDY

Lighting & General
Electrical Engineer

_____ St., LEEK, Staffs.

MOTORS
ELECTRIC
LIGHTING
HOUSE & FACTORY
WIRING
TELEPHONE
BELLS· Etc.
BELTS & PULLEYS
Etc. Etc.

Feb. 11th/

Mr. W. Wardle Sales. Leek.

		@	£	s.	d.		£	s.	d.
1932.									
Nov. 28th.	1. 100 Watt. 230 Volt Gasfilled Lamp							6	0.
	2. 20 Watt. 230 Volt Vacuum Lamps.	2/9						5	6.
								11	6.
		Less 2½%							3
								11	3

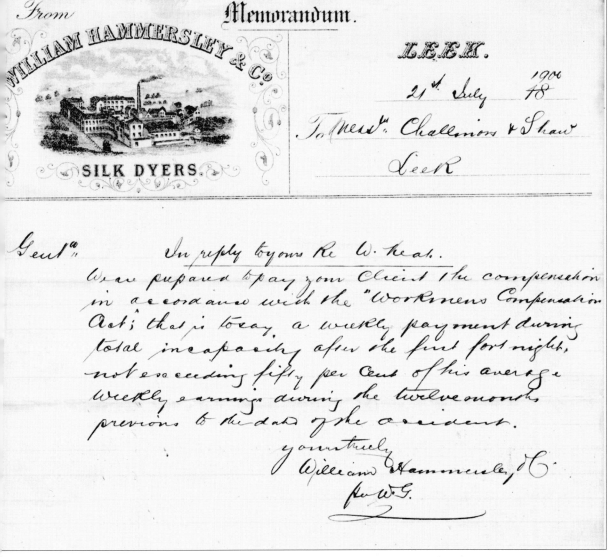

From

Memorandum.

WILLIAM HAMMERSLEY & Co.

SILK DYERS.

LEEK.

21st July 1900

To Messrs. Challinors & Shaw

Leek

Gentn

In reply to yours Re W. Keat.

We are prepared to pay your Client the compensation in accordance with the "Workmens Compensation Act; that is to say, a weekly payment during total incapacity after the first fortnight, not exceeding fifty per Cent of his average weekly earnings during the twelve months previous to the date of the accident.

yours truly
William Hammersley & Co.
per W.G.

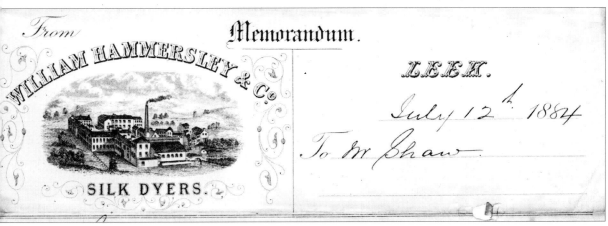

From

Memorandum.

WILLIAM HAMMERSLEY & Co.

SILK DYERS.

LEEK.

July 12th 1884

To Mr Shaw

William Hammersley's Dye Works were at the bottom of Mill Street.

P. J. HAMMERSLEY AND SON, PORK BUTCHERS

PORK PIES
Any Size to Order.

Our Celebrated Sausages are the best in Town.

We claim to have the most Up-to-date and Hygienic Premises in North Staffordshire.

Address :—

Gaunt Buildings, Derby St., Leek.

STANDARD CARS for 1933
ARE BETTER than ever.

Prices of COACHBUILT SALOONS.

Little NINE	4 cyl.	£159
Little TWELVE	6 ,,	£189
Big NINE	4 ,,	£205
Big TWELVE	6 ,,	£215
SIXTEEN		£235
TWENTY		£325

FOUR SPEED TWIN TOP GEAR BOXES, PRE-SELECTIVE GEARS £25 extra.

District Agents :

The Harris Motor Co. Ltd.

'Phone 262   **LEEK.**   Manager : D. H. Hope.

THE HARRIS MOTOR CO LIMITED.

HIGH ST. & SALISBURY ST. LEEK

WE SPECIALISE IN CAR MAINTAINANCE & 'CASTROL LUBRIQUIPMENT SERVICE.'

SEND YOUR CAR
Repairs to the
GARAGE that
DOES THE WORK

WE ALSO DELIVER The GOODS

Any make of Car can
be supplied, including
**Austin, Morris, Rover,
Riley, Essex, Chrysler.**

**ALBION,
MORRIS,** } **Commercial**
CHEVROLET

Buy the Car you like
From Deal"
" The Firm.

The Harris Motor Co. Ltd.
LEEK. - - Phone 262

Manager - Mr. D. H. HOPE.

World's greatest value
altogether or part by part

ESSEX siner

A first
to which there is no second
HAVE A TRIAL RUN & PROVE IT.
PRICES from £245
to £275

FOR FULL PARTICULARS and SPECIFICATION
Apply to :—
MAIN AGENTS FOR NORTH STAFFS.

THE HARRIS MOTOR CO. LTD.
Phone
226   **LEEK.**   Manager
Mr. D. H. Hope.

The Harris Motor Company was still present in Leek at the end of the 1960s, with large premises on the corner of High Street with Salisbury Street (still there), and with a larger presence in the Potteries as well.

ELECTRICAL
GIFTS
WILL PLEASE EVERYONE.

The most acceptable gift is
one that can be put to
practical use. That is why
you should give electrical
gifts this year. Electric
kettles, saucepans, toasters
electric irons and heaters,
table lamps, Radio Sets.
You will find amongst these a
gift to please everyone. Something they can use every day in
the ensuing year. Call and see
our display of electrical gifts.

FRANCIS W. HARRIS & Co., Ltd.,
High St., Leek.   PHONE 133

Members of
ELECTRIC CONTRACTORS' ASSOCIATION,
NATIONAL REGISTER INSTALLATION CONTRACTORS.

ESTABLISHED 1874.   MILL Nos:- TAMESIDE, 483. COLLYHURST, 482. WINKHILL, 998.

ALSO AT
Tameside Mills.
STALYBRIDGE.
AND
Winkhill Mills.
NEAR LEEK.

JOHN HARGREAVES.

PAPER MAKER,

Collyhurst Mills, *Manchester* *Feb 4 1905*

Telephone 273 STALYBRIDGE.

Todhope Challinor & Shaw

Cawdry Buildings are seen in the middle of this
picture towards the bottom of Fountain Street. They
remain much the same today.

Wellingtons,
Slippers,
Leggings,
Gaiters,
Spats,
&c.   &c.

Boots & Shoes for every occasion.
See our special XMAS Display.

R. HARROP,

THE ORIGINAL BOOT SHOP,

Cawdry Buildings.

Agent for the famous Portland,
Marie and Alfreta Brands.

T. HARRIS,
BAKER AND CONFECTIONER

Milk Bread and Sweet Bread a Speciality.
First Prize Winner for Milk Bread, Leek Agricultural Show, 1908.

Bakehouse :—72, Portland St. Residence :—9, West St

Memorandum.

FROM *Harris, Sanders & Pilkington,*
SILK MANUFACTURERS,
Leek, STAFFORDSHIRE.

Apl 21 1897

To Mr Robinson

Dear Sir

We do not want the 1100£ untill the expiration of 6 mos so let it stand untill the end the term

Your Truly

THE SWAN FAMILY AND COMMERCIAL HOTEL,

LEEK, Nov 29 1897
STAFFORDSHIRE.

Messrs Challinor & Shaw

DR. TO WILLIAM HARRISON,
BEER, WINE, AND SPIRIT MERCHANT.

Sep 9/97 To Use of Assembly Room for Property Sale conducted by Ferguson & Son	10	6
To refreshments Served	14	2
	1. 4.	8

POSTING & FUNERAL ESTABLISHMENT,
Stockwell Street,
LEEK, *May 7* 1891

M͞ʳ *Grofellow*

Dr. to G. T. Harrod,

Post Horses, Wedding & other Carriages
FOR HIRE ON THE SHORTEST NOTICE.

Terms Cash.

May	*To Shelibre to Rushton Church & Back*	*1 = 10 = 0*

POSTING AND FUNERAL ESTABLISHMENT,
STOCKWELL STREET, LEEK, ...188 4

M͞ *The Executor o Late John Plant*
Easing Farm

Dr. to G. T. HARROD,
(LATE SLATER.)

POST HORSES, WEDDING AND OTHER CARRIAGES FOR HIRE
ON THE SHORTEST NOTICE.

June 5	*To Hearse & Pair In Coach to b Leek Cemetery*	

POSTING AND FUNERAL ESTABLISHMENT,
Stockwell Street, Leek, ... *Oct* 188 8

M͞ʳ *The Executor 4 Late M͞ʳˢ Grosvenor*

Dr. to G. T. HARROD, *wetley Rocks*

Post Horses, Wedding and other Carriages for Hire
ON THE SHORTEST NOTICE.

Terms Cash.

POSTING ESTABLISHMENT,

Roe Buck Yard, Leek, *Aug 31* 188 9

Mr *Burnett*

DR. TO W. HARROD.

Post Horses, Wedding and other Carriages
for Hire on the shortest notice.

All orders promptly attended to.

Aug 23	Horse & Trap Ashcombe	~	4	0
28	Horse & Trap Endon	~	5	0
	Do Smithenley	~	6	0

Leek, *Jan 15* 1895

M A Shaw Eq

Dr. to W. HARROD,

Roebuck Hotel Livery Stables.

First-class Wedding and Party Carriages on the shortest notice.
Mourning Coaches, &c.

Jan 14	To Carriage & Pair		
	Bradley Green	£ 1	0 0
	Driver		5
	Ostler		1
	H. Malkin	£ 1	6
	Paid 16th 1-95		

Posting and Funeral Establishment,

Stockwell St., Leek, _____ 189**3**

Lot: Mr Prince Woodcroft

Dr. to

G. T. HARROD.

POST HORSES,

Wedding and other Carriages for
hire on the shortest notice.

Terms Cash.

Feb 9	Cab Town Hall	1,6
Ap 10	Do 2	2 -
July 10	Landau	5
11	Do Rushton	5
27	Do Spare Buxton	1 0
Aug 8	Do	1 0
19	Do	
29	Horse + Trap Do	
Sep 4	Landau Road	
7	Two Cabs	
14	Landau	

Receipt

Harrod's basketware shop was on the corner of
Dog Lane in Stanley Street. No billhead available.

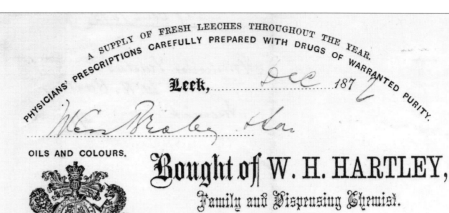

A SUPPLY OF FRESH LEECHES THROUGHOUT THE YEAR.

PHYSICIANS' PRESCRIPTIONS CAREFULLY PREPARED WITH DRUGS OF WARRANTED PURITY.

Leek, _____ Dec _____ 187_

OILS AND COLOURS.

Bought of W. H. HARTLEY,

Family and Dispensing Chemist.

GENUINE FAMILY and PATENT MEDICINES.

Foreign and English Perfumery.—Hair, Nail, and Tooth Brushes.

HORSE & CATTLE MEDICINES OF EVERY DESCRIPTION.

W. H. HARTLEY,

DISPENSING CHEMIST,

(BY EXAMINATION.)

MARKET PLACE, LEEK.

SOLE PROPRIETOR

OF THE CELEBRATED

"TIC DOLOREUX POWDERS."

W.H. Hartley's chemist was
succeeded by Cousins (p. 123).

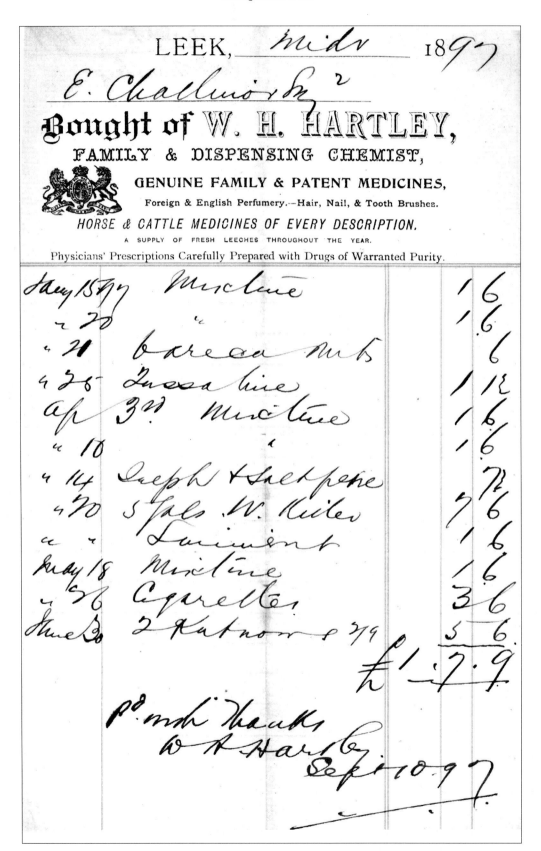

LEEK, _Midr_ 1897

E. Challinor

Bought of W. H. HARTLEY,

FAMILY & DISPENSING CHEMIST,

GENUINE FAMILY & PATENT MEDICINES,

Foreign & English Perfumery.—Hair, Nail, & Tooth Brushes.

HORSE & CATTLE MEDICINES OF EVERY DESCRIPTION.

A SUPPLY OF FRESH LEECHES THROUGHOUT THE YEAR.

Physicians' Prescriptions Carefully Prepared with Drugs of Warranted Purity.

Jany 15/97	Mixture		1	6
" 20	"		1	6
" 21	borax &c			6
" 25	Emulsion		1	12
Ap 3rd	Mixture		1	6
" 10	"		1	6
" 14	Sulph & Saltpetre			7½
" 20	5 Gals. W. Killer		7	6
" "	Liniment		1	6
May 18	Mixture		1	6
" 26	Cigarettes		3	6
June 30	2 Katnox @ 2/9		5	6
		£1	7	9

Pd with Thanks
W H Hartley
Sept 10 97

8, MARKET PLACE, LEEK,

Bought of E. HASSALL,

Milliner and Artificial Florist.

MADE-UP MILLINERY, DRESS CAPS, &c.
Straws, Ribbons, Feathers, Flowers, &c.

To The Exers of The Late Mrs Wilm Prince

		£		
1893			1	
Aug. 28	Set Spray	"	1	"
31	Set d Trimmings	"	10	"
Sept. 30	Set d Trimmings	"	11	6
	Set Cleaning string		3	6
		£1	10	"

Received by Cheque
with Thanks

Gould

EDWARD HASSALL,

Monumental &
General Mason.

DESIGNS PREPARED FREE.

ESTIMATES ON APPLICATION.

Mural Tablets, Chimney Pieces, Tiled
Hearths, Mosaic Work, &c.

Works: HAYWOOD STREET, LEEK.

Central Stores:— 57, DERBY STREET,   Branches — 45, WEST STREET.
19, BROAD STREET.

LEEK, *Nov 30 19*

Bo.t by Mrs Ferns

OF *Arthur Hay.*

Wholesale & Retail Grocer.

NOTED FOR FINEST BAKING POWDER.

✓	2 Butter		2	6
✓	3 lbs Cheese 8d		2	0
Gone	6¼ Ham		3	1½
✓	2 Milk Loaves			10
✓	2 Large Currant Loaves		2	0
✓	1/2 Coffe			10
✓	1/2 Tea		1	0
✓	2 lb Sugar Lump			4
✓	2 Sugar (Small)			4
✓	¼ Tabocca		1	0
			13	11½
	e of %		10	4½
	£	1	4	4

8th 1900

F. A. Hay.

The Executors of the late   May 1909

Mr Tymsey Coach House

Bought of ARTHUR HAY,
Grocer & Provision Merchant,
57, Derby Street,   Only Branch—45, West Street, LEEK.

CROSS OF LEGION OF HONOUR.   PURVEYORS OF MUSTARD, AND STARCH TO THE KING.
THE LARGEST MUSTARD MANUFACTURERS IN THE WORLD.

COLMAN'S
N^o1 STARCH
MUSTARD

BY SPECIAL APPOINTMENT TO THE KING

Colman's
BULL'S HEAD
Mustard
DOUBLE SUPERFINE

COLMAN'S
N^o1 AZURE BLUE

COLMAN'S CORN FLOUR

COLMAN'S SELF RISING FLOUR.

ASK FOR COLMAN'S D.S.F. MUSTARD.

ARTHUR HAY, in addition to his main Derby Street shop (now Bargain Booze), had a branch at 45 West Street, and also a shop in Cheadle. He sold out to George Mason in the late 1920s, and lived to be about 100 years old.

Arthur Hay, GROCERY AND PROVISION DEPÔT,

57, DERBY STREET, ✤ ✤ LEEK. ✤ ✤

Noted for **FINE COFFEE.**   *Delicious Teas*
Freshly Roasted Daily.   *1/6, 1/8 and 2/-*

The Best and Freshest Provisions.

Tinned and Dried Fruits and Fish.

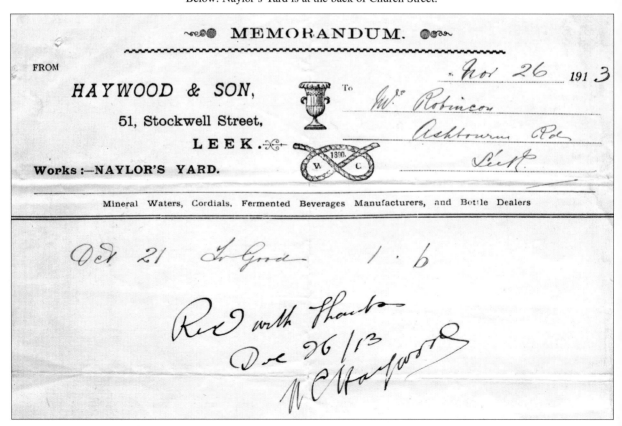

This old-established Wine Merchant was in Spout Street (now St. Edward Street). The business was carried on for some time by Mrs Frances Hayward, following the death of her husband.

Below: Naylor's Yard is at the back of Church Street.

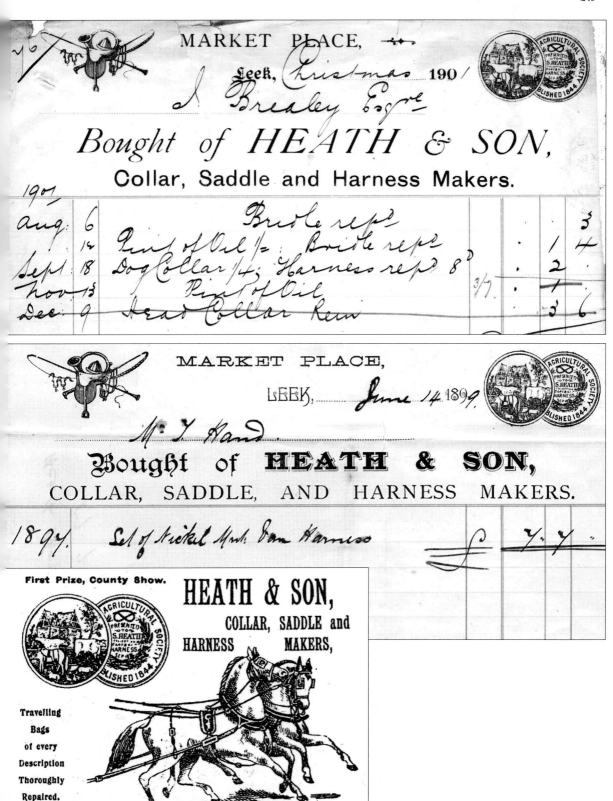

MARKET PLACE,

Leek, *Christmas* 190*1*

J Brealey Esqre

Bought of HEATH & SON,
Collar, Saddle and Harness Makers.

1901					
Aug.	6	Bridle reps			3
Sept.	14	Pint of Oil /- ; Bridle reps		1	4
	18	Dog Collar /4 ; Harness reps 8d		2	
Nov.	15	Pint of Oil	3/7	1	
Dec.	9	Head Collar Rein		3	6

MARKET PLACE,

LEEK, *June 14 1899*

Mr T Hand

Bought of HEATH & SON,
COLLAR, SADDLE, AND HARNESS MAKERS.

1899	Set of Nickel Mtd. Van Harness	£	7 . 7 .

First Prize, County Show.

HEATH & SON,
COLLAR, SADDLE and HARNESS MAKERS,

Travelling
Bags
of every
Description
Thoroughly
Repaired.

MARKET PLACE, LEEK.

RAILWAY APPROACH, RUDYARD.

Sep 30   189 7

Mr S Wood

Dr. to G. T. HEATH,

Coal & Coke Merchant.

TERMS CASH.

PETROLEUM OIL IN CASKS.   Agent for WALLGRANGE BRICK & TILE CO.

TONS	CWTS.	QRS.	DESCRIPTION	at	£	s.	d.
March 1897			To a/c Rendred for Coal		1	0	2

55

COAL WHARF,   *Leek,*   OCT 31 1916   19

STAFFORDSHIRE.

Miss Pickford

Mill St.

To Robert Heath & Sons, Ltd., Dr.

DATE.	SPECIES.	TONS	CWTS.	QRS.	PRICE.	AMOUNT.
Oct 6	H Lane Coal	1			30/-	110
"	"	1			"	110

ISAAC HEATH,

House and Estate Agent

57, DERBY ST., LEEK.

Property Purchased or Disposed of.   Rents Collected.

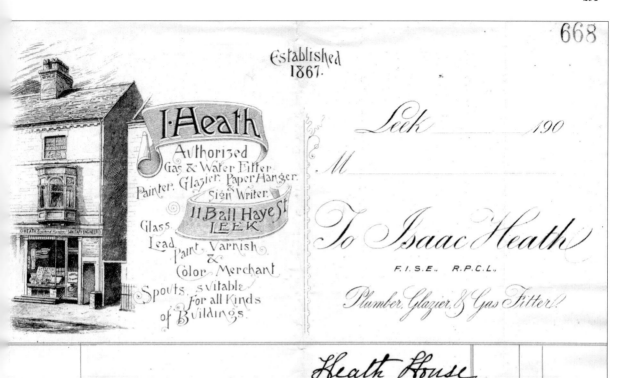

Established
1867.

I·Heath
Authorized
Gas & Water Fitter.
Painter, Glazier, Paper Hanger,
& Sign Writer.
11 Ball Haye St
LEEK
Glass, Lead, Paint, Varnish
& Color Merchant
Spouts, suitable for all kinds
of Buildings.

Leek _____ 190

M _____

To Isaac Heath
F. I. S. E.,   R. P. C. L.,
Plumber, Glazier, & Gas Fitter.

Heath House
Layton Lane
Blackpool
Oct 22th 1915.

Mr Wardle
Dear Sir.

We received your letter this morning.
& Mr Heath has decided for Mr Ferguson to
sell & raise as much money, as he possibly
can. Mr Heath is thinking of asking the
building Society to lend him two or three
hundred pounds to buy property here. The
house he is living in at the present time.
Mr Heath thinks Mr Ferguson prices are
too low. But he hopes you will raise as
much as possible.

I remain.
Yours Sincerely
E Heath.

Isaac Heath.

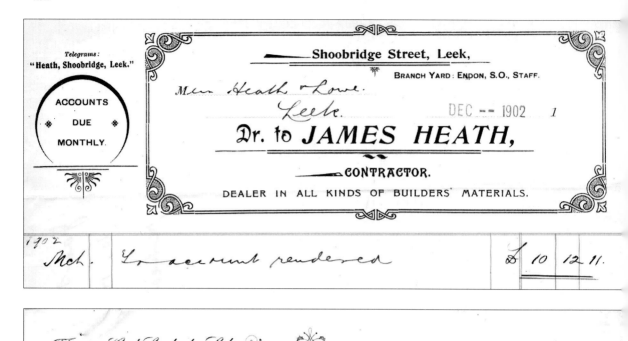

Telegrams:
"Heath, Shoobridge, Leek."

ACCOUNTS
DUE
MONTHLY.

Shoobridge Street, Leek,
BRANCH YARD: ENDON, S.O., STAFF.

Mess Heath & Lowe.
Leek.   DEC —— 1902   1

Dr. to JAMES HEATH,
CONTRACTOR.
DEALER IN ALL KINDS OF BUILDERS' MATERIALS.

1902				
Mch.	To account rendered	£	10	12	11.

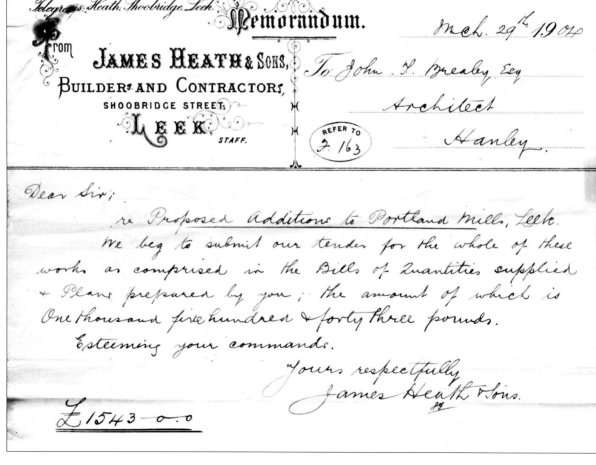

Telegrams Heath, Shoobridge, Leek.   **Memorandum.**   Mch. 29th 1904

From
JAMES HEATH & SONS,
BUILDERS AND CONTRACTORS,
SHOOBRIDGE STREET,
LEEK, STAFF.

To John F. Brealey, Esq
Architect
Hanley.

REFER TO
F. 163

Dear Sir,

re Proposed Additions to Portland Mills, Leek.
We beg to submit our tender for the whole of these
works as comprised in the Bills of Quantities supplied
& Plans prepared by you; the amount of which is
One thousand five hundred & forty three pounds.
Esteeming your commands.

Yours respectfully
James Heath & Sons.

£1543 – 0 . 0

James Heath won the contract to build All Saints' Church, and earned high praise from the architect,
Richard Norman Shaw, for the high standard of their work (1884).

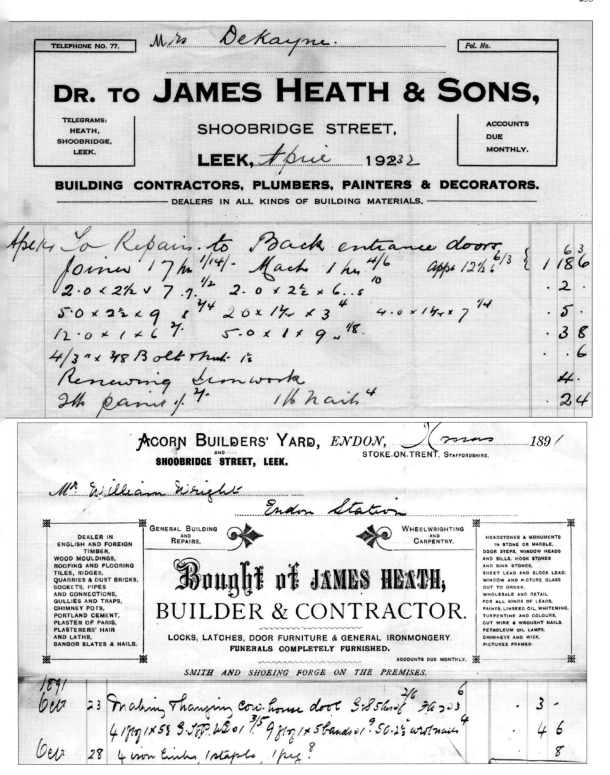

James Heath also operated from Acorn Builders Yard at Endon. George Heath, the Moorland Poet, was of this family, and he served his apprenticeship as a joiner with them. While he was working on the restoration of Horton Church he contracted a chill which eventually led to his early death from consumption.

Like many builders and joiners, Heaths also offered their services as undertakers. The business continued in Shoobridge Street, under the management of Mr. Stanley Smith, local councillor, until the 1970s.

ENDON,
Near Stoke-on-Trent, *June 30 / 1879*

Mr Joseph Challinor Esqr

BOUGHT OF JAMES HEATH,

JOINER, BUILDER, WHEELWRIGHT

AND CONTRACTOR IN ALL KINDS OF WOOD WORK.
REPAIRS PROMPTLY ATTENDED.

May 17	4	4 Setts of Sash Fasteners 1/	-	6	"
		4 Rack pulleys 4/ 1 Doyn Screws	-	4	4½
		Time Man 5½ h.	-	2	7½
Do 28	1	1 Kind Guara Chimney pot	-	5	6
June 25		2 - 1 - 14 of Sheet Lead for Flashing 39/	3	0	11½
		plumber 37 h. 1/1½	1	3	1½
		Mason Chasing for Lead Fixing			
		Chimney pot & pointing Flashing			
		&c 28½ h. 7½	-	17	9½
		Cement 3/6 Mortar 1/	-	3	6
		Received at the Office July 4/9/79	£ 6	3	5½
		from John Bentley Aug 28th 3/79	Disct	0	5½
		Totals	6	0	0
		James Heath			

Works:
CRUSO STREET.

CRUSO STREET,

LEEK, *Nov 11th* 189 9

Mr S Turnock

Dr. to HEATH & LOWE,

Joiners, Builders, and Undertakers.

New Window for Dun Lee Farm		
5 ft 6 of 4½ × 3 Oak 1/	5	6
5 ft 6 × 3½ × 3 Deal 2d		11
16 ft × 3½ × 2 Do 1½	2	0
Mans Time 10 hrs @ 9d	7	6
Machining	1	0
Settled with thanks	16	11
Nov 15th 1899 J Heath		

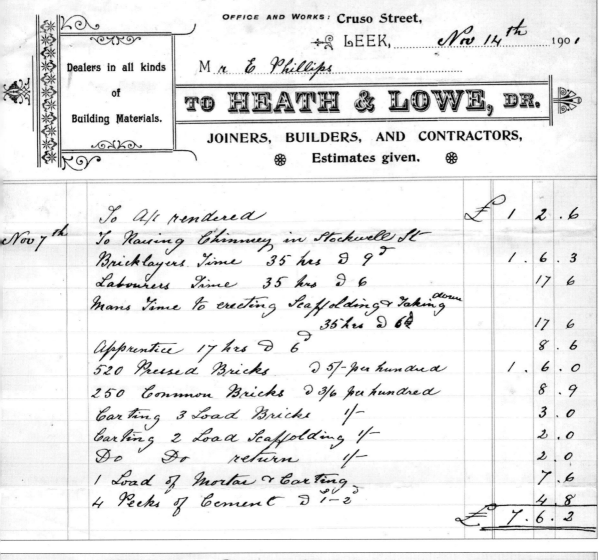

OFFICE AND WORKS: Cruso Street,

LEEK, _Nov 14th_ 190 _1_

M r E Phillips

TO HEATH & LOWE, DR.

JOINERS, BUILDERS, AND CONTRACTORS,

Estimates given.

Dealers in all kinds of Building Materials.

		£	s	d
	To A/c rendered	1	2	6
Nov 7th	To Raising Chimney in Stockwell St			
	Bricklayers Time 35 hrs @ 9d	1	6	3
	Labourers Time 35 hrs @ 6		17	6
	Mans Time to erecting Scaffolding & Taking down 35 hrs @ 6¼		17	6
	Apprentice 17 hrs @ 6d		8	6
	520 Pressed Bricks @ 5/- per hundred	1	6	0
	250 Common Bricks @ 3/6 per hundred		8	9
	Carting 3 Load Bricks 1/-		3	0
	Carting 2 Load Scaffolding 1/-		2	0
	Do Do return 1/-		2	0
	1 Load of Mortar & Carting		7	6
	4 Pecks of Cement @ 1-2		4	8
	£	7	6	2

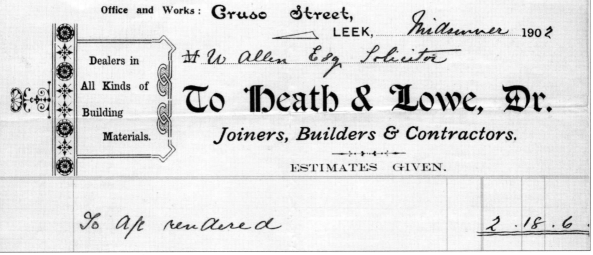

Office and Works: Cruso Street,

LEEK, _Midsummer_ 190 _2_

H W Allen Esq Solicitor

To Heath & Lowe, Dr.

Joiners, Builders & Contractors.

ESTIMATES GIVEN.

Dealers in All Kinds of Building Materials.

		£	s	d
	To A/c rendered	2	18	6

J. E. HEATH

(Late C. E. Mitchell,)

HIGH-CLASS

GROCER & PROVISION MERCHANT,

23, Market Place, Leek

TEA & COFFEE A SPECIALI...

Try our noted (Moorland) Tea !

TEL. 280.

The presence of so many Heaths is not surprising.
It is very much a North Staffordshire name

Right: Henshaw 1892.

M. J. HENSHAW

(Late Yates & Henshaw)

GENERAL DRAPER,

MILLINER, AND DRESSMAKE...

60 B, ST. EDWARD STREET, LEEK.

LADIES & CHILDREN'S UNDERCLOTHIN...

A large Assortment of fancy Aprons & Pinafores
always in stock.

Mourning made on the shortest notice.

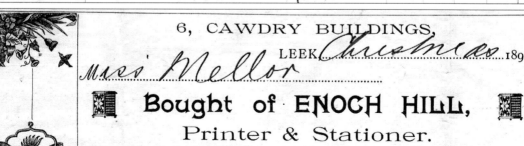

THE NORTH STAFFORD CONSERVATIVE NEWSPAPER CO. LIMITED,

OFFICES: 8, HAYWOOD STREET,

Leek, March 31   188*8*

Mr Holland, Macclesfield

Dr **To the Proprietors of THE LEEK POST,**

PUBLISHED EVERY SATURDAY. PRICE ONE PENNY.

DATE.	TITLE OF ADVERTISEMENT.	No. Insertions	No. of Inches.	Price per insertion	£	s.	d.
Feby 11 to March 31	*Exchange Drapery*	8		1/6		12	"

6, CAWDRY BUILDINGS,

LEEK *Christmas* 189*1*

Miss Mellor

Bought of ENOCH HILL,

Printer & Stationer.

The only Printer in Leek who holds the Certificate, given by the City and Guilds of London Technical Institute, of efficiency in Typography.

Lithographer, Bookbinder, Bookseller, Newsagent, Paper and Paper Bag Merchant, &c.

NOCH HILL was born in one of the small houses in
Milk Street, Ball Haye Green. As a young man he was
diligent in his studies and took an active part in the
religious, social and municipal life of Leek, being
closely attached to St Luke's Church and the Ball Haye
Green Mission Church. For many years he was a
Sunday School teacher and lay reader. Virtually self-
taught, his perseverance was exemplary. He became
acquainted with Mr John Sykes, headmaster of the
Leek Grammar School, under whose influence and
guidance he undertook a further course of private
tuition.

He began printing in a shed behind his Milk
Street home, and later went to work for Edward
Hallowes, printer and stationer, in Stockwell Street.
Printing became his first commercial enterprise. He
moved into a shop in Cawdry Buildings (Kelly's
Directory 1892) where he established a stationery and
printing business.

But his great work was still to come. In 1895 he
was appointed Secretary to the Leek United Building
Society, a position he held for seven years. During that
time he was elected to the Leek Urban District Council,
on which he served for the remainder of his time in
Leek. He played a major part as secretary of the
Catering & Entertainment Committee for the local
celebrations of the Coronation of King Edward VII.

In 1902 he was appointed secretary of the
Halifax Permanent Building Society, and his career
went from strength to strength. He became prominent
in the building society movement nationally, presiding
at the Annual Building Societies Conference for
several years. He earned considerable distinction in
banking circles, and was rewarded in 1928 with a
knighthood.

When Enoch Hill entered the Building Society
profession, his printing business had to be offloaded, so
he transferred his interest to his brothers, forming the
firm of Hill Brothers (Leek) Ltd. The firm left Derby
Street and took new premises in Haywood Street (now
'Genies') in 1900 and it was here that the Leek Post
was printed for many years. The Leek Post and the
Leek Times, of M.H. Miller, ran concurrently for a
number of years. At first the Leek Post was less
successful, the Leek Times enjoying a much larger
circulation. Because of this, it charged a higher rate for
advertisements, and this ultimately led to a reversal.
The Leek Post, in spite of its poorer financial position,
installed new and more efficient machinery, while the
Leek Times became less efficient and more unreliable.
Ultimately the Times was incorporated into the Post to
form the Leek Post and Times in 1934.

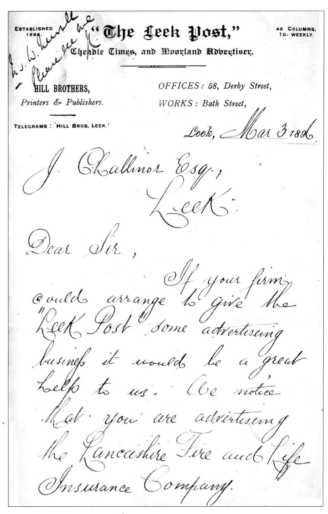

The Leek Post,
CHEADLE TIMES & MOORLAND ADVERTISER.

ADVERTISE IN THE POST

By far the largest circulation in the district.

CALL OR PHONE 96.

No. 2205   REGISTERED AT THE GENERAL POST OFFICE AS A NEWSPAPER.   SATURDAY, AUGUST 25, 1928.   PRICE TWOPENCE.

DISTRICT BANK
LIMITED

ESTABLISHED 1829.

PERSONAL and BUSINESS ACCOUNTS.

TRAVELLERS' CHEQUES AND LETTERS OF CREDIT issued payable throughout the British Isles and Abroad.

Ask for particulars at the Local Branch

Sales by Public Auction.

By S. MOTTRAM & SONS

LEEK CATTLE MARKET.

WEDNESDAY NEXT at 11 o'clock prompt.

100 DAIRY, FAT AND STORE CATTLE.

50 FAT AND YOUNG CALVES.

Usual Prices.

Entries respectfully solicited

HULME END MONTHLY STOCK SALE.

will be held on

THURSDAY, NEXT, AUGUST 30th, at 12-30.

100 DAIRY and STORE CATTLE, SHEEP, PIGS and CALVES.

Further Entries Solicited.

Good buyers will attend.

SEPTEMBER 13th.

THE COTTAGE, CALTON.

SALE OF HOUSEHOLD FURNITURE and EFFECTS for Mr. Constantine.

FREEHOLD RESIDENCE, known as "The Cottage," Calton, with Vacant Possession on completion; also FIELD of ACCOMMODATION LAND, 3 roods, called "Little Stantion."

LEEK ANNUAL SHEEP SALES.

LAMBS: 10th Sept. Entries solicited to 12th Sept.

SHEEP: 3rd October.

Auction Offices:—
Waterhouses, Stoke-on-Trent.

Sales by Public Auction.

By Messrs. FERGYSON & SON.

Removed from Rock House, Bridge End, Leek.—Three Days Sale of Attractive and Valuable Modern and Antique Furniture.—About 300 ozs. of Silver, Silver plate, Antique China, Oil Paintings, Water Colours, Etchings, Broadwood Pianola, Dining, Drawing room and Boudoir Furniture, Inlaid Mahogany Bedroom Suites, Spanish Mahogany Walnut and Pitch Pine ditto, more particularly described in Catalogues, and being the contents of Hall, Drawing and Dining Rooms, Boudoir, 5 Bedrooms and Domestic Offices.

FERGYSON and SON, instructed by the Exors of the late Mrs. Jessie Hiller, will sell without reserve, as above the Valuable Furniture and Effects at the SWAN ASSEMBLY ROOMS, LEEK, on THURSDAY, AUGUST 30th, at 1 p.m., and on FRIDAY and SATURDAY, August 31st and Sept. 1st, 1928, at 1 and 6 p.m. each day.

On view by Catalogue on Wednesday, August 29, from 10 to 12 and 1 to 4 p.m. Catalogues may be obtained at the Auction Offices, 4, Church Lane, Leek, 10 days before the sale; between 10 a.m. and 4 p.m. only, price 6d. Saturday 10 a.m. to 1 p.m.

THORNCLIFFE, Near LEEK.

VACANT POSSESSION.

For Sale by Auction by MESSRS. J. OAKES ASH & SON, at the RED LION HOTEL, LEEK, on WEDNESDAY NEXT, 29th AUG., 1928, at 3 p.m., prompt, subject to conditions.

AN ATTRACTIVE FREEHOLD DAIRY FARM known as "QUARRY BANK FARM," occupying a pleasant and convenient position in the Village of Thorncliffe, 2½ miles from Leek, comprising an excellent Homestead and an area of 44 Acres 1r. 9p., or thereabouts of Sound Old Turf Land, at now occupied by the Vendors, Exors. of the late Mr. William Felthouse, who will give Vacant Possession on Completion and not make any charge for tenant right.

The farm enjoys good roads, and there is an excellent water supply, which is subject to the House and adjoining lands, two of which pay an annual rent of £1 each.

To view, apply on the premises, and for further particulars, and to inspect Plan, to the Auctioneers, 43, St. Edward

By Messrs. J. OAKES ASH & SON.

LEEK CATTLE MARKET.

WEDNESDAY NEXT at 11 o'clock.

220 CATTLE.

150 CALVES.

Also SHEEP PIGS and Sundries.

Usual Prices. Entries Solicited.

Public Notices.

LONGSDON
(STAFFS)

HORTICULTURAL SOCIETY.

THE NINTH ANNUAL

SHOW

OF HORTICULTURAL PRODUCE, POULTRY, PIGEONS, ETC.

will be held in the MEMORAL HALL AND GROUNDS, LONGSDON, on SATURDAY, AUGUST 25th, 1928.

will be opened at 3 o'clock.

SCHEDULE AND BYELAWS.

OVER £60 IN PRIZES.

Admission to Show:
3 to 5 p.m., Adults, 1s., Children 6d. 5 to 8-30, Adults 6d., Children 3d.

THE BIG THREE

14 GNS.

14 Guineas

14 Guineas

Extended Terms if desired

THREE LARGE FACTORIES are concentrating on home production in the manufacture of these goods, giving the highest grade in both materials and workmanship. Inspection invited.

14 GUINEAS EACH SET.

LEEK'S PREMIER FURNISHING HOUSE,

CAMPBELL'S

Russell St. - LEEK.

Phone 317.   Send for Illustrated Catalogue FREE

The Homes of Britain

No. 8. No. 10 DOWNING STREET.

This plain looking house was built at about the time of the Fire of London, and became the official residence of the Prime Minister in 1731 by the gift of George II.

IF you have to live in a town your house may look plain from the outside, but you can always make it cosy and attractive within.

If your home is your own you can go on making one little improvement after another, with the prospect of your outlay coming back to you should you ever decide to sell.

So be wise and buy your home now, through The Leek & Moorlands Building Society, who will lend you a large part (usually about three-quarters) of its value, which you can repay in small monthly instalments.

Write for particulars to:—

LEEK & MOORLANDS
BUILDING SOCIETY.

THE LARGEST STAFFORDSHIRE BUILDING SOCIETY.

HEAD OFFICE:
15, STOCKWELL STREET, LEEK.

FRANCIS BILLING, Secretary.

Messrs. Challinors & Shaw, Solicitors, Leek.

WE MAKE ALL OUR OWN

BEDROOM SUITES & SIDEBOARDS

AND ARE NOW MAKING A SPECIAL OFFER OF A

3ft. OAK BEDROOM SUITE

COMPRISING

3ft. Wardrobe, 3ft. Dressing Chest, 2ft. 6in. Chest. 4ft. 6in. Bedstead, Wire Mattress & Wool Mattress.

COMPLETE AT £17-10-0

J. NOKES & SONS
OVERTON BANK, LEEK.

BIDDULPH
AND
DISTRICT
Agricultural Society
LIMITED.

61 Derby St., Leek.

WE HAVE NOW IN STOCK AT ALL DEPOTS:—

A.O.M. and B.O.C.M. Compounds; Mill Offals; Linseed Cake and Meal; Egyptian Cotton Cake; "B" Pure Cotton Cake; Grass Nuts; Flaked Maize; Nitrate of Soda; Superphosphate; Sulphate of Ammonia; Kainit.

For prices and samples apply at Depots:—

LEEK, BIDDULPH, WINKHILL, and IPSTONES.

All Varieties of CHICK and POULTRY CORNS and MEALS; DOG CAKES; HOUND MEAL; BIRD SEED; PIGEON CORNS (separate and mixtures).

FOR ALLOTMENT HOLDERS: Nitrate or Soda; Sulphate of Ammonia; Superphosphate; Kainit; Bone Meal in small quantities to suit purchasers at the shop.

Bath Street, Leek.

"MAGIC NOTES"

MAGIC Notes! Magic Notes, indeed. Music's magic that Paul Whiteman draws from his world famous orchestra are now recorded exactly "like life.

PAUL WHITEMAN

exclusive

Columbia
Record Artist

16 Feby 1911

Messrs Challinors & Shaw Leek

Dr. to THE PROPRIETORS OF THE "LEEK POST."

CHEADLE TIMES & MOORLAND ADVERTISER.

The most influential and most extensively circulated Paper in the district.

Best medium for Advertisers.

REMITTANCES PAYABLE TO HILL BROTHERS (LEEK) LIMITED.   OFFICES: HAYWOOD STREET, LEEK.

1911	FOR ADVERTISING :—	NO. OF INSERTS	AT EACH.	£	s.	d.
Jany to 28	Rudderton Ladderedge &c Property Sale 2nd	4	26/		5	4
" 21 & 28	Ashborne Road Pply Sale 2nd	2	13/6		1	7

From
GEORGE HILL,
Printer
Stationer & B
8, STANLEY
LEE

April 10 1891

To A. H. Shaw, Esq

⚘8, STANLEY STREET,

Leek, Midsummer 1895

Messrs Challinors & Shaw

To GEORGE HILL,

Letter-press & Lithographic Printer, Bookbinder,

STATIONER, PATTERN CARD MANUFACTURER, AND NEWS AGENT.

1895.

8, STANLEY STREET,
Leek, *Xmas* 190

Mrs Brealey

To GEORGE HILL,

LETTER-PRESS & LITHOGRAPHIC PRINTER, BOOKBINDER,

Stationer, Pattern Card Manufacturer, and News Agent.

Printing of every description executed with promptitude. Bookbinding in every style, and best workmanship.

| Sep | 18 | Repairing Book "Monte Christo | 1 | 3 |

NEW GENERAL

Printing Establishment,

8, STANLEY STREET, LEEK.

GEORGE HILL,

(For upwards of 20 years with the late Mr. Rider, and Mr. Samuel Rider,)

s to inform the Gentry, Manufacturers, Tradesmen, and Inhabitants of Leek District, that he has commenced Business at the above address, and respectfully cits a share of their patronage and support.

Having had long practical experience as a Printer, and possessing New Type it Modern Appliances, he is able to execute all orders promptly and efficiently,

---

Printing of every Description,

INCLUDING

Sermons, Pamphlets, Reports and Rules of Public Institutions and Societies, Posting Bills, Handbills, Circulars, Invoices, Memorandum and Delivery Notes, Business Cards, &c., &c.

ESTIMATES GIVEN.

✦MEMORY✦CARDS✦PRINTED✦ON✦THE✦SHORTEST✦NOTICE✦

✦BOOKBINDING✦IN✦ALL✦ITS✦BRANCHES✦

CHARGES STRICTLY MODERATE.

ANNOUNCEMENTS INSERTED IN LOCAL AND OTHER NEWSPAPERS.

George Hill, General Printer and Stationer,

8, STANLEY STREET, LEEK.

12th OCTOBER, 1881.

8, Stanley Street, Leek,

Dec. 31 1907.

Messrs Challinors & Shaw

To G. Hill & Sons,

Printers, Stationers, Bookbinders, & News Agents.

Publishers of the "Photographic" Series of Local View Post Cards.

1907.

Date	Description			
July 10	36 Notices Special Sessions		3	6
" 29	200 Forms. Description of property as Mortgage Deed	1	4	.
Aug 16	300 " Conviction for Penalty recoverable by Distress		12	6
" 27	110 D'Demy posters Houses & Land in Mill St. end	1	5	.
" 30	75 copies, particulars & conditions of Sale of ditto end	1	17	6
" 31	100 Summonses, Poor Rate, 50 end. 50 plain		15	.
Sep. 21	150 Informations under Leek Improvement Act		7	6
Oct 22	500 Forms, Instructions for Summonses		9	9
Nov 7	300 " Summons to Witness		16	6
" "	300 Informations Staffs. County Council		12	.
" 14	300 Forms Biddulph Order, General Dist. Rate		14	.
Dec 23	200 " Notice of Special Petty Sessions		7	.
" "	100 Sheets, Sessions List 1908.		16	.
		£ 10	.	3

24/2/08

Paid with thanks

G Hill

G. HILL & SONS. In addition to running his business as a printer and stationer, George Hill was a keen and prolific photographer. He produced a very wide selection of local views which were sold as picture postcards in the Stanley and Photographic series. Being a local man, he had an eye for the unusual and obscure parts of the town and moorlands, often able to divert from the main highways and byways to seek out the views that the major postcard publishers neglected. George Hill's business as a letterpress printer and stationer was established in 1881, and became George Hill & Sons in 1920. Mr. John Myatt bought the business in 1940, and continued trading until the 1970s.

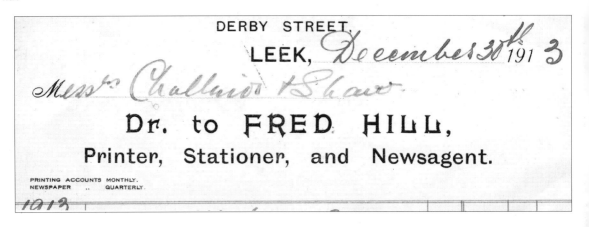

In 1901 Mr Fred Hill commenced business as a stationer and bookseller, and established a printing shop in a section of Haywood Mill, Haywood Street. John Maycock, a life-long friend of Mr. Hill, was the printer.

After the end of the First World War Mr Hill purchased three cottages in Getliffes Yard, just off Derby Street, almost opposite his shop premises at 58 Derby Street. The cottages were three storeys high, and he made the three into one long building, removing an upper floor to make a more lofty building with a goods entrance opening on to York Street. The printing was done on the ground floor, and the upper floor was the paper store, cutting room and finishing department. The machinery was letterpress, and the staff were two journeymen, with assistance from newsboys from the book shop, as their time allowed. Some of these boys became apprentices, and transferred to the print works, where they were able to learn the trade, from composing type and printing, to folding, numbering and finishing. The firm undertook a wide variety of jobbing work for the textile industry and other commercial enterprises in the town, as well as social printing and funeral work.

He was for many years a member of the Leek Urban District Council, and Chairman in 1934/5. He became involved with the annual Leek carnivals which were held in the 1930s (mainly raising money for local hospitals). Later he became a director of the Leek United and Midlands Building Society.

The combination of his experience in the printing trade, his strong connections with the public life of the town and his

The Outstanding Gift
A Good Book

- Fiction -

WITCH WOOD—*John Buchan.*
NO OTHER TIGER—*A. E. W. Mason.*
SIR PERCY HITS BACK—*Baroness Orczy.*

- Belles-Lettres -

THE CHARM OF BIRDS—*Viscount Grey.*
LAW, LIFE AND LETTERS—*Earl Birkenhead.*
ARTHUR MEE'S BOOK of EVERLASTING THINGS
ON LEAVING SCHOOL. and the choice of a career-
                                    Sir Charles Wakefield

THE IMPATIENCE OF A PARSON—*by the Rev*
        H. R. L. Sheppard, until recently Vicar o
        S. Martin's-in-the-Fields.

All these and hundreds of other books
——— may be seen at ———

FRED HILL'S, The Bookseller
Derby Street, LEEK.

involvement with the Leek Chamber of Trade, put Fred Hill in a unique position to produce *Leek News*. *Leek News* was a advertising journal - a well-produced and well-illustrated journal containing numerous articles of local interest. The cost o production was covered by revenue from the advertisements, enabling it to be distributed free each Christmas. Printed in his ow workshop in Getliffes Yard, every word was set by hand composition and the work would have to start in late October to ensur it would be out by Christmas. Much of the material in *Leek News* was the direct work of Fred Berrisford, who was employed b Mr Hill in the office. He did most of the proof-reading and wrote many of the unsigned articles, long and short. An army o delivery men and boys delivered it free to every household in Leek.

Each year a small *de luxe* edition of about 500 copies would be produced with a better quality cover, printed on art pape and sold for 3d each. About 5,000 copies of *Leek News* were printed each year for the 14 years between 1925 and 1938.

A major contribution for several years was the article by 'The Small Boy in the Market Place' - the *nom-de-plume* of M W. Warrington. He played a leading role in the public life of the town as a member of the Leek Urban District Council.

One of the factors guaranteed to disrupt a printer's working day was a sudden in-rush of funeral work. This was alway wanted very quickly, and could include a fully-printed order of service. If a "funeral notice" was wanted, this would be don immediately, and distributed round the shops for display in their windows, often within an hour or so.

Fred Hill at the door of his shop with Mr William Pedley, the furniture dealer. M & S Hill (advert below photo) were Fred Hill's wife and sister, and their shop was next door.

The Misses H. & M. HILL,

XMAS ANNUALS,

WONDER BOOKS,   BUMPER BOOKS

——AND——

Games to make a Happy Xmas for the Children.

Bibles and Hymn & Prayer Books
in Large Variety.

....

Extensive Stock of

NOVELS BY
Popular & Famous Authors

5, High Street, LEEK.

WB
CORSETS

• • • Your Xmas frock must look its best !

. . Christmas parties—family gatherings—you naturally want to look your very best, why not let your frock take the place it should do, in bringing about this desirable result ? It will do, you know, if you give it a chance.

A. W. B. Foundation Garment is fashioned with a dual purpose : it controls your figure-lines, giving them a beauty of curve, and at the same time provides a modish foundation over which your frock will set to the very best advantage

Here are just three W. B. models out of a widely varied range which we can show you, and our assistants are trained to help you in your selection.

W.B. Youthline. Model 1504. (Two-way-Stretch) A step-in, fashioned entirely from peach "two-way-stretch" elastic.
Sizes 24-32. **18/11**

W. B. CORSET. Model 1318. For figures developed slightly beyond the average : side-hook model in peach shadow-striped coutil, hip-panels of rayon elastic; false busk affords additional support. Sizes 26-36. **10/11**

W. B. CORSET. Model 1412. Front-lacing foundation, lightly fashioned in peach brocade, with insets of fancy elastic at bust. Sizes 24-34. **10/11**

M. & S. HILL,
LADIES' and CHILDREN'S OUTFITTERS
60, DERBY STREET, LEEK. - - -

Messrs. William Hill and Co.,   **Wellington Mills, Leek,**
Successors to the late S. Gibson, **And at 47, Gutter Lane, Cheapside, E.C.**
Manufacturers of Sewing Silks, &c.,

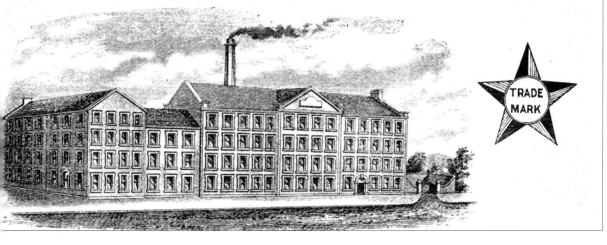

TRADE MARK

141

VETERINARY ESTABLISHMENT,

LEONARD STREET, LEEK Midsummer 1898

Mr Oliver Upper Hulme   Swinmore

To Robert Hill, M.R.C.V.S. London,

(MEMBER OF THE ROYAL VETERINARY COLLEGE MEDICAL SOCIETY, LONDON)

VETERINARY SURGEON.

HORSE, CATTLE, SHEEP AND DOG MEDICINES.

HORSES EXAMINED AS TO SOUNDNESS.

1898

			£	s	d
March 16	½. Dog Powders			3	
April 27	½. Dog Powders			3	
				6	0

Received with thanks
Richd Hill
Jany 4th 1899

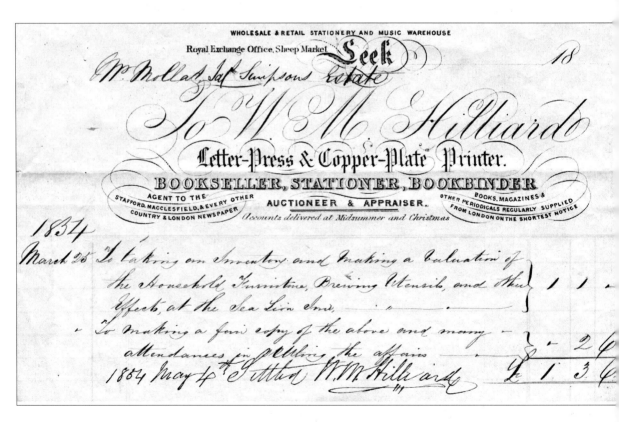

WHOLESALE & RETAIL STATIONERY AND MUSIC WAREHOUSE
Royal Exchange Office, Sheep Market **Leek**   18

Mr Mollat Jas Simpsons Estate

To W. M. Hilliard

Letter-Press & Copper-Plate Printer.

BOOKSELLER, STATIONER, BOOKBINDER

AGENT TO THE
STAFFORD, MACCLESFIELD, & EVERY OTHER
COUNTRY & LONDON NEWSPAPER

AUCTIONEER & APPRAISER.

BOOKS, MAGAZINES &
OTHER PERIODICALS REGULARLY SUPPLIED
FROM LONDON ON THE SHORTEST NOTICE

Accounts delivered at Midsummer and Christmas

1854

		£	s	d
March 25	To taking an Inventory and making a Valuation of the Household Furniture, Brewing Utensils, and other Effects, at the Sea Lion Inn,	1	1	.
	To making a fair copy of the above and many attendances in settling the affairs		2	6
1854 May 4th Settled W. M. Hilliard		£ 1	3	6

Midd 1834.

WHOLESALE AND RETAIL STATIONERY AND MUSIC WAREHOUSE.

Plain and Elegant
BOOKBINDING.

ROYAL EXCHANGE OFFICE, SHEEP-MARKET, LEEK.

Mr Gascoyne, Union Inn,

TO W. M. HILLIARD,

Letter-Press and Copper-Plate Printer,

BOOKSELLER, STATIONER, BOOKBINDER, MUSIC SELLER,

General Newspaper Agent, Auctioneer, Appraiser, &c.

7.44

Leek, _____ 186

Miss Ferriar

Bought of W. M. Hilliard,

Licensed Wholesale Dealer in

PORTER, BITTER BEER, LIGHT & STRONG ALE.

☞ Please to put a Cork and Vent-Peg in the Cask when empty, and return it as soon as possible.

Leek, _____ 185

Miss Ferriar

Bought of W. M. Hilliard,

Licensed Wholesale Dealer in

PORTER, BITTER BEER, AND PALE ALE.

☞ Please to put a Cork and Vent-Peg in the Cask when empty.

Sale by Auction, at *late Miss Gardner* 187

Mr John Wardle

Bought of W. M. Hilliard,

AUCTIONEER, APPRAISER, &C., 5, STOCKWELL STREET, LEEK.

LOT.		£.	s.	d.
191	Clock	1	0	0
206	Mahy Chest of drawers	3	12	0
210	Pair of Sheets	,	3	3

WHOLESALE AND RETAIL STATIONERY AND MUSIC WAREHOUSE.

Royal Exchange Office, Sheep-Market, Leek, _____ 186

Mess.rs Challinor & Co Magistrates' Clerk's account,

To W. M. HILLIARD,

LETTER-PRESS & COPPER PLATE-PRINTER,

BOOKSELLER, STATIONER, BOOKBINDER.

Agent to the Stafford, Sentinel, Derby, Macclesfield, & every other Country and London Newspaper,
New Books, Magazines, and other Periodicals regularly supplied from London on the shortest notice.
AUCTIONEER, GENERAL APPRAISER, ESTATE AND HOUSE AGENT,
SOLE AGENT IN LEEK FOR THE SALE OF MILNER'S PATENT FIRE-PROOF SAFES.

10-226
1865   Terms 1865

Date	Description		£	s	d
July 15	To Printing 25 copies Application for Licence Mr Derbyshire	✓		4	6
" 21	" Printing 100 Summonses Leek Town Act	✓	"	7	6
" "	" Printing 100 ditto endorsed (2 workings)	✓	"	12	6
" "	" Printing 75 copies Appeals against Rates	✓	"	4	6
Aug 18	" Printing 100 Summonses for Poor Rates	✓	"	7	6
" "	" Printing 100 ditto ditto endorsed	✓	"	12	6
Sep.t 4	" Printing 100 copies Commitment for Penalty & costs	✓	"	7	6
" 16	" Printing 150 copies orders in Affiliation and costs	✓	"	10	6
" 23	" Printing 40 copies Receipts for Revision of Jury lists	✓	"	2	6
" 26	" Printing 50 copies Summons in Bastardy	✓	"	5	.
" "	" Printing 50 ditto ditto endorsed	✓	"	7	6
Oct.o 7	" Printing 100 copies Summonses for Poor Rate	✓	"	7	6
" "	" Printing 100 ditto ditto endorsed	✓	"	12	6
" 14	" Printing 100 copies Appeal against Rates	✓	"	4	6
Nov 7	" Binding "General Statutes" as before	✓	"	4	6
Dec.r 11	" Printing 100 Recognizances both sides Printed	✓	"	12	6
" 30	" Printing 100 copies Commitments Punishment &c	✓	"	7	6
" "	" Printing 50 copies Special Session F.cap folio		"	4	6
1866 Jan.y 8	" Printing 100 copies Special Sessions F.cap 4.to	✓	"	6	.
			£7	1	6

Correct W.H.

1866 March 5.th Settled
W. M. Hilliard

ONE PENNY

With W. M. Hilliard's best thanks

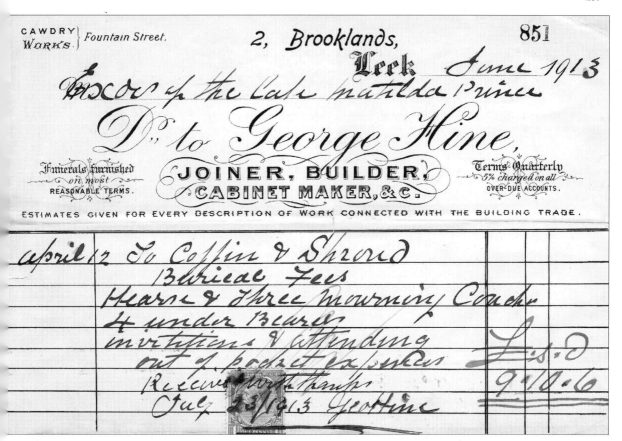

CAWDRY WORKS. Fountain Street.

2, Brooklands,

Leek June 1913

851

Exco~ of the late Matilda Prince

D~ to George Hine,

Funerals furnished on most REASONABLE TERMS.

JOINER, BUILDER, CABINET MAKER, &c.

Terms Quarterly 5% charged on all OVER-DUE ACCOUNTS.

ESTIMATES GIVEN FOR EVERY DESCRIPTION OF WORK CONNECTED WITH THE BUILDING TRADE.

	£ s d
April 12 To Coffin & Shroud	
Burial Fees	
Hearse & Three Mourning Coaches	
4 under Bearers	
invitations & attending	
out of pocket expenses	
Received with thanks	9 18 6
July 23/1913 Geo Hine	

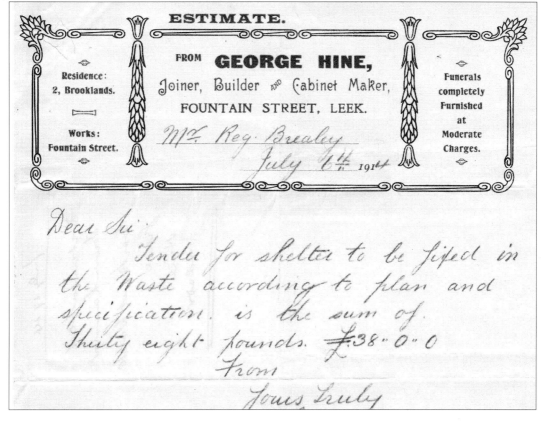

ESTIMATE.

FROM **GEORGE HINE,**

Joiner, Builder and Cabinet Maker,

FOUNTAIN STREET, LEEK.

Residence: 2, Brooklands.

Works: Fountain Street.

Funerals completely Furnished at Moderate Charges.

Mr Reg. Brealey

July 6th 1914

Dear Sir

Tender for shelter to be fixed in the Waste according to plan and specification. is the sum of. Thirty eight pounds. £38 0 0

From

Yours Truly

Dain's Mill, Upperhulme, near Leek.

_____ 189 8

Mr. M. Oliver. Executors. Swainsmoor

Bought of THOMAS HINE,

CORN ✠ DEALER ✠ AND ✠ MILLER.

TERMS—Cash, 5 per cent charged on all Accounts over due.

			£	s	d
Feby	7	To L Hom 10/6 & cwt Gd Cake 9/6	1	0	0
	15	L Hom 11/- & 10 st flour 16/-	1	7	0
		60 lbs Meal		7	0
	26	cwt Gd Cake		9	6
March	5	L Hom		11	0
	12	L Hom 11/- & 2 cwt Gd Cake 19/-	1	10	0
		Bag Bran 4/6 & Bag Combs 3/3		7	9
	24	L Hom 11/- & 60 lbs Meal 7/6		18	6
April	7	L Hom 10/6 & L Hom 4/-	1	0	6
		2 cwts Gd Cake		19	0
	15	L Hom 10/6 & 4 Bags Combs 3/3	1	3	6
	28	L Hom 13/- & 2 cwts Gd Cake 19/-	1	12	0
		Bag Bran 4/9 & 2 Bags Combs 3/3		18	3
May	10	L Hom 13/- & L Hom 12/6	1	5	6
		10 st flour 2/9 & 3 olbs Meal 4/-	1	4	0
	21	2 cwts Gd Cake 19/- & 2 Bags Bran 4/9	1	8	6
	23	L Hom		12	4
June	2	do		12	0
	9	½ L Galaty		6	0
	21	L Hom 10/- & Bag Bran 4/9		14	9
		10 st flour 19/- & 3 olb Meal 4/-	1	3	9
		1 cwt 3 qrs 10 lbs botton cake 9/-		13	0
July	1	2 cwts Gd Cake 19/- & Bag Bran 4/6	1	3	6
		2 cwts 5 lbs botton cake 9/- & Bag Sharps 9/6	1	4	10
	7	L Hom 10/6 & L Hom 10/-	1	0	6
Aug	4	L Hom 10/6 & L Hom 10/-	1	0	6
		10 st flour 15/6 & Bag Bran 4/3		19	9
			£ 25	5	4

W. HINE,

House Furnisher,

13 & 15
St. Edward Street,
LEEK.

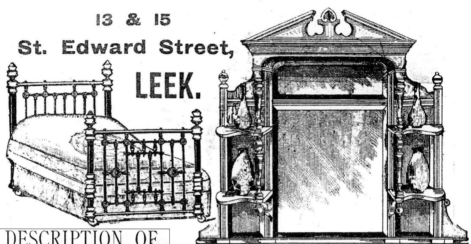

FOR EVERY DESCRIPTION OF
Household Furniture,
GO TO
HINES,

Good & Cheap Feathers, flocks, Tickings, Bedsteads, palliasses,
Oilcloths, Linoleum Hardware &c.

WRINGING & MANGLING MACHINES.

A large and well selected stock of

BOOTS AND SHOES

To suit all classes,

Repairs promptly attended to.

13, & 15, St. Edward St, Leek.

(20 Oct 1909)

WETLEY ROCKS,

STOKE-ON-TRENT.

Aug 2nd 1909

Mrs Unwin Pool House Farm Bucknall widow.

Bought of G. HOCKNELL,

GROCER, CORN AND PROVISION DEALER.

Leek, 16th April 1887

Mr H Y Russell

To SANDEMAN & HODGSON
Photo Artists.

To 6 Imperial Photos of Wm Simsons House	12	-
To Oak Frame & Mount	3	6
To 6 Cabinet Photos of self 1/6	6	-
To 2 Brackets 2/6	5	-
To Oak Frame & Mount for Mr Aylmer	3	6

THE OLD ESTABLISHED
FURNITURE SHOP,
Next Door to the Commissioners' Offices,
8, RUSSELL STREET, LEEK.

PHILIP HODGSON,
CABINET & PICTURE FRAME MANUFACTURER
HAIR, WOOL, COTTON, & STRAW MATTRESSES
MADE TO ORDER.
VENETIAN SHADES
Made to any size or colour.

DEALER IN FURNITURE, IRON BEDSTEADS, GLASS,
China, Earthenware, Cutlery, Hardware, Brushes, &c.

FURNITURE NEATLY REPAIRED.

Mrs Allsup   Leek 14 Nov. 1829

BOUGHT OF WILLIAM HOLLAND,

Grocer, Tea Dealer, Tobacconist & IRONMONGER,

Fine Flavored Fresh Roasted Coffee

Chocolate Cocoa Spices & Foreign Fruits

Teas Genuine as Imported by the East India Company.

1 doz Moist Sugar 7/9	1 do Coffee 1/10	" 9 " 7
1 doz Yell. Soap 6/3	1/2 doz White do 3/9	" 10 " 0
1 doz Dipd Candles 18 & 8		" 6 " 3
1/2 doz Lump Sugar 10/6		" 5 " 3
2 do Mould d do 8/		" 1 " 4
one sett fire Iron 3/6	1 p Bellows 2/3	" 5 " 9
1 Band Brush 1/6	1 Broom & Handle 1/11	" 3 " 5
sett Shoe Brushes 3/-	Scouring Do 1/3	" 4 " 3
Blklead Do 1/3	Saucepan & Cover 1/8	" 2 " 9
Italian Iron 1/-	Dust Pan 1/-	" 1 " 8
Pair Candle Stick 1/4	p Sugar Tongs 1/9	" 3 " 1
2 Iron Spoons 3 1/2	1 Iron Stand 3/-	" 3 " 3 1/2
Iron Fender 4/6	Iron Pott 5/6	" 10 " 0
		3 " 6 " 7 1/2

Settled   Wm Holland

Charles Hollins, Mill Street Garage, was one of the earliest pioneers of motoring in Leek. He also offered driving tuition and a car hire service.

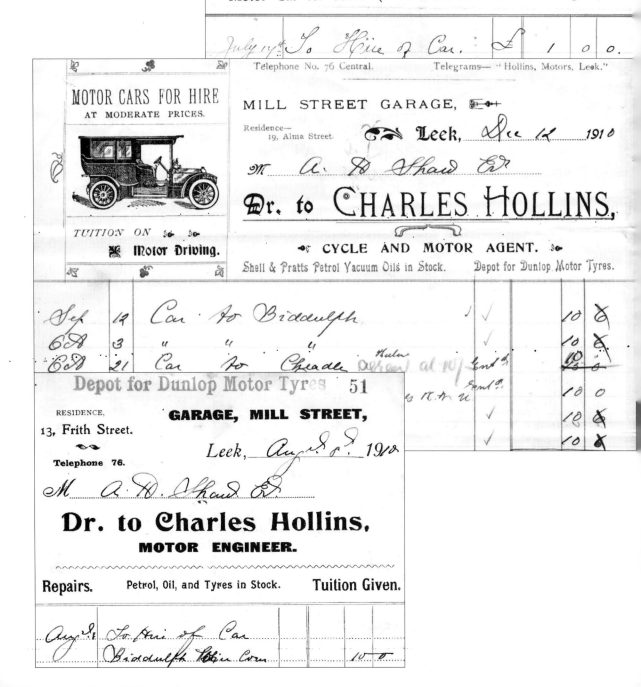

13, Frith Street.

LEEK, Aug 4th 1909.

M A. H. Shaw, Esq.

Dr. to Charles Hollins,
CYCLE & MOTOR AGENT.

Motor Car for Hire. ⚬ Tuition on Motor Driving.

July 14th To Hire of Car. £ 1 0 0.

MOTOR CARS FOR HIRE
AT MODERATE PRICES.

TUITION ON
Motor Driving.

Telephone No. 76 Central.   Telegrams— "Hollins, Motors, Leek."

MILL STREET GARAGE,
Residence— 19, Alma Street.   Leek, Dec 12 1910

M A. H. Shaw Esq

Dr. to CHARLES HOLLINS,
CYCLE AND MOTOR AGENT.

Shell & Pratts Petrol Vacuum Oils in Stock.   Depot for Dunlop Motor Tyres.

Sep	12	Car to Biddulph		✓	✓	10	8
Oct	3	" " "			✓	10	8
Oct	21	Car to Cheadle					
						18	0
					✓	18	8
					✓	10	8

Depot for Dunlop Motor Tyres **51**

RESIDENCE, 13, Frith Street.

GARAGE, MILL STREET,

Leek, Aug 8 1912

Telephone 76.

M A. H. Shaw Esq

Dr. to Charles Hollins,
MOTOR ENGINEER.

Repairs.   Petrol, Oil, and Tyres in Stock.   **Tuition Given.**

Aug 1 To Hire of Car
Biddulph Robin Corn   10 0

Mount Pleasant Works,

LEEK Dec 21st 1899

Mr A. G. Fisher Leek

To the HOME Confectionery Co.,

ROBERT P. THOMPSON & Co.,
Proprietors.   *Folio*

LEEK,

Staffs., Apr. 1902

F. Stanton Smith.

Dr. to H. HOOD & SON,

Practical Tailors & Breeches Makers.

And at ASHBOURNE, DERBYSHIRE.

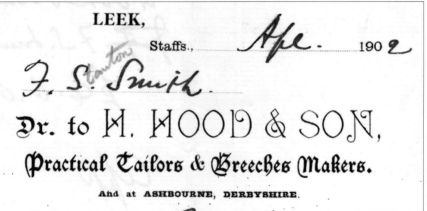

69, DERBY STREET,
LEEK, January 14th 1890

Mr Russell

DR. TO W. H. HORNE,

PHOTOGRAPHER.

PHOTOGRAPHS DONE ON PORCELAIN, IN PLATINOTYPE, IN CARBON, AND IN EVERY PROCESS CONNECTED WITH THE PHOTOGRAPHIC ART.	OUT-DOOR PHOTOGRAPHY. RESIDENCES, LANDSCAPES, GROUPS, &c.	PERMANENT ENLARGEMENTS ON PORCELAIN OR PAPER. THIS BRANCH A SPECIALITY.

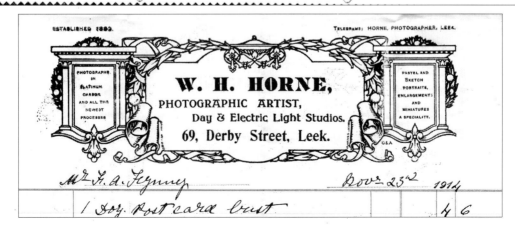

ESTABLISHED 1882.   TELEGRAMS; HORNE, PHOTOGRAPHER, LEEK.

PHOTOGRAPHS IN PLATINUM CARBON AND ALL THE NEWEST PROCESSES

W. H. HORNE,

PHOTOGRAPHIC ARTIST,
Day & Electric Light Studios.
69, Derby Street, Leek.

PASTEL AND SKETCH PORTRAITS, ENLARGEMENTS AND MINIATURES A SPECIALITY.

Mr F. A. Fynney   Nov 23rd 1914

1 doz. post card bust   4 6

W.H. HORNE, 69 Derby Street, Leek

William Henry Horne started work as a newsboy, but later became a picture framer. This led to his interest in the growing art of photography. He founded his business in 1880 and it continued until about 1955, several years after his death.

W.H. Horne was a very prolific photographer. His photographs of local scenes were used on a wide selection of picture postcards, and he illustrated books, magazines and guide books.

He was also in great demand for family photographs, groups and portraits and his shop in Derby Street also sold art materials.

W.H. Horne described himself as a "photographic artist", and these headings indicate the variety of his services - photographs reproduced on porcelain, pastel portraits and miniatures. His studio was clearly well equipped, enabling him to provide a comprehensive photographic service to his many customers, private and commercial.

Market Place, Leek, Xmas _____ 1861

M & John Pimlott

BOUGHT OF J. & W. HOWARD,
IRONMONGERS, AGRICULTURAL IMPLEMENT DEALERS,
COPPERSMITHS, BRAZIERS, ZINC AND TIN PLATE WORKERS.

1861 229

		£	s	d
Octr 23	Spittoon 8 Stove 2 " " Piping for dr 14/8	2 "	15	4
	Making 2 Elbows 1/	"	1	
	Stove Shovel	"	"	4
Nor 14	Watering Pot	"	1	"
26	Flower Scofel	"	1	"
Dec 13	New Grid	"	"	6
18	3 Scofes at 4 & 2 at 6	"	2	4
	Goods 3 . 1 . 2			
	2 . 6 . 1	**3** "	**1**	**2**
	15 . 1			

JOSEPH HOWARD was one of several local ironmongers who also stocked sporting guns and ammunition. First appearing in the 1860 Directory.

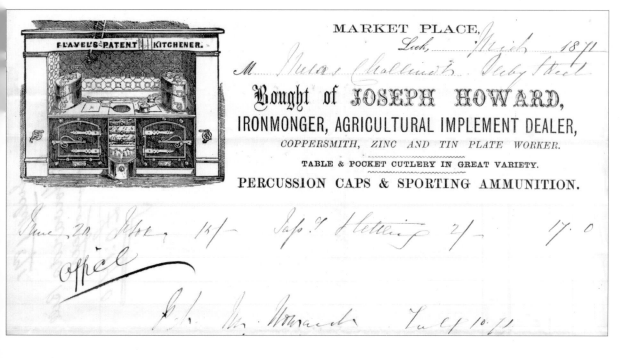

MARKET PLACE,

Leek, March 1871

M Thomas Challinor, Derby Street

Bought of JOSEPH HOWARD,
IRONMONGER, AGRICULTURAL IMPLEMENT DEALER,
COPPERSMITH, ZINC AND TIN PLATE WORKER.
TABLE & POCKET CUTLERY IN GREAT VARIETY.
PERCUSSION CAPS & SPORTING AMMUNITION.

FLAVEL'S PATENT KITCHENER.

June 20 Stove, 15/- Taps & Fitting 2/- 17 . 0

Recd

J. W. Howard July 10/71

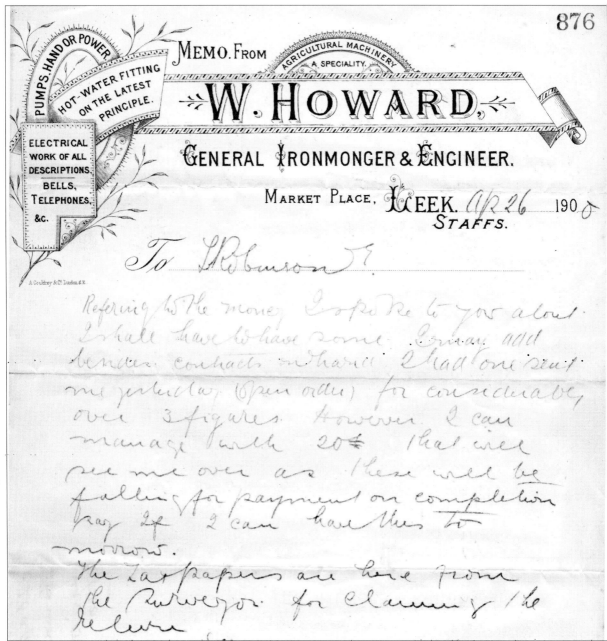

W. HOWARD,

Furnishing Ironmonger,

IMPLEMENT DEALER,

METAL WORKER, &c.,

24, MARKET PLACE, LEEK.

MAKER OF

RAILWAY MILK CANS,

CHEESE KETTLES,

And other Dairy Appliances.

Awarded Silver Medal      *Agricultural Show*

at Staffordshire   *for Dairy Utensils.*

Hot Water and Electrical Work of every description.

A Large Stock of Mowing Machines, Horse Rakes, Hay Rakes, Mowing Machine Fittings, Scythes, Pikels, &c.

SPORTING AMMUNITION OF EVERY KIND.

GALVANIZED ROOFING SHEETS, FENCING WIRE, BEDSTEADS, &c.

W. H. has supplied Agricultural Implements and Dairy Appliances of all kinds to a large number of the leading farmers in the surrounding district, which have given every satisfaction.

W. H. has sold and repaired twice as many Mowing Machines as all the other Iron-mongers put together ; this is a convincing proof who is the practical man.

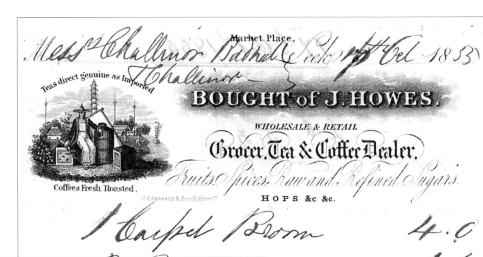

Mess Challinor Bathal Leek 17th Oct 1853
J Challinor

Market Place.

BOUGHT of J. HOWES,

WHOLESALE & RETAIL

Grocer, Tea & Coffee Dealer,

Fruits, Spices, Raw and Refined Sugars,

HOPS &c &c.

Teas direct genuine as Imported

Coffees Fresh Roasted.

1 Carpet Broom   4.0
                                        1.3
                                    £ " 5.3

Sud 6d of 9/53

J Howes

FAMILY GROCERY LIST.

ALL GOODS OF THE BEST QUALITY.

S. HOWES,

Family Grocer & Provision Dealer,

2, MARKET PLACE, LEEK.

TEAS.	SUGARS.	
Black, Green, or Mixed.	Lump	Preserves (all kinds)
Sound Congou 2s. 0d.	Raw	Miller's Baking Powder
Good useful 2s. 6d.	Refined	Symington's Pea Flour
Fine „ 3s. 0d.		Hemmingway's Dry Soap
Finest „ 3s. 8d.	**SOAPS.**	Carbonate of Soda
	Pale	Split Peas
COFFEE.	Brown	Green Peas
	Soft	Saltpetre
Fine Plantation	Toilet	Soda
„ Jamaica		Vinegar
	SUNDRIES.	Linseed
COCOAS.	Rice	Blacking
	Pearl Barley	Black Lead
Taylor's Soluble	Sago, small	Blues
„ Homœopathic	„ large	Cigars
„ Maravilla	Tapioca	Tobacco
Epp's Pearl	Arrowroot	
	Corn Flour	
SPICES.	Ground Rice	
	Starch, Colman's	
Mace	„ Glenfield	
Cinnamon	„ Reckett's	
Cloves	Candles, dips	
Nutmegs	„ composite	
Pepper White	Maccaroni	
„ Black	Vermicelli	
„ Clove	Lobsters	
Ginger	Salmon	
Ground Ginger	Sardines	
	Pickles	
FRUITS.	Sauces	
	Capers	
Currants	Salad Oil	
Raisins, Valencia	Mustard, Colman's	
„ Muscatel	„ Keen's	
„ Sultana	Peel, Lemon	
Figs	„ Orange	2lb. Tins
Almonds	„ Citron	4lb. Tins
		Corned Beef.

Agent for the Finest Wiltshire Smoked Bacon, & Huntley & Palmer's
Celebrated Biscuits. Parcels forwarded to any part of the Town.

BY ROYAL WARRANT

TO HIS MAJESTY THE KING.

BOVRIL

Mrs Gould   May 1st 1901

M rs Gould

BOUGHT OF

Samuel Howes,

Family Grocer and Provision Dealer,

2 MARKET PLACE

LEEK.

A splendid first-hand impression of Samuel
Howes appears in 'The Small Boy in the
Market Place' in 'Leek News'.

14 BATH STREET, LEEK,

January — 18*83*

Mrs Bradshaw, Compton Terrace

DR. TO JOSEPH HUDSON,

Joiners and Builders.
— etc —

£ s d

1883			£	s	d
June 29th	To 1 pair of back flaps & screws, time to lock doors & windows		·	1	6
			·	3	-
Decr 19th	1 strong brass sash fasten, &screws			1	6
	repairing front &back door lock – new Spring &screws		·	1	4
	2 brass screw hooks, &brass nails & screws to door handles,		·	·	9
	time to sundries W. H Hudson 5½ hours		-	3	-
	Settled with thanks	£	·	11	1

January 30th 1883

W H Hudson
Pro Joseph Hudson.

The Leek Public Baths are seen on the right just before Bath Street. they were built in 1854 and demolished c. 1980. Joseph Hudson and his workshop and house were a short distance down on the right, in Bath Street.

PARSON AND BRADSHAW 1818

NEW DIRECTORY

OF THE

County of Stafford.

A LIST

OF

Professions, Trades, &c.

IN LEEK

Attornies.
Copeland Charles, Spout street
Cruso John, sen. Market place
Cruso John, jun. Spout street
Jones Henry, Market place
Kilminster and Challinor, Derby street
Porter Sinclair, Derby street
Prime Joseph, Market place

Auctioneers.
Barnes Jonathan, Stockwell st.
Davenport William, Derby st.
Wright Thomas, Derby street

Bakers and Flour Dealers.
Bloor Thomas, Derby street
Bull Richard, Sheep market
Davenport Joseph, Church st.
Gatcliff Simon, Derby street
Hunt Robert, Mill street
Joinson Charles, Bread street
Leason John, Custard street
Maskery Samuel, Spout street
Phillips John, Derby street
Tatton William, Mill street

Blacksmiths and Farriers.
Bold George, Mill street
Dale Daniel, Mount pleasant
Hargreaves Samuel, Leek moor
Hughes Thomas, Mill street
Lambert William, Derby st.
Watts Daniel, Sheep market

Booksellers and Stationers.
Hope William, (and binder) Custard street
Lowe Charles, Sheep market
Smith John, Market-place

Boot and Shoemakers.
Allen John, Back of Church
Bott Ralph, Mill street
Bowcock Samuel, Gaunt's yard
Davenport Joseph, Spout st.
Davenport Joseph, jun. Stockwell street
Fallows Richd. Scolding bank
Hall John, Clark's bank

Lownds James, Spout street
Mason Thomas, Sheep market
Walwyn James, Derby street
Walwyn John, Sheep market
Williams and Co. Spout street

Braziers & Tin plate Workers.
Goodwin Joseph, Spout street
Travis Samuel, Market street

Brewer.
Smith Edward, Cheddleton

Butchers.
Challinor James, nr. Derby st.
Critchley James, Custard st.
Critchley Wm. Sheep market
Mycock Thomas, Mill street
Stubbs Richard, near Spout st.
Smith Thos. Back of Church

Joiners and Cabinet Makers
Clewlow Wm. Stockwell st.
Davenport Uriah, near Derby street
Davenport William, Derby st.
Emerson Robert, Sheep mkt.
Furnihough Jas. Church street
Hide Ralph, Stockwell street
Joinson Thomas, Stockwell street
Wright Thomas, Derby street

Carver and Gilder.
Shufflebotham Jesse, Custard street

Cheesemongers.
Birch John, Spout street
Brown Joseph, Derby street
Crompton Peter, Mill street
Gatcliff Simon, Derby street
Johnson William, Spout st.
Leason John, Custard street
Lees Anne, Clark's bank

Chemists and Druggists.
Challinor Benjamin, Market place
Challinor Jesse, Custard street
Smith John, Druggist

Coal Merchants.
Gould Sampson, Wharf
Hammersley Nathan, Wharf
Johnson William, Wharf
Tatton John, Wharf

Confectioners.
Allcock Samuel, Sheep market
Birch Elizabeth, Derby street

Coopers.
Clowes Thomas, Custard st.
Titterton Thomas, Market pl.

Corn Millers.
Bassett and Sons, Winkhill
Crompton Peter, Mill street
Smith Edward, Cheddleton

Curriers and Leather Sellers.
Large William, Spout street
Young Samuel, Spout street

Dyers.
Badnall Richard, High field
Badnall Joseph, Mill street

Fire Offices.
Eagle, Agent, Charles Lowe, Spout street
Phoenix, Agent, Edward Hordern, Sheep Market
Shrewsbury, Agents, Kilminster & Challinor, Derby st.

Gardeners and Seedsmen.
Oakden Ralph, Derby street.
Wallbanks Job, Market pl.

Glass and China Dealers.
Redfern George, Custard st.
Shufflebotham Wm. Spout st.

Grocers and Tea Dealers.
Ash William, Stockwell st.
Bourne Sarah, Spout street
Bullock Thomas, Sheep market
Hulme William, Sheep market
Hunt Robert, Mill street
Lees Anne, Clark's bank
Pegg William, Compton
Smith John, Market place
Wain William, Market place
Wooliscroft George, Market place

Hatters.
Fox James, Sheep market
Howard William, Derby st.
Howard Samuel, Derby street

Inns and Taverns.
Angel Inn, Daniel Nixon, Market place
Bird in Hand, John Mould, Market place
Blackamoor's Head, Thomas Hine, Bottom of Market p.
Black Swan, William Thompson, Sheep market
Blue Ball, Samuel Hunt, Mill street
Butcher's Arms, Joseph Bullock, Derby street
Bowling Green, Edward Tatton, Abbey Green
Bull's Head, Thomas Machin Spout street
Coach and Horses, William Crichley, Sheep street
Cock, Robert Nixon, Derby street
Cock, Henry Beard, Market place
Cross Keys, George Crichlow, Custard lane
Crown Inn, John Walmsley, Church street
Duke of York, Jonathan Jackson, Derby street
George Inn, James Rideout, Spout street
Golden Lion, John Lownds, Church street
King's Head, Timothy Beresford, Market place
Nag's Head, Mathew Lees, Mill street
New Bridge, George Fielding, Bridge end
Plough, Mark Emerson, Spout street
Queen's Head, Anne Barlow. Custard street
Quiet Woman, Uriah Davenport, Spout street
Red Lion, William Stubbs, Market place
Roe Buck Inn, John Lownds Derby street
Swan Inn, John Redfern, Spout street
Talbot Inn, John Taylor, Derby street
Wheat Sheaf, Joseph Pickford, Custard street
Wilkes's Head, Thomas Sutton, Spout street

Iron Founders.
Bassett and Sons, Winkhill

Lace Manufacturer.
Rose William, near Derby st

Linen and Woollen Drapers.
Birch William, Market place
Carrington Thomas, Custard st
Harrison William, Market pl
Moxon J. Sheep market
Stoddard William, Spout st.

Liquor Merchant.
Lownds John, Church street

Milliners and Dress Makers
Andrew Elenor, Spout street
Bamfield Mary, Derby street
Black and Walker, Spout st.
Clewlow Eliza, Derby street
Johnson Betsey, Spout street
Marshall Anne, Spout street
Mountford Margaret, Church st
Shelley Lucy and Catharine, Clark's bank

Paper Makers.
Bassett and Sons, Winkhill
Hope Peter, Winkhill

Plumbers and Glaziers.
Clee William, Custard street
Goodwin Joseph, Spout street
Hulme George, Spout street
Redfern George, Custard st.

Printer (Letter-press)
Hilliard Francis, Scolding bank

Rope and Twine Manufacturers.
Barratt Thomas, Stockwell st.
Frost John, Derby street
Goldstraw Joseph, Derby street
Mountford Ralph, Derby st.

Saddlers.
Griffin John, Derby street
Johnson Joseph, Market pl.
White Benjamin, Church st.

Schools.
Bell Miss, Spout street
Bentley Revd. Richd. Clark's bank
Hobson Robert, Clark's bank
Taylor James, Derby street

Silk Manufacturers.
Alsop John, Derby street
Baddeley and Brough, Stockwell street
Badnell Richd. & Co. Spout st.
Carr and Thompson, Derby st
Carr William, Spout street
Cutting Richard, near the Methodist Chapel
Fynley and Ward, Derby st.
Goodwin and Abbott, Derby street
Gaunt Josiah, and Co. Spout street
Gaunt and Lucas, Derby st.
Phillips S. W. and Co, Barn gates.
Sleigh John, Spout street
Sutton and Co. Custard street
Sterling Edward, Clark's bank
Tomlinson and Turner, Derby street

Slaters and Plasterers.
Acton William, Leek moor
Stonehewer Samuel, Church street
Stonehewer Wm. (and stone cutter), Mill street

Stamp Office.
Hordern Edwd, Sheep market

Stone Masons.
Barlow Benjamin, Leek moor
Eyres Thomas, (and builder), Leek moor
Holroy Joseph, (and builder,) Mill street
Saunders Samuel, Clark's bank

Surgeons.
Chadwick Chas. Clark's bank
Flint Charles, Stockwell street
Fynney A. A. Spout street
Fynney S. B. Custard street
Fynney G. A. Spout street
Lamb William, Market place
Lees John, (veterinary) Market place

Tailors.
Armitt Hiram, Mill street
Barker John, Market street
Barker Charles, Stockwell st.
Braddock S. Scolding bank
Clewlow John, Spout street
Clewlow William, Spout st.
Cumming John, Market street
Fowell Thomas, Spout street
Plant James, Mill street
Scotton Henry, spout street
Stoddard Wm. (and draper,) Spout street

Tallow Chandlers.
Allen John, Custard, street
Pegg William, Sheep market

Timber Merchants.
Ash William, Stockwell st.
Emerson Robert, Sheep mkt.
Wright Thomas, Abbey st.

Turners in Wood and Chair Makers.
Barnes Jonathan, Stockwell st
Bassett William, (turner, &c.) Spout street
Booth William, Spout street

Watch and Clock Makers.
Ashton John, Sheep market
Travis William, Market pl.
Winterbotham Kenyon, Derby street

Wheelwrights.
Poynton Thos. Spooner's In.
Salt Samuel, Leek moor

Woolstapler.
Warrington John, Spout st.

COACHES
The MAIL, to London, by way of Derby, Leicester, an
Dunstable, every morning at half past six o'clock.

*From the **RED LION INN**, Market place.*
The DEFIANCE, through Derby, every evening, at twent
minutes past eight o'clock to London. To Manchester, ever
afternoon, at half past two o'clock.

*From the **ROE-BUCK INN**, Market Place.*
The TELEGRAPH, through Derby and Leicester, ever
evening, at twenty minutes past eight o'clock to London. T
Manchester, every afternoon at half past two o'clock.
The EXPRESS, to Birmingham daily, at half past twelve a
noon. To Manchester, at half past four in the afternoon.

CARRIERS.
T. and M. PICKFORD, by Boats and Waggon, daily to Londo
Manchester, Ashburne, Derby, Leicester, and all parts of th
kingdom.
JOSEPH BENNETT, daily to Manchester, Macclesfield, an
Congleton.

WHITE'S DIRECTORY 1834

POST OFFICE, Custard street; Miss Catherine Williams, Postmistress. Letter bags are despatched to London and the South at 20 min. bef. 1 noon; and to Manchester, and the North and West at 1/4 before 11 mg. daily. A Horse Post to Longnor, Warslow, Flash, Hartington, &c. every Monday, Wednesday, and Friday, at half-past one afternoon, from the Red Lion Inn.

The CONTRACTIONS *used for the names of streets, &c. are - Ard. for Ashbourn road; Ast. Albion street; Bln. Ballhaye lane; Bst. Ballhaye st.; Bgn. Ballhaye green; Brd. Buxton road; Cbk. Clerk's bank; Cht. Church st.; Chn. Church lane; Cst. Custard st.; Cpt. Compton; Dst. Derby street; Fst. Fountain st.; Kst. King st; Lmr. Leek moor; Lst. London st.; Obk. Overton bank, sometimes called Schooling bank; Mkp. Market place; Mst. Mill st.; Nst. New st.; Qst. Queen st.; Rst. Regent street; Skt. Sheep market; Spt. Spout street; Sst. Stockwell street; Spn. Spooner's lane; Ust. Union st.; and Wst. West st. The abbreviation mfr. signifies silk manufacturer.*

MISCELLANY - *Including the Addresses of Gentry, Clergy, Partners in Firms, and others, not arranged in the Classification of Trades and Professions.*

Abbott Geo. cowkpt. Ashbourn road
Abbott Jph. mfr. Kst.
Alcock Wm. constab. Church lane
Ashton Mrs. Chn.
Atkinson Miss Mary, Spout street
Ball Chas. bookkpr. West street
Ball Chas. bookkpr. Bridge end
Birch Mr. Saml. Sst.
Booth Mrs. Ann, Sst.
Bourne Rev. Wm. P. (Ind.) Compton
Brandreth Rev. Jno. Mount pleasant
Brassington Chrsphr. bookkeeper, Brd.
Brealey Thos. attorney's clerk, Dst.
Brentnall Mrs. Sar. Church lane
Brooks John, wood handle dlr. Mill st.
Brooks Samuel, rake maker, Mill st.
Brough Mrs. Ann, Spout street
Brunt Isc. mfr. Lmr.
Brunt Josiah, mfr. Queen street
Brunt Wm. mfr. King st.
Bullock Thos. gent. Clerk's bank
Challinor Wm. solr. sheriff's replevinor, clk. to comssrs of taxes;
Chorley Toft, Esq. Spout st. & Haregt.
Clowes Mrs. Jenny, West street
Clowes John, bookpr. Ballhaye street
Crompton Miss Eliz. Stockwell street
Cruso John, sen. Esq. land agent, Mkp.
Cruso Mr. Fras. Mkp.
Cruso Mich. Daintry, solr.; h. Spout st.
Cutting Mr. Rd. Kst.
Daniels Thos. overlooker, Union st.
Davenport John, Esq. M. P. Westwood hl.
Davenport Urh, Mst.
Dix Jas. agent, Bst. Edge Thos. cowkpr. Ballhaye lane
Ellis Lilley, mfr. Kst.
Fearnside Rev. Josh. (Meth.) Mount pl.
Fowler Mrs. Sar. Mkp.
Gaunt John, Esq. banker, Sst.

Gaunt Josiah, mfr.; h. Ballhaye street
Gaunt Josiah, jun mfr. h. Market pl.
Gaunt Rd. Esq. Dst.
Glendining Rt. Witting, mfr. Union st.
Goodwin Misses Ann & Mary, Daisy bk.
Griffin Mr. John, Brd.
Griffin Thomas, high constable for Totmonslow, Cbk.
Grosvenor Mary, Sst.
Hall Jph. gov. Works.
Hammersley George, warehouseman, Ast.
Harrison Miss Mary, Spout street
Heathcote, Rev. Thos. Henry, Vicarage
Hine Jph. bookr. Queen st.
Hilliard Fras. parish clerk, Overton bank
Horn Joseph, swine dealer, Buxton rd.
Ibbert John, overlooker. Ashbourn road
Jackson Geo. cowkeeper, King st.
Johnson Mr. Jph. Derby st.
Johnson Jas. warehouseman, Queen st.
Keates Geo. magistrates' clerk, Spout st.
Killmister Geo. Ridgway, solicitor; h Regent street
Keen M. Jas. Bgn.
Knight Mrs. Martha, Spout street
Lea Thos. glover, Spt.
Leason Mrs. Ann, Bst.
Leech John, land agt. and road surveyor, Wall bridge
Lees Mattw. bailiff & furniture broker, Sheep market
Lucas Allan Key, mfr. Spout street
Marshall John, Spt st.
Mien John, Queen st.
Mears Jas. letter carrier, New street
Morley Richd. hatter, Custard street
Moss Jph. whsman. King street
Moss Ralph, mfr. Union st.
Moulton Rev. James Egan, (Meth.) Bst.
Nixon Allan, cabinet maker, Mill street
Nixon Mattw. warehouseman, Lmr.
Nixon Wm. gas wks.
Phillips Saml. & Wm. Esqrs. The Field
Poingister John, professor of music and French, King st.
Pointon Elijah, paver, Leek moor

Pratt Mrs. Ann, Cbk.
Prince Peter, Bgn.
Rathbone Etchells, overlooker, Nst.
Rawlins Wm. architect and assistant overseer, Lst.
Roe Mrs. Margt. Spt.
Rogers Miss Elz. Spt.
Russell John, mfr. Spout street
Scholfield Richard, overlooker, Ard.
Sharratt Miss Mary, Derby street
Sharratt Jerh. cowkeeper, Mill street
Sharratt Mr. Wm. Cpt.
Shenton Sml. grindr. Ashburn road
Slack Mr. Benj. Qst.
Sleigh Mr. Richard, Spout street
Sleigh Mr. John, Spt.
Squire John, manager, London street
Stirling Mr. Rbt. Sst.
Stonehewer Samuel, sexton, Clerk's bk.
Stubbs Edw. Ball haye gn.
Sutton Miss Mary, Spout street
Tatton Edw. Kiln ln.
Tomlinson Mr. Rd. Fountain street
Turner John, gent. Sheep market
Turnock Edw. warehouseman, Fst.
Wain John, traveller, Leek moor
Walker Chas. warehouseman, King st.
Wamsley Jas. warehouseman, Kst.
Wamsley Philip, mfr. Church lane
Wardle Jas. mfr. King st.
Welsh John, warehouseman, Albion st.
Whitaker Rev. Saml. (Cath.) Fountain st.
Willock Mrs. Cath. Fountain street
Winton Thos. excise officer, Bst.
Woolliscroft Joseph, coach maker, Mst.
Young George, gent. Clerk's bank

*Academies. Marked * take brdrs.*
* Babington Ann and Martha, Queen st.
Brumby Corns. Lst.
·* Etches Mary, Bst.
Free Grammar, Rev. Jeremiah Barnes, B. A. Clerks bank
Smith Eliz. Spout st.
Morrow Rev. Jas. Derby st.
Shufflebotham W. M. Mill street
Wamsley Uriah, Kst.

Attorneys.
Condlyffe Wm. Dst.
Doupland Chas. Sst.
Cruso John, jun. Spt.
Gaunt Mattw. Sst.
Heathcote John, Dst.
Hilliard Ths. Harvey, Stockwell street
Killmister & Challinor, Derby Street
Killmister Abm. Kershaw, Regent st.
Redfern Thos. Cha.

Auctioneers, &c.
Barnes Jonth. Sst.
Fergyson Rt. Kst.
Hilliard Wm. Ml. (& genl. agent & printer) Church st.
White George, Sheep mkt.; h. Alstonfd.

Bakers, Flour dlrs. &c.
Alcock Wm. Spn.
Brunt Micha, Sst.
Bull Rd. Spout street
Clowes Thomas, Mst.
Caley Geo. Cbk.
Davenport Jph. Cht.
Davenport Uriah, Clerk's bank
Gettliffe Peter, Dst.
Holroyde Olive, Mst.
Hunt Saml. Mst.
Maskery Saml. Spt.
Smith Joseph, Cst.
Smith John, Brd.
Smith Saml. Dirty ln.

BANKS.
Fowler, Gaunt, & Co. Stockwell st. (draw on Rogers,
        Towgood, & Co.)
Manchester & Liverpool Dist. Branch, Spout st. (open ev.
        Wed.; John Stupart, manager)

Basket maker.
Smith Reuben, Skt.

*Blacksmiths. * are Whitesmiths.*
Beardmore Sl. Skt.
Bold George, Mst.
Bradley John, Brd.
Hargreaves Geo. Lmr.
Hargreaves Jph. Spt.
*Heath Jas. Spt.
Lambert Wm. Dst.
*Plant Jthn. Mst.

Bookseller & Stationer.
Nall Geo. (stamp off. & subs. & cir. library) Sheepmkt.

Boot & Shoe makers.
Barlow Lewis, Cst.
Birtles John, Spt.
Bott Ralph, Mst.
Challinor Wm. Lmr.
Davenport Jph. Spt.
Davenport Jane, Cst.
Done Joseph, Bgn.
Forrister Saml. Mst.
Hudson Thos. Spt.
Knight Wm. Sst.
Lovatt John, Sst.
Rigby Jph. Mkp.
Rutland John, (smallware, &c. dlr.) Skt.

Sharp Thomas, Mst.
Shelley Eliz. Kst.
Tipper Thomas, Cst.
Walwyn Ellen, Skt.
Walwyn Jph. Ard.
Wood John, Brd.

Braziers & Tinmen.
Fisher John, Skt.
Howard Jph. Mkp.
Travis Thomas, Spt.

Bricklayers.
Barlow Jas. Lmr.
Eyres Thomas, Lmr.
Fogg Varnam, Bkd.
Holroyd Jph. Mst.
Mellor James, Fst.
Rowley James, Obk.
Stretch Saml. Lmr.

Butchers
Bullock Ralph, Spn.
Critchlow John, Cst.
Critchlow Jas. Cst.
Critchlow Wm. (flour & cheese dlr.) Cht.
Godwin Jph. Dst.
Keates John, Sst.
Thorpe Geo. Mst.
West Francis, Mkp.

Button Mould Trnrs.
Sharratt Wm. Dst.
Sharratt Charles, Fst.

Cabinet Makers.
Joinson Thomas, Sst.
Turnock Danl. Dst.

Chair mkrs. & Turners.
Booth Wm. Spout st.
Harrison Saml. Mst.
Wain Rd. Derby st.

Coal dealers.
Burrows Thos. Spt.
Gould Sampson, Whf.
Woodhead Colliery Co.; John Clark, agent, Spn.
Johnson Wm. Spt.
Twigg Jno. Derby st.

Clog & Patten maker.
Goodwin Ralph, Mst.

Confectioners.
Nixon & Birch, Nst.
Smith John
Smith Joseph, Cst.

Coopers.
Deakin Saml. Dst.
Slater Thomas, Cst.

Corn Miller.
Getliffe Simon, Mst.

Curriers, & c.
Large Wm. Spout st.
Young Saml. & Wm. (& tanners) Spt.

Druggists.
Dale John, Mkp.
Johnson Thos. Dst.
Sutton George, Mkp.
Wardle Hugh, Cst.

Dyers.
Clowes John, (late) Mill street
Hammersley Wm. Bridge end

Eating Houses.
Birch Frances, Dst.
Gould Sarah, Spt.

Farmers.
Bagshaw Isc., Lowe
Birch Thomas, Lowe
Brough John, Brd.
Brassington Wm., Lowe
Dale Joseph; Lowe
Dale Richard Lowe
Hocknell Thos., Big Birchall
Johnson Rph., Lowe
Marsden Anty., Lowe
Millward John, Bgn.
Oulsnam Benjamin, Bridge end
Rowley Wm. Sheep hs.
Smith Thos. Nibden
West Hy. Wall grange

Fire & Life Office Agents.
Atlas, John Heathcote, Derby st.
Manchester Guardian T. Johnson, Dst.
County, T. H. Hilliard, Stockwell st.
Nowich Union, Wm. Challinor, Dst.
Royal Exchange, Geo. Keates, Spout st.
Sun Life & Salop Fire, G. R. Killmister, Derby street

Gardeners, &c.
Leadbetter Jno. Thos. Wm. & Edward, Little Birchall
Nunns Wm. (nursery & seedsman) Mkp.
Twigg John, Spt.
Wallbank Job, Spt.

Glass Dealers.
Clee Wm. Cst.
Redfearn Frances, Spt.
Woollen Charles Spt.

Grocers & Tea dlrs.
Bull Geo. Derby st.
Bull Rd. Spout st.
Colgrave Geo. Hy. Dst.
Fisher John, Skt.
Hammersley Wm. Market place
Hine Wm. Mkp.
Hope & Bolshaw, Mkp.
Mountford Ralph, Cst.
Wittles Saml. Bower, Market place
Williams Ann & Wm. (& coffee roasters) Spout street
Woolliscroft Geo. Skt.

Gun Maker.
Jones Thos. Cst.

Hair Dressers.
Ball Saml. (register office) Cst.
Hassell Saml. Dst.
Mace Adam, Skt.
Mycock Josiah, Mst.
Pilkington Wm. Spt.

Hat manfrs.
Morley Ths. Spout st.
Wigley Hy. Spout st.

INNS & TAVERNS
Angel, Martha Sutton, Market place
Ball Haye Tav. Wm. Davenport, Bgn.
Bird-in-hand, Benj. White, Mkp.
Black's Head, Joseph Chell, Custard st.
Black Swan, Wm. Allen, Sheep market
Blue Ball, Jonathan Plant, Mst.
Bull's Head, Thomas Hine, Spout st.
Butchers' Arms, Jno. Chappell, Dst.
Cheshire Cheese, Ths. West, (malt & hop dealer) Skt.
Cock, Wm. Glover, Market place
Cock, Saml. Lassetter, Derby st.
Cross Key, George Critchlow, Cst.
Crown, Isaac Hammond, Cht.
Dog & Partridge, Jp. Perkin, Dst.
Dun Cow, Wm. Pipes, Ashbourn road
Duke of York, Jonathan Jackson, Dst.
Fountain, Sar. Kirkham, Fountain st.
George Inn, (empty)
Globe, Vernon Hulme, Spout street
Golden Lion, Thos. Hulme, Church st.
Gate, Thomas Hidderley Brd.
Green Man, Joseph Jackson, Compton
King's Arms, Eli Plant, Mill st.
King's Head, John Walker, Mkp.
Nag's Head, Wm. Rider, Mill st.
Plough, Geo. Gould, Spout street
Queen's Head, Geo Walker, (agent for Cheddleton brewery)
                                        Custard st
Quiet Woman, John Maskery, Spt.

Red Lion Inn, & excise office, John Barlow, Mkp.
Roe Buck Inn, & posting house, John Lowndes, Derby st
Royal Oak, Eliz Dale, Buxton road
Swan Inn, Thos. Tatler, Spout st.
Talbot, Rd. Ratcliffe, Leek moor
Unicorn, Wm. Mellor, Spout street
Union Inn, Adam Hawksworth, Sst.
Wheat Sheaf, Thos. Burrows, Cst.
White Lion, John Hawkins, Bdg. end
Wilke's Head, Joseph Pickford, Spout st.
Wm. IV., Jno. Hulme, Church street

BEER HOUSES.
Barley Mow, Joseph Martin, Spt.
Blacksmiths' Arms, Chrpr. Walmsley, Mill street
Britannia, Jn. Clowes, Spout street
Crispin's Arms, Jph. Davenport Spt.
Dyer's Arms, George Thorp, Mst.
Earl Grey, Wm. Jackson, Ashbourn rd.
Green Dragon, Job Wallbank, Spt.
Hargreaves Jph. Spt.
Hare & Hounds, Isaac Johnson, Lst.
Heapy John, Kiln ln.
Navigation Inn, Chas. Sheldon, Spn.
Nag's Head, Edward Murfin, Sst.
Pig & Whistle, Benj. Wilson, Brd.
Rising Sun, Hannah Goodwin, Kst.
Twisters' Arms, Geo. Prince, Bgn.
True Blue, Richard Smith, Mst.
Vine, John Phillips, King street
White Hart, John Gillman, Sst.
Weavers' Arms, Thos. Johnson, Lmr.

Ironmongers.
Fisher John, (bar iron mercht nail mfr & whitesmith) Skt
Woolfe Benjamin, (& nail maker) Mkp.

Joiners. See also Cabinet mkrs.
Davenport Jas. Mst.
Eyre John, Regent st.
Fernyhough Jas. Chn.
Hide Joseph, Sst.
Hide Ralph, Bln.
Hunt Saml. Regent st.
Nixon Wm. & James, Stockwell street
Weston Wm. Ard.

Linen & Wllns. Drprs.
Birch Thomas, Mkp.
Etches George, Skt.
Mellor Wm. & Thos. Custard street
Rogers George, Mkp.
Smith Charles, Cst.

Milliners, &C.
Ball Emma, Cst.
Brough Sarah, Mkp.
Machin J. & S. Kst.

Mellor M. A. Mst.
Morley & Dale, Bst.
Morley Mary A. Spt.
Robinson Hanh. Bird.
Scotton J. & S. Bst.
Shelley Mary, Kst.
Vickerstaff Ann & Eliz. Derby st.
Walker Ann, Spt.
Walker Mary, Dst.
Wardle Sarah, Spt.

Music Dealer.
Wheatley John, (organ bldr. &C.) Mkp

Nail makers. (See Ironmongers.)
Deaville Wm. Dst.
Henshaw Wm. Mst.

Painters, Plumbers, and Glaziers
Clee Wm. & Edm. Cst.
Gell Sampson, Sst.
Goodwin Joseph, Spt.
Holmes George, Spt.
Johnson Wm. Spt. & Stockwell st.
Osborne Wm. Brd.
Simon Charles, Dst.
Stafford Edward, Sst.

Pawnbroker
Barlow Lewis, (& shoe warehouse) Cst.

Plasterers.
Crompton Wm. Kst.
Staniforth Wm. Chn.
Stonehewer Wm. Wst.

Printers.
Hilliard Wm. M. Cht.
Nall George, Skt.

Rag Merchants.
Deaville Wm. Ds.
Nall George, Skt.

Rope & Twine mkr.
Mountfort Ralph, Cst.

Saddlers.
Allen George, Mkp.
Street John, Dst.
White Benj. Mkp.

Shopkeepers. See also Bakers.
Abbott James, Mkp.
Barlow James, Lmr.
Bermingham Henry, Leek moor
Bott Ralph, Mst.
Bradley Mary, Skt.
Brown Joseph, Dst.
Crompton Wm. Kst.

Davenport Jas. Mst.
Deaville Geo. Brd.
Gettliffe Eliz. Dst.
Gettliffe Simon, Mst.
Gillman John, Sst.
Goldstaw Elizabeth, Derby street
Gratton Wm. Bgn.
Hall Wm. Spout st.
Harrison James, Bgn.
Haynes Henry, Sst.
Henshaw Wm. Mst.
Hulme George, Dst.
Johnson Wm. Spt.
Jones Sarah, Mst.
Murfin George, Sst.
Robinson Wm. Spt.
Rogers Elizabeth, Spt.
Steers Thomas, Mkp.
Tharme Ann, Sst.
Walwyn Hanh. Dst.

SILK MFRS.
Barnes Jonathan, Sst.
Bowcock James, (ribbons) Kiln lane
Brough Joshua, Jas. & Co. Union st.
Brunt Jsh. & Co. Dst.
Carr Thos. & Co. Dst.
Colquhoun Daniel, Clerk's bank
Davenport Nathan, Mill street
Ellis, Russell, and Clowes, West st.
France Brothers, & Co. Leek moor; h. Stockwell street
Gaunt, Wardle, & Wamsley, New st. (& 111 Wood st. London)
Glendinning & Gaunt, Union street
Goodwin Saml. & Co. Black's head yard, (& Manchester)
Goostrey John, Portland street
Heywood Benj. Fanshaw, Spout street
Hudson John, Kst.
Milward Saml. Cht.; h. Park cottage
Morley Sampson, Spt.
Moss & Brunt, Black's head yard
Rushton Richd. Spn.
Thompson Geo. Leek moor; h. Dst.
Tomkinson Edward, Queen's square
Ward Anthony & Co. Albion Mill; h. Derby street
Wreford John, Lst.

Stone Masons.
Alcock Wm. Spn.
Heath Robert, Kst.
Ratliffe Richard, Leek moor
Sanders Thomas, Derby street

SILK TWISTERS, *(by commission.)*
Astles Jonah, Lst.
Broster Samuel, Mst.
Gibson Silas, Lst.
Haywood Jph. Obk.

Balkin Benj. Spt.
Ridgway James, Kst.
Swindells Samuel, (throwster,) Sst.
Worthington Wm. Overton bank

Straw Hat makers. See also Milliners.
Ball Susan, Kst.
Critchlow Ann, Cst.
Webberley Sarah, Sst.

Surgeons.
Chadwick Chas. Obk.
Cooper Richard, Dst.
Flint Chas. Compton
Robins James, Sst.

Tailors.
Armitt Hiram, Mst.
Ball Samuel, Brd.
Bradley Joseph, Spt.
Eaton Wm. spt.
Fowel Thomas, Spt.
Hall Rupert, Spt.
Hudson James, Lmr.
Magson John, Ust.
Plant Wm. Cst.
Plant James, Mill st.
Scotton Henry, Spt.
Sheldon Thomas, Derby street
Smith Jas. Mill st.
Wooding Wm. Cpt.
Wood Wm. Derby st.

Tallow Chandlers.
Hammersley Wm. Market place
Tharme Ann, Sst.

Timber Merchants.
Brooks Wm. Brd.
Nixon Wm. & James, Stockwell street

Watch & Clock mkrs.
Ashton John, Skt.
Travis Wm. Mkp.

Wheelwrights.
Ball Ths. Bridge end
Fowler Samuel, Mr.
Pimlett John Lomas, Leek moor
Pointon Thomas, Spooner's lane

Wine & Spirit mert.
Hayward Frances, Spout street

COACHES.

From the Red Lion.
　Mail, to London, 1 aft. and to Manchester, 12 noon
　Defiance, to London, 11 night, and to Manchester, 1/2
　past 12 noon.

From the Swan.
　Magnet, to London, 11 night, and to Manchester, 1/2 pas
　12 noon.

From the Roe Buck.
　Express, to Birmingham & London, one noon, & to
　Manchester, 1/2 past 3 aft.

CARRIERS.

Sampson Gould, wharfinger, and agent to the fly-boats, &c.,
which sail twice or thrice a week to all parts of the kingdom,
from the Canal Wharf, Spooner's lane.

Pickford and Co.'s Van, daily at 1/2 p. 12 night, to Ashbourn,
Macclesfield, Manchester, London, &c., from Benj. Woolfe's,
Market place. And *canal boats* to London, Liverpool, &c.,
every Tues. & Fri. from the Wharf.

CARRIERS FROM THE INNS

*who arrive in the morning and depart in the afternoon, on
Wednesday, unless otherwise expressed. Marked * go from the
Butchers' Arms, and + from the Black Swan.*

* Ashbourn, John Johnson.
+ Burslem, John Wooton
* Butterton, Peter Harrison
Buxton, Cock, Thos. Brunt, Wed. & Sat. 5 evening
Congleton, Red Lion, Peter Johnson, Sat. 5 evening
　　+ Flash, Wm. Wood, Eaton, Black's Head, John Smith,
　　Wed. and Sat.
Grindon, Cross Keys, James Stoddart
Hanley and Shelton, Black Swan, Eml. Forrester; Unicorn,
　　Wm. Jeffery; and Butchers' Arms, Henry Brereton
　　+ Harding's-booth, John Haynes, Wed. and Sat.
　　+ Lane-end, Wm. Daniels, Wed. & Sat.
Longnor, (see Sheffield & Buxton)
Macclesfield, King's Head, R. & S. Malkin, and Butchers'
　　　　　　　　　　　　　　Arms, Thos. Nixon
Newcastle, Bird-in-Hand, John Findlay; & Black Swan, Mr.
　　　　　　　　　　　　　　Worral

* Sheffield & Bakewell, Isaac Gillman